Filled with thoughtful insights of Jewish history, Perry Stone's new book, *Breaking the Jewish Code*, is sure to reveal hidden truths that will cause you to live the blessed life.

—JENTEZEN FRANKLIN
Senior Pastor, Free Chapel
New York Times best-selling author of *Fasting*

D0974042

BREAKING THE JEWISH CODE

PERRY STONE

CHARISMA
HOUSE

Most CHARISMA HOUSE BOOK GROUP products are available at special quantity discounts for bulk purchase for sales promotions, premiums, fund-raising, and educational needs. For details, write Charisma House Book Group, 600 Rinehart Road, Lake Mary, Florida 32746, or telephone (407) 333-0600.

BREAKING THE JEWISH CODE by Perry Stone
Published by Charisma House
Charisma Media/Charisma House Book Group
600 Rinehart Road
Lake Mary, Florida 32746
www.charismahouse.com

Unless otherwise noted, all Scripture quotations are from the New King James Version of the Bible. Copyright © 1979, 1980, 1982 by Thomas Nelson, Inc., publishers. Used by permission.

Scripture quotations marked KJV are from the King James Version of the Bible.

Scripture quotations marked NIV are from the Holy Bible, New International Version. Copyright © 1973, 1978, 1984, International Bible Society. Used by permission.

Scripture quotations marked THE CHUMASH are from The Chumash: Stone Edition, copyright © 1997, 1994 by Mesorah Publications, Ltd., 4401 Second Avenue, Brooklyn, NY 11212, (718) 921-9000. Used by permission.

Cover design by Amanda Potter
Design Director: Bill Johnson

Visit the author's website at www.voe.org.

International Standard Book Number: 978-1-61638-494-4
E-book ISBN: 978-1-59979-842-4

The Library of Congress has catalogued the previous edition as follows:
Stone, Perry F.
  Breaking the Jewish code / Perry Stone.
    p. cm.
  Includes bibliographical references.
  ISBN 978-1-59979-467-9
  1. Christian life--Church of God authors. 2.
Judaism--Relations--Christianity. 3. Christianity and other
religions--Judaism. 4. Bible. O.T.--Criticism, interpretation, etc. I.
Title.
  BV4509.5.S8473 2009
  231.7′6--dc22   2008050649

While the author has made every effort to provide accurate telephone numbers and Internet addresses at the time of publication, neither the publisher nor the author assumes any responsibility for errors or for changes that occur after publication.

This publication is translated in Spanish under the title Se descrifa el código judio, copyright © 2009 by Perry Stone, published by Casa Creación, a Charisma Media company. All rights reserved.

13 14 15 16 17 — 9 8 7 6 5 4 3 2 1
Printed in the United States of America

Dedication

I N 1985 I EXPERIENCED MY FIRST PILGRIMAGE TO ISRAEL, WHERE I met my tour guide, Gideon Shor, who has served as my main guide during my thirty-one trips to the Holy Land. Gideon is a master at explaining Jewish history, customs, and culture and blending them with his superior knowledge of the Bible. His on-location teaching birthed a spiritual hunger within me to understand the Hebraic roots of the Christian faith.

Since 1985 I have spent literally thousands of hours swimming into the deep river of Hebraic understanding to bridge the Jewish knowledge of God and the Torah with the Christian understanding of the New Testament. I learned that the roots of Christianity run deep in Hebraic soil. This book, *Breaking the Jewish Code,* is the fruit of those many years of research concerning amazing spiritual, practical, and life-changing revelations of the Torah Code. They have been followed by observant Jews who have preserved them through centuries of tribulation, bringing them back to Israel after nineteen hundred years. Believing Gentiles can now understand how these codes not only apply to Jews—but are also a part of our own root system and spiritual development.

Contents

Introduction

THOSE STUDYING BIBLICAL PROPHECY IN THE LATE 1930s believed an evil power of darkness had been unleashed in Europe. A charismatic German dictator and tyrant named Adolf Hitler, like a demon on assignment, was initiating his "solution" to the world's problems by planning what historians would later identify as the Jewish Holocaust. To Jews, especially those in Europe, the word *Nazi* brings a haunting image of death trains on which Jewish families took their last ride before stepping into eternity. Others visualize ghostly images of concentration camps where starving Jews' physical frames resembled skeletons covered with a layer of skin as they shivered on cold, splintered bunks. Like sheep going to slaughter, many would be marched to gas chambers created to resemble innocent stalls of showers. To Hitler, all *problems* in the world were caused by the Jews. Americans did not believe this lie, according to the *Miami Daily News*. It published a blistering message to the Nazis in their paper:

> A Nazi who has syphilis must not allow himself to be cured by Salvarsan, because it is the discovery of the Jew, Ehrlich. He must not even take steps to find out whether he has syphilis, because the Wasserman reaction used for the purpose is the discovery of a Jew....A Nazi who has heart disease must not use digitalis, which use in heart disease was developed by a Jew, Ludwig Trabo....Typhus must not be treated, for he will have to benefit by discoveries of Jews, Widall and Weill. If he has diabetes, he must not use insulin, because of the research work of a Jew, Minkowsky. If he has a headache, he must shun ovarmidon and antipyrin, discovered by Spiro and Eiloge. Anti-Semites who have convulsions must put up with them for it was a Jew, Oscar Leibreach, who thought of using chloral hydrate....[1]

When 1948 arrived, the world was missing six million Jews, including 1.5 million innocent children who had perished during the Nazi "Final Solution." Most Holocaust survivors were without a permanent home, had few if any possessions, and had watched their paintings, antiques, gold and silver jewelry, and money being seized by Hitler's godless goons. The survivors had one flame of hope burning in the void of their spirits—a homeland in Palestine. On May 14, 1948, at midnight, the British Mandate over Palestine ended, and a new Jewish nation with the name *Israel* was resurrected from the grave of history.

There is a famous story in which the German kaiser asks Bismarck, "Can you prove the existence of God?"

Bismarck replied, "The Jews, your majesty, the Jews."[2]

The Jews comprise less than 1 percent of the world's population, yet 176 Nobel Prize winners have been Jews.[3] Twenty-five percent of the organizations receiving the Nobel Peace Prize were founded or cofounded by Jews.[4] While 67 percent of American high school graduates attend college,[5] 80 percent of Jewish high school graduates go to college,[6] with 23 percent attending Ivy League schools.[7] Studies have shown the Ashkenazi Jews (those from Northern Europe) are highly intelligent with a verbal IQ of 117–125[8] and score 12–15 points higher than Gentile groups, thought to be accredited to two thousand years of emphasizing verbal scholarship.[9] The number-one-rated economically productive small group is Israeli-Americans, who are "seven times more likely to have the highest concentration of higher incomes and lowest rate of dependency upon public assistance."[10]

Some identify these phenomena as a *genius factor,* and others as some mysterious *success factor* deep in the Jewish culture that fosters such accomplishments. From a spiritual perspective, the ancient Hebrew shepherd Moses gave us the Torah, and inspired Hebrew prophets penned the Old Testament scriptures. The majority of writers in the New Testament, along with the founder of Christianity, were raised and educated in Jewish families. Historically, the Jewish people have been both the most successful and the most persecuted of any ethnic group on earth. Their business expertise has exalted them to the highest positions in the global business community, producing top lawyers, skilled doctors and surgeons, and successful civic leaders.

They are the only people who were 1,939 years without a nation, a united language, or a capital. Yet today they have returned to their original land (Israel), speak their original language (Hebrew), and pray at their original capital (Jerusalem). I call this unique ability the Jewish DNA of success and survival—and it all began with one man, Abraham.

Abraham the "Hebrew" (Gen. 14:13) left the city of Ur (in Mesopotamia) with his wife, Sarah, and numerous servants, settling in a large, desolate, desert land called Canaan. He dug wells, built a massive livestock portfolio, amassed commodities in gold and silver, and eventually turned the barren landscape into a blossoming desert. He made peace with surrounding tribes, who honored him as a man of God (Gen. 20). Over four hundred years later, the descendants of Abraham had produced six hundred thousand men of war (Exod. 12:37) who marched out of Egypt to reclaim the land called Israel, which God promised Abraham's children they would possess (Gen. 15:18).

This piece of Middle East real estate was named "Israel" in recognition of the new name God gave to Abraham's grandson Jacob (Gen. 32:28). After the Israelites left Egypt, they arrived at the Promised Land, dividing it among nine and a half tribes who settled in the land, leaving two and a half tribes (Reuben, Gad, and half of Manasseh [Josh. 22:9]) on the east side of the Jordan River. The Israelites were marked as God's covenant people, and their daily guide for living was the *Torah*, the first five books in our Bible, written during Moses's forty years in the wilderness. This divine revelation became the *God Code* for social, moral, ceremonial, sacrificial, and civil laws and requirements that would forge the Hebrews' living standards and mold their moral ethics. By following this *rule book of heaven*, the Hebrew nation would enjoy abundance and success, and they would rise in influence above the surrounding tribes and nations.

Devout religious Jews, often identified as *Torah-observant Jews*, have followed God's Torah Code for thirty-five centuries, enriching their personal lives, families, health, and, in many instances, their finances. For centuries, Gentile Christians have ignored or simply not studied the many important practical applications of the Torah Code. Many of its truths are actually important for our time, such as the significance of physical rest one day a week, the importance of eating the proper types of food, the blessing of moral standards, and the life cycles for raising children. We need to examine these codes to understand why devout Jews often build strong families, live long lives, and celebrate life.

Books have been written about Jewish wealth and why Jews have been successful, but many secular books leave out the significance of the *Torah* and the *covenant* as the spring from which all Jewish blessings flow. The purpose of *Breaking the Jewish Code* is to discover the hidden secrets encoded in the Torah, the Abrahamic covenant, and the divine revelations in the Old Testament that have molded Jewish thinking and lifestyles, making the Jews an undefeatable people, a blessed ethnic group, and a nation that survives against all odds.

Devout, religious Jews understand God's laws, and Christians understand God's grace. Both have knowledge of the Almighty's covenant book, the Bible. Rabbis have amazing knowledge of the Torah and the Prophets, which Christians call the *Old Testament* and Jews call the *Tanakh*.[11] Christians understand the twenty-seven books identified as the *New Testament*. By merging the rivers of knowledge and building a bridge of understanding, Christians will comprehend the Torah mysteries, and Jews will understand the redemptive covenant established by Christ and experienced and taught in the Christian faith.

It is my desire that unlocking these twelve Jewish codes will reveal fresh insight and practical illumination that will enlighten Gentile believers' understanding of the divine revelations God gave to the Jewish people. Many aspects of the Torah Code can provide important instruction for practical, daily living, including keys to wealth, health, celebrating life cycles, and raising successful and gifted children. Let's unlock the code.

—PERRY STONE

Note to readers:

The terms *Jewish* and *Hebraic* are used throughout the book. I use the terms *Jew* and *Jewish* in a contemporary sense, alluding to the natural descendants of Abraham from a Jewish family or a person who has a Jewish mother. The term *Hebrew* will be used to allude to the early patriarchs of the Jewish faith, and *Hebraic* in relation to the customs, traditions, and culture of the Israelites and early Jewish people. Judaism is identified as the religion and culture of the Jewish people.

I will not be following the Jewish custom of writing God's name G-d, as this is often confusing to Gentile readers. Also I have used B.C. to identify time frames before Christ and A.D. (Latin for *anno Domini*) meaning "in the year of the Lord," as a time frame following Christ's birth. These are the time frames most readers will be familiar with. Jews will use BCE, meaning "before the common era," and CE, meaning "of the common era."

Chapter 1

LIVING BY HEAVEN'S RULE BOOK

CODE 1:
Devout Jews have known and lived by the God Code in the Torah.

And Moses called all Israel, and said to them: "Hear, O Israel, the statutes and judgments which I speak in your hearing today, that you may learn them and be careful to observe them. The LORD our God made a covenant with us in Horeb.... The LORD talked with you face to face on the mountain from the midst of the fire."

—DEUTERONOMY 5:1–2, 4

FOR TWENTY-FIVE CENTURIES, MESSAGES FROM HEAVEN WERE scarce. From the time when God created Adam until the revealing of the Torah (the Bible's first five books) to Moses is slightly over twenty-five hundred years. After Adam was expelled from Eden, intimate, face-to-face communication between God and man ceased. Occasionally, God revealed a plan or His will through a vision or a dream. The first reference to a vision in the Scripture is Genesis 15:1: "...the word of the LORD came to Abram in a vision." Later, God spoke to Abraham's descendants in dreams and occasional angelic visitations (Gen. 31:10; 37:5). From Adam to Moses, men possessed no written revelation from God except one incident recorded by the Jewish historian Flavius Josephus. This ancient writer records a prophetic revelation that Adam received, passing it on to his son Seth. Speaking of the sons of Seth, Josephus wrote:

> They also were the inventors of that peculiar sort of wisdom which is concerned with the heavenly bodies, and their order. And that their inventions might not be lost before they were sufficiently known, upon Adam's prediction that the world was to be destroyed at one time by the force of fire, and at another time by the violence and quantity of water, they made two pillars, the one of brick, the other of stone: they inscribed their discoveries on them both, that in case the pillar of brick should be destroyed by the flood, the pillar of stone might remain, and exhibit these discoveries to mankind; and also inform them that there was another pillar of brick erected by them. Now this remains in the land of Siriad to this day.[1]

This prediction of two global catastrophes is one of the first known *written prophecies*. For ten generations from Adam to Noah, information was passed down orally, by word of mouth. In pre-Flood times, men lived very long lives—between 365 and 969 years (Gen. 5:23, 27), giving them the ability to pass down information from generation to generation. Ten more generations passed from Noah's son Shem to Abraham. Twenty generations after Adam's failure, God selected Abraham to birth a new nation and become God's *covenant representative* on Earth. The children of Abraham, identified early as Israelites, would carry the name *children of Israel* and later be identified globally as *Jews*.[2]

Abraham was first called a *Hebrew* in Genesis 14:13. It is the word *Ivri*, meaning, "one from the other side," alluding to God bringing Abraham from Ur (the other side of the river Euphrates) to the Promised Land. Abraham, at age one hundred, and Sarah, at age ninety, bore Sarah's only son, Isaac (Gen. 21:5). Isaac, whose Hebrew name *Yitzchak* means "laughter," would marry at age forty (Gen. 25:20), and his wife, Rebekah, would birth twins, Esau and Jacob (Gen. 25:25–26). God Himself eventually changed Jacob's name to Israel. Jacob's twelve sons would produce offspring, growing into twelve tribes, becoming the *nation of Israel*.

Moving Them Out to Move Them In

To survive a massive famine, Jacob's family loaded the wagons, traveled to Egypt, and settled in a region in Egypt called Goshen (Gen. 45:10). After several hundred years, Israel grew into a multitude, striking fear in the heart of a new Egyptian king who was concerned that the Hebrew men could eventually overrun the Egyptian empire. The Hebrew people were forced into slavery to build treasure cities for the Egyptians (Exod. 1:11).

The time came for God to move them *out* of Egypt and move them *into* the Promised Land. Thus, along came Moses! As a newborn infant, he survived a death threat against the Hebrews' firstborn sons by being hid in a basket. Pharaoh's daughter discovered the floating ark among the reeds of the Nile River. She chose to adopt the baby as her own, and for forty years Moses was raised in Pharaoh's palace and educated in Egyptian art and military. He wore an Egyptian uniform but carried a Hebrew's heart, as demonstrated when he killed a fellow Egyptian for beating a Hebrew slave (Exod. 2:11–12). Fearing Egyptian retaliation, Moses fled from Egypt into the Midian desert. The baby who survived in a basket was now himself a forty-year-old *basket case!*

After forty years of watching his father-in-law's sheep, Moses received a revelation at a burning bush (Exod. 3:2). Being raised in Egypt, Moses had been familiar with Ra, the Egyptian sun god; Apis, the bull god of prosperity; Amun; Ptah; Khnum; Aten; and numerous other Egyptian gods and goddesses.[3] When the Almighty spoke to Moses from the bush, Moses asked, "Who are You?" Before the day concluded, Moses had met the God of Abraham, Isaac, and Jacob. The instructions were clear: *bring Israel out of Egypt back to the Promised Land.*

Returning to Egypt, Moses and his brother, Aaron, witnessed ten plagues that were an assault against the ten major gods of Egypt. On the fifteenth of Nissan, Moses directed six hundred thousand men and an estimated total of 1.5 million people, counting women and children, across the Red Sea into the wilderness. This exodus was the beginning of God preparing a people and preparing to reveal for the first time a message from heaven that would be written down for all men to read and see.

THE GOD CODE REVELATION

Fifty days after departing Egypt, Moses ascended to the top of Mount Sinai in the Arabian Desert and returned forty days later with the most detailed message from God in mankind's history (Exod. 24:16–18). The words, carved on stone tablets, were spoken from God in the same fashion as when a secretary types a letter, word for word, for her boss. Later, the instructions were penned by scribes using large animal skin scrolls. Called the *Torah* (meaning "teaching"), these instructions were the *rule book of heaven*, revealed to the Hebrew people.

> Then the LORD said to Moses, "Come up to Me on the mountain and be there; and I will give you tablets of stone, and the law and commandments which I have written, that you may teach them."
>
> —EXODUS 24:12

The Torah (called the *Pentateuch* in Greek) consists of the first five books in the Bible, which were all written by Moses during his forty-year wilderness journey with the children of Israel. Each handwritten Torah scroll contains 79,847 words and 847,304,805 individual Hebrew letters.[4] The themes of these five books are as follows:

- **Genesis** is the history of creation to the time when the twelve sons of Jacob and their families went down to Egypt.

- **Exodus** is the call of Moses, the departure from Egypt, and the establishment of the priesthood and tabernacle.

- **Leviticus** details the sacrificial, ceremonial, and moral laws of God and instructions for following them.

- **Numbers** details a census of the twelve tribes and the failures of the nation to obey God in the wilderness.

- **Deuteronomy** is a summary of Israel's wanderings, new guidelines, and prophecies about Israel's future.

While the Torah contains history, much of it reveals specific guidelines and instruction for spiritual, social, and moral living; sacrificial procedures; and ceremonial applications. The divine instructions in the Torah are often divided into four categories: the law, the commandments, the statutes, and the judgments. Students of Scripture often merge these four divisions into one package and call it *the Law of Moses* or *the Law of God*. It is God's law given to Moses, but, more importantly, it is the revealed mind of the Creator concerning how His people should live, treat one another, eat, and think, and how to be successful in the journey of life. *This was literally the God Code.*

One tribe from among the sons of Jacob, Levi, was chosen to teach this code and pass it from generation to generation. Jacob's son Levi, whose name means "joined," was the third son of Jacob's wife Leah (Gen. 29:34). Levi became a "connecter," helping join the Israelites to God. When the tabernacle of Moses was constructed, the Levites were the full-time ministers, directed by the high priest Aaron and his sons, all of whom were Levites. This tribe carried a unique *God gene*, as proven in recent DNA testing. Human DNA is called a genetic book of life that encodes detailed information linked to human physical development. Your looks, personality, strengths or handicaps, and much more are encoded in your DNA. A number of Jewish men living in Israel had a special genetic test conducted, proving they were from the lineage of the ancient Hebrew priesthood. The gene test was developed by an American geneticist in 1997. Geneticists began studying variations in the Y chromosome from 306 Jewish men, including 106 self-identified *Kohanim* from Israel, Canada, and England.[5]

The Hebrew word for *priests* is *Kohanim*. If a Jewish person has the surname Levi, Levee, or Levin, it indicates they are linked to the tribe of Levi. If their Jewish surnames are Cohen, Kahn, Kane, or a similar variation, the name indicates a connection to the ancient priest, although not all men with such surnames are Kohanim. David Goldstein reported that of seventeen Kohanim tested in Israel, thirteen tested positive with this *priestly gene.*[6] Researchers also tested three thousand Jewish men from a tribe in India and another group in Africa. Several men in each group have tested positive for this priestly DNA gene.

The amazing success of Jewish people has been a mystery pondered and studied for many generations. Of the many books and articles written, many ignore or omit the central heart of all Judaism—studying, reading, and following the Torah Code. The Torah reveals detailed information that, when followed, can help extend your life, increase physical health, bring emotional stability, build strong families, and provide wisdom for wealth opportunities.

HOW MUCH DO YOU KNOW?

You can't follow what you can't see, can't listen to what you've never heard, and can't obey what you don't know. The Orthodox Jews and children of religious Jews are taught to read, learn, and observe the Torah, along with the Talmud.[7] From an early age, children become familiar with the ceremonies, rituals, and precepts in this Torah Code. The Gentile Christian community has, for the most part, remained uninformed concerning the many amazing discoveries and principles for practical living revealed in the Torah. Most believers who attend church hear messages from the four Gospels or the New Testament epistles. Occasionally, ministers preach from Genesis or mention the Exodus, but they seldom expound on the everyday moral and social instruction found in Leviticus, Numbers, and Deuteronomy.

Yet, the very founding documents of America, including the Declaration of Independence, the Constitution, and the Bill of Rights, are national documents that have moral principles founded in the Torah. America's Founding Fathers and original leaders were very much aware of the consequences of disobeying the Word of God. Therefore, special emphasis was placed upon the commandments of God in the first five books of the Bible. Just because Christians teach from the New Testament, or *New Covenant*, does not indicate that God changed His moral commandments to accommodate liberal thinkers of future generations. In other words, God continues to require obedience to His commandments, even though they originate in the Old Testament.

First, "All Scripture is given by inspiration of God" (2 Tim. 3:16). Some Christians are unaware of the numerous times New Testament writers quote directly from the Tanakh—what Christians call the Old Testament. When the four Gospels, Book of Acts, and epistles mention the "Scriptures," they are referring to the Torah, the Prophets, and writings (wisdom literature) of the Old Testament. (See Luke 24:27; Acts 17:2; 2 Timothy 3:15.) The twenty-seven books of the New Testament were not compiled in book form until the fourth century. Today there are sixty-six books in the English translation of the Bible. However, "all Scripture"—both the Tanakh (Old Testament) and the New Testament—is inspired.

Some liberal Christians reject the entire Old Testament, especially the Torah, as an outdated, primitive document. Part of this misunderstanding stems from a verse that says, "Do not think that I came to destroy the Law or the Prophets. I did not come to destroy but to fulfill. For assuredly, I say to you, till heaven and earth pass away, one jot or one tittle will by no means pass from the law till all is fulfilled" (Matt. 5:17–18). Jesus did not destroy the Law, but He fulfilled messianic predictions and the types and shadows that were hidden in the Law of the prophesied Messiah. He was the "Lamb of God" (John 1:29) crucified near the time of Passover, which fulfilled the image of the Passover lamb offered in Exodus 12. Christ hung on a cross between heaven and Earth, similar to Moses's brass serpent on the pole in Numbers 21 (John 3:14). The sacrifice of the red heifer in Numbers 19 speaks of wood, hyssop, and scarlet, which were used during this ancient ritual. All three items were part of the crucifixion of Christ fifteen hundred years later. (See John 19:17, 29; Matthew 27:28.)

So how does a person equate the New Testament fulfillment of parts of the Torah with the practical moral and social commandments that we should continue following today? Understanding the Torah's three main codes helps us to understand what was fulfilled through Christ and what remains intact.

The Torah Code can be divided into three main categories:

1. The sacrificial code
2. The ceremonial code
3. The judicial-moral code

THE SACRIFICIAL CODE

Animal sacrifices were initiated after the fall of Adam. God cut the skins from two animals, covering the nakedness of Adam and Eve (Gen. 3:21). Noah, Abraham, and Jacob built stone altars from which they offered sacrifices during their lifetimes. By Moses's time, the sacrificial offerings atoned for the sins of the priests and the Israelites. Blood sacrifices were important since "the life of the flesh is in the blood" (Lev. 17:11). An innocent victim was offered in place of the guilty. Each offering was a preview of the final and ultimate sacrifice that would complete the redemption process once and for all.

At Passover, the Hebrews discovered the protective and redemptive power of the lamb's blood (Exod. 12). The three marks on the outer door of the Hebrew homes restrained the death angel from entering the houses. The blood of a lamb defeated the destroying angel in the same manner that the blood of God's lamb, Jesus Christ, would also defeat the power of death (Rev. 12:11).

The sacrificial code included a lamb in the morning and in the evening, and bulls, rams, goats, pigeons, and turtledoves for sin, trespass, thanksgiving, and atonement offerings. (See the Book of Leviticus.) It is clear that the sacrificial requirement of the animal offerings in the Torah was *fulfilled* through the complete and vicarious sufferings of Christ. His death provided forgiveness from our sins and trespasses. Christ *fulfilled* the pattern of the sacrifices through His death on Calvary. There is now no more need for sacrificial animal blood (Heb. 9:11–12). Thus the secrets of the sacrificial code were unlocked through Christ.

THE CEREMONIAL CODE

The second facet of the Law is the ceremonial division. These ceremonies include seven yearly festivals known as the seven feasts. The English names are:

- Passover
- Unleavened Bread
- Firstfruits
- Pentecost
- Trumpets
- Day of Atonement
- Tabernacles

These seven are celebrated each year at specific appointed times on the Jewish calendar. Other ceremonies and special seasons included a weekly Sabbath of rest (Exod. 20:10), new moon celebrations (Ps. 81:3), and Jubilee rest cycles (Lev. 25:9–52). Throughout time, other major events in the history of the Jews would be remembered and added to these yearly festivals.

Paul wrote that these unique biblical celebrations and ceremonies were all a preview (a shadow) of the coming Messiah and His kingdom:

So let no one judge you in food or in drink, or regarding a festival or a new moon or sabbaths, which are a shadow of things to come, but the substance is of Christ.

—COLOSSIANS 2:16–17

The chart below reveals how the Exodus Passover was a detailed preview of what would occur fifteen hundred years later at Christ's crucifixion.

The Old Testament Passover	The Crucifixion of Jesus on Passover
A lamb was taken into the house on the tenth of Aviv.	Jesus entered the temple on the tenth of Aviv.
The lamb was a young male without blemish.	Pilate "found no fault [blemish]" in Christ.
The lamb was examined for four days.	Jesus was tested by leaders for four days.
The lamb was slaughtered on the fourteenth of Aviv.	Jesus was crucified on the fourteenth of Aviv.
The lamb was killed at 3:00 p.m. (between the evenings).	Jesus died at 3:00 p.m. (the ninth hour, Mark 15:25–38).
The lamb was tied to a wooden pole.	Jesus was crucified on a wooden cross.

Pentecost is identified as the time when Moses received the Law on Mount Sinai and Israel became married to God. The first Pentecost was a reflection of the future Day of Pentecost when the Holy Spirit came and the church was born in Jerusalem.

The Pentecost in Moses's Time (Exod. 19)	The Pentecost in Peter's Time (Acts 2)
God spoke in seventy languages so all could hear.	They spoke in the tongues of sixteen nations.
Moses was on Mount Sinai.	Believers were on Mount Zion.
God's voice issued forth as a flame of fire.	Tongues of fire descended upon them.
The mountain shook and quaked.	A sound came like a rushing mighty wind.
Three thousand were slain for worshiping an idol.	Three thousand were converted to the Messiah.

Christ was crucified at Passover and placed in the tomb during the Feast of Unleavened Bread. He was raised during the time of Firstfruits. The church was born on the Day of Pentecost (Acts 2:1–4). Many scholars believe that the three fall feasts will be fulfilled at the coming of Christ, the Tribulation, and the future thousand-year reign of Christ (Rev. 20:4).[8]

The first appearing of Christ fulfilled the three spring feasts, and the church was birthed at the fourth feast, Pentecost. Christ's return will fulfill the prophetic patterns of the three fall feasts. Thus, the ceremonial aspect of the Law saw partial fulfillment during the first coming of Christ and will see complete fulfillment when He returns.

THE JUDICIAL-MORAL CODE

The judicial-moral code in the Torah reveals the code of moral-ethical conduct and civil law decisions involving family, neighbors, civic authority, and business transactions. The social-ethical-judicial commandments and guidelines discuss responsibilities to follow, blessings for obedience, and penalties for breaking these laws. The family codes enable a person to understand sexual purity, marriage, and raising children. For example, these codes teach:

- You were not to see the nakedness of nearest kin or family members (Lev. 18:6–18).

- You were not to have sexual relations outside of marriage (Lev. 18:20).

- You were not to offer your children to idol gods (Lev. 18:21).

- Men were not to have sexual relations with men or with a beast (Lev. 18:22–23).

- You were to honor and respect your parents and rest once a week (Lev. 19:3).

- You were to leave the corners of your field unharvested to allow the poor to eat (Lev. 19:9–10).

- You were not permitted to lie or steal (Lev. 19:11).

- If you hired a person for work, you must pay them the agreed-upon wage (Lev. 19:13).

- You must show respect for those who are deaf and blind (Lev. 19:14).

- You were to honor the older among you and not vex a stranger (Lev. 19:32–34).

- There were cycles of rest every seventh day, seventh year, and seven times seven years (Lev. 25:1–55).

- Judges and officers were to be established in every city (Deut. 16:18).

- Judicial leaders could not take gifts lest they pervert judgment (Deut. 16:19).

- You must have two or three witnesses to establish guilt in a crime (Deut. 17:6).

If the above *laws* sound familiar, they should. Numerous state, federal, and local laws in America have their roots in the soil of the Torah! When Christians imply that the "Law was done away with in Christ," they misunderstand that the moral and ethical instructions, guidelines, and restrictions God put in place in the time of Moses were never altered or changed by Christ. Adultery and fornication are forbidden in both Testaments (Exod. 20:14; Rom. 13:9). Lying, cheating, and bearing a false witness are forbidden in both Testaments. Honoring God each week in worship and setting aside a time for rest (a Sabbath) are in both Testaments. Following God's moral and ethical guidelines create strong communities free of crime, emotionally strong families, and an emphasis on spiritual commitment to God.

To demonstrate that the moral laws continued during the New Testament era, compare the Ten Commandments in the Torah with the instructions written by the New Testament apostles regarding how Christians should conduct themselves:

The Commandments in the Torah	The Same Commandments in the New Testament
Have no other gods.	Matthew 4:10
Do not make idols or images.	1 John 5:21

The Commandments in the Torah	The Same Commandments in the New Testament
Do not take the name of the Lord in vain.	1 Timothy 6:1
Remember the Sabbath.	Acts 13:42
Honor your father and mother.	Ephesians 6:1–3
Do not kill.	Romans 13:9
Do not commit adultery.	Galatians 5:19–21
Do not steal.	Ephesians 4:28
Do not bear false witness.	Romans 13:9
Do not covet.	Colossians 3:5–6

Because other nations surrounding ancient Israel practiced sexual immorality, idolatry, child sacrifices, and unclean living, God revealed the rules of heaven in the Torah Code, instructing the children of Israel to separate themselves from the practices of the heathen nations. They were to be a peculiar and chosen people (Deut. 7:6). Other nations had ceremonies and sacrifices. However, the Hebrews had a moral and ethical code that marked them as a nation for God. Under the new covenant, if we love God and love our neighbor, we will keep the moral instructions of the Almighty (Matt. 22:34–40).

WHY THE JEWS?

Four thousand years ago, why didn't God raise up a nation or a tribe already in existence to be His chosen people? Because most of the tribes were rooted in idol worship and were a mixture of intermarriages among the Gentile nations. God desired a new nation of monotheistic people who would maintain their tribal purity by marrying among themselves, keeping the same religious beliefs, and following the laws of the Creator.

The first house of worship built by divine revelation for the true God was revealed to Moses and constructed by the Hebrews in the wilderness. Called the *tabernacle*, this inspired structure was created by men who were building on Earth what God had built in heaven. It was a pattern of the heavenly temple and a place where the high priest could communicate with God each year in the holy of holies on the Day of Atonement (Heb. 8:5; Lev. 16:1–22).

Why the Jew? Paul wrote:

> What advantage, then, is there in being a Jew, or what value is there in circumcision? Much in every way! First of all, they have been entrusted with the very words of God.
>
> —ROMANS 3:1–2, NIV

God entrusted the Jews to record, copy, read, and live by His Word from generation to generation. This enabled them to maintain a pure and complete lineage, traceable back to Abraham and traceable forward to the Messiah (Matt. 1:1–25; Luke 3:23–38). Obedience to the Torah Code helped devout Jews to maintain ethnic purity and integrity in the genealogies.

THE AMAZING SUCCESS OF THE JEWS

This God Code laid out in the Torah has been handed down from Jewish father to son for over forty generations. This unbroken link of reading, teaching, and instructing each generation has brought success in secular, social, civil, and spiritual life. Yet, there must be particular keys that unlock the doors or foundation stones upon which religious Jewish society was built. When examining the Torah, one essential key becomes visible— understanding the message, meaning, and manifestation of having a *covenant with God*. The Abrahamic covenant is the spring that feeds the river, the beam that supports the building, or, simply, the secret to understanding why the Jewish people have amazingly endured centuries of persecution and grow where they are planted.

WHAT *God* KNEW

After the fall of Adam, sin would be passed on through the spiritual DNA in all mankind. Mankind would have an evil inclination, subjecting them to temptation and carnal desires that would pollute their minds, corrupt their spirits, and eventually destroy their bodies. The laws, commandments, statutes, and judgments in the Torah, if followed, would guarantee loving and caring family relations, success in building business wealth, and help to maintain personal physical and emotional health.

WHAT DEVOUT *Jews* KNOW

The Hebrew nation understood that blessings of health, wealth, and prosperity were contingent upon *obedience* to the words of the law and covenant. By following God's Code, they were promised generational blessing and favor in all they set their hands to do. Only by breaking the law and covenant did they experience natural disasters, agricultural ruin, and disorder in their lives. The numerous promises of divine favor and blessings became the motivation for walking in obedience (Isa. 1:19).

WHAT *Christians* SHOULD KNOW

Christians must understand that the moral, ethical, and judicial code penned in the Torah was not removed through the new covenant. While Christ fulfilled certain ceremonial and sacrificial aspects of the law, the same Torah principles for daily living were practiced and refined in the first-century church, which began with an all Jewish *membership* in Acts chapter 2. By searching the Scriptures, we will better understand and bridge the concepts of the Torah with the revelation of the new covenant. The roots of Christianity are in the justification by faith that began with the Abrahamic covenant, the Torah, and the Prophets. Paul taught that the Gentiles were wild olive branches grafted into the Jewish olive tree and that we receive nourishment from the root of the tree. That root is the Torah and the Prophets, and we need to examine the root to enjoy the Hebrew fruit. (See Romans 11.)

Chapter 2

THE SECRET IN THE COVENANT

CODE 2:
*All blessings are linked to the
Abrahamic covenant.*

*And the LORD said, "Shall I hide from Abraham what I am
doing, since Abraham shall surely become a great and mighty
nation, and all the nations of the earth shall be blessed in him?
For I have known him, in order that he may command his
children and his household after him, that they keep the way of
the LORD, to do righteousness and justice, that the LORD may
bring to Abraham what He has spoken to him."*

—GENESIS 18:17–19

I N A GENTILE (NON-JEWISH) SOCIETY, BUSINESSMEN SPEAK OF
contracts and agreements. However, the word *covenant* was used in
ancient times and was more than just a binding agreement signed on a parchment or sealed with a wax impression from a signet ring. To the ancient
cultures, a covenant was sealed in blood. To the Hebrews, the biblical covenants are also connected to blood covenants.

The first time the word *covenant* is used in the Torah is in Genesis 6:18

when God made a covenant with Noah to spare him and his family during the Flood. The second reference is with Abraham (Gen. 17:1–2). Originally named Abram (meaning "high father"), he lived in Ur of the Chaldeans, located six miles from the Euphrates River. He was the third of three sons born to Terah (Gen. 11:27).

Jewish tradition reveals that Abram's family had served idol gods (Josh. 24:2, 14–15). The almighty God appeared to Abram in a vision, instructing him to leave Ur and move to the land of Canaan. At age seventy-five, Abram followed this vision. During Abram's journey, God progressively appeared to Abram, revealing His divine purpose for Abram and his future children.

- God told Abram he would become a "great nation" (Gen. 12:2).

- God told Abram he would be a "father of many nations" (Gen. 17:4).

- God told Abram that nations and kings would come out of him (Gen. 17:6).

- God told Abram he would become a "mighty nation" and bless all nations (Gen. 18:18).

- God told Abram that "all nations of the earth shall be blessed" (Gen. 22:18).

With each step of obedience that Abram took, God increased the magnitude of His promises—from just a nation, to a *great* nation, to nations of *kings*, to a nation that would bless the *entire world*! The master key to release the fulfillment of these promises was obedience to the instructions demanded by God in His covenant.

THE SECRETS IN THE COVENANT

The secret of the LORD is with those who fear Him,
And He will show them His covenant.

—PSALM 25:14

> On the same day the LORD made a covenant with Abram, saying: "To your descendants I have given this land, from the river of Egypt to the great river, the River Euphrates."
>
> —GENESIS 15:18

The Hebrew word for covenant is *b'rit*, and it is used 280 times in the Old Testament. According to *W. E. Vine's Expository Dictionary of Old and New Testament Words*, the word *b'rit* is frequently the object of the verb *karath*, "to divide or to cut in two."[1] In Genesis 15, when God and Abraham "cut covenant," Abraham provided a heifer, a female goat, a ram, a turtledove, and a young pigeon as offerings, dividing the larger animals into two halves (Gen. 15:9–10). This was an ancient ratification ceremony, which invoked oaths and binding agreements. God passed between the pieces, sealing the covenant in the sacrificial blood.

> And it came to pass, when the sun went down and it was dark, that behold, there appeared a smoking oven and a burning torch that passed between those pieces. On the same day the LORD made a covenant with Abram.
>
> —GENESIS 15:17–18

From the arrangement of the dividing of the parts of the sacrifice came the expression that literally denoted "to cut covenant" (similar idioms are found in Greek and Latin).[2] The very Hebrew word for covenant, *b'rit*, carries the implication of an agreement made with blood since the cutting symbolism involves a cutting and dividing of an animal sacrifice. The division of the animals into two parts represented the agreement between the two parties.

Ancient legal contracts (or covenants) had an official seal attached to the parchment. From the time of the Egyptians to the Roman Empire, rings with specific emblems (called *signet rings*) were used to seal legal documents by pressing the ring onto hot wax.[3] In Genesis 15, God entered a binding covenant with Abraham and sealed the agreement when a flaming torch passed between the pieces of the sacrifices.

The Jewish commentaries note that in the ancient East, normally the weaker party in a covenant would walk between the pieces, indicating that person's fate if he violated the conditions of the covenant. Yet it was God, the stronger one, who was sealing the covenant with Abraham, the weaker, by passing between the sacrifices![4] According to one rabbi I spoke with years ago, during the ancient Middle East marriage covenants the father would hold a torch, indicating that breaking the marriage vows would lead to a fiery conclusion to the unfaithful partner (as seen in Judges 15:4–6). God was revealing that He was sealing the covenant at that moment, and if a descendant of Abraham broke the covenant, that person would be "cut off" from God and His covenant (Gen. 17:14). This "cutting off" theme was revealed to Abraham in Genesis 17:14.

From Genesis 12 to Genesis 17, the Abrahamic covenant was ratified and fully established. However, the real *secret* of Abraham's covenant with God was hidden from Abraham for twenty-four years. This *seal* involved the shedding of blood, making this covenant an official *blood covenant*.

If the secret to all spiritual and material blessings originated in the Abra-hamic covenant, then the secret of all covenants is linked to blood. Many ancient nations recognized blood pact agreements. In pre-Islamic times, ancient Syria acknowledged a blood pact called *M'ahadat ed-Dam*, or Brotherhood of the Covenant. In the agreement, each party must provide guard from treachery, protection in time of danger, and provision for the wants of the others' family members if one covenant partner passes away prior to the other.[5] Many African tribes have used covenants for centuries.

Dr. David Livingstone, the famous missionary to Africa, witnessed numerous covenant rites in Africa. He himself made a covenant pact in July 1854 with Queen Manenko of the Balonda tribes. In some instances, incisions were made in the wrist and afterward rubbed in gunpowder. The tribal chief pronounced curses if the covenant was broken, and both parties exchanged gifts, which was a common aspect of the ancient covenant rites.[6]

In 1871, Henry Stanley traveled to Africa looking for Livingstone. He encountered the most feared tribal leader who controlled ninety thousand square miles. Stanley was warned to avoid the leader, named Mirambo. Stanley eventually encountered the chieftain on April 22, 1876. They agreed to make a "strong friendship." Once a covenant was ratified, the entire tribe became friends with the chieftain's new covenant partner, and every inch of land controlled by the chieftains was now open for travel without danger to the chieftain's new friend (Stanley) as a result of the covenant. Stanley wrote that his arm was used to draw blood fifty times to cut covenant with tribal leaders in Africa![7]

Often a tribal leader would send his chief representative to shed his blood on behalf of the chief. This is the imagery of the new covenant, in which: "God so loved the world, that he gave his only begotten Son" (John 3:16, KJV). Christ was God's representative, using His own blood to redeem mankind, thereby giving redeemed man access to God.

> Not with the blood of goats and calves, but with His own blood He entered the Most Holy Place once for all, having obtained eternal redemption.
> —Hebrews 9:12

BLOOD-STAINED TREES

According to author H. Clay Trumbull in his book *The Blood Covenant*, in various parts of the East a tree was used in the rite of forging a blood covenant. Among some nations, planting a tree was a symbol of the covenant. In ancient Timor, a young fig tree bore a portion of the blood of the covenant. In both instances, the tree was a visible and continually growing sign of the covenant.

Trumbull points out that the covenant Abraham made with a neighboring tribal leader named Abimelech involved trees. "Then Abram...dwelt in the plain of Mamre" (Gen. 13:18, KJV). In Hebrew the word 'elown is the root word translated as "plain" in the English Bible but means "oak." There were three men in this covenant, with Abraham being the fourth (Gen. 14:13).[8]

The olive tree, fig tree, mustard tree, and pomegranate tree are common trees in Israel and are mentioned throughout Scripture. The oak, however, is mentioned in numerous passages involving unusual settings. Rebekah's nurse was buried under an oak (Gen. 35:8). In Shechem, Joshua wrote God's Word on a stone, erecting the memorial under an oak tree (Josh. 24:26). Gideon fed an angel of the Lord under an oak tree in an area called Ophrah (Judg. 6:11–19). A "man of God" was found sitting under an oak (1 Kings 13:14), and the bones of Saul and his sons were buried under an oak (1 Chron. 10:12). Israel had made a covenant with the men of Jabesh in a time of war (1 Sam. 11). Oak trees served as the token or public sign of the covenant that had been made between Israel and the men of Jabesh. Ezekiel witnessed that idol worshipers burned incense under thick oak trees (Ezek. 6:13). It seems the oak trees were an important symbol of a covenant made in the land of Israel. This may be due to the oak being a symbol of strength and endurance, since a covenant was to remain strong and endure from generation to generation.

The tree as a living symbol of a covenant is important. The rod of Aaron, used to perform miracles in Pharaoh's court, was cut from an almond tree (Exod. 7:12). This dead branch later produced leaves and almonds, a sign God had chosen Aaron and his sons for the priesthood (Num. 17:8). The bitter waters of Marah were sweetened when Moses threw the branch from a tree into the waters (Exod. 15:23–25).

All of the imagery of ancient covenants being cut under trees, the use of a tree branch (rod) blossoming as signaling the priestly covenant, along with the tree branch making bitter waters sweet, is a preview of the tree on which the Messiah would suffer, initiating a new priesthood, and turning the bitter waters of life sweet through His suffering on the cross.

Abraham's Covenant Sealed by Blood

God promised Abraham that his seed would create a new nation. But there was a problem—Abraham had no children because his wife, Sarah, was barren. At age seventy-five, he left Ur and journeyed to Canaan with his sixty-five-year-old wife, Sarah.[9] It is interesting that God never revealed the visible sign or *token* of His covenant to Abraham until Abraham was ninety-nine years of age. The secret sign of the covenant was circumcision, which involved removing the foreskin from the male child. The practice of circumcision was known in Abraham's day among the Egyptians and other Semitic groups. However, the Almighty's sign was different for two reasons. The ancient Semites would often cut a mark in the male foreskin, but God said the foreskin must be completely removed. Secondly, performing circumcision must be done on the eighth day after a son's birth:

> This is My covenant which you shall keep, between Me and you and your descendants after you: Every male child among you shall be circumcised; and you shall be circumcised in the flesh of your foreskins, and it shall be a sign of the covenant between Me and you. He who is eight days old among you shall be circumcised, every male child in your generations, he who is born in your house or bought with money from any foreigner who is not your descendant.
>
> —Genesis 17:10–12

Why did God wait for twenty-four years until revealing the sign of the covenant to Abraham? I believe it was because of Ishmael. After Abraham failed for eleven years to have a child through Sarah, Sarah finally suggested that Abraham impregnate Hagar, her Egyptian handmaid. Hagar conceived and bore Abraham a son named Ishmael, meaning, "God has listened." Abraham was eighty-six when Ishmael was born (Gen. 16:16). At age ninety-nine, God revealed that circumcision was the sign of the covenant (Gen. 17:10–12).

God waited until Ishmael was thirteen years of age before the revelation of circumcision was given to Abraham. In Judaism, the age of thirteen is considered the *coming of age* for boys. Jews conduct a bar mitzvah for young boys turning age thirteen, a special ceremony indicating the child is now responsible for his own actions.[10] God waited until Ishmael was thirteen, indicating that Ishmael was now responsible for his own spiritual walk with God.

Consider this. If at age seventy-five Abraham had known that circumcision was the sign of the covenant, then eleven years later the son of the bondwoman would have been "marked" for God's covenant promise, thus disrupting God's plan of a Hebrew nation through Abraham and Sarah. Thus God waited until Ishmael could take personal responsibility for his own moral and spiritual destiny (age thirteen). Then at age ninety-nine, Abraham received the seal of the covenant. One year later Isaac was born (Gen. 21:3–5). The mark of circumcision is important to the Jewish people, since those who are unborn are considered the "seed" of future generations. The term "seed" is often used in the Torah to identify unborn children, since conception occurs after the seed (sperm) of the man passes through the covenant "mark" (on the foreskin).

Circumcision on the eighth day is interesting for several reasons. First, Jewish tradition believes that the first seven days of an infant's life represent the finished creation of the physical world in seven days. The number eight (representing new beginnings) transcends the physical world and initiates the child into the Abrahamic covenant. Also, a newborn was to experience one Sabbath before being circumcised. Muslims choose the seventh day based upon statements in the Islamic traditions called the *hadith*.[11] In America, circumcision is usually performed at a parent's request within two days of the child's birth, but Torah-observant Jews keep the commandment to circumcise on the eighth day.

Medical research has discovered two unique blessings linked to circumcision. The *British Journal of Cancer* reported that certain cancers of the cervix appear lower in Jewish women in Israel than among other female ethnic groups. Some have suggested that circumcision assists in actually preventing cervical cancer in Jewish women.[12] The second feature is a blood-clotting factor, vitamin K, that contains prothrombin. It appears (based on data) that on the eighth day after birth, an infant baby has more available prothrombin than on any other day of his life, making the eighth day the best time for circumcision.[13] Thus, God knew the physical and medical significance for eighth-day circumcision.

After Isaac was weaned, Ishmael was removed from the household of Abraham, which gave full covenant rights to Abraham and Sarah's promised son (Gen. 21:10–14).[14]

THE COVENANT—SEALED BY A MEAL

It was customary to seal a covenant deal with a meal. This ritual dates back to ancient empires and tribes long before the Torah. Some primitive tribes would prepare an animal, or more primitive groups would literally mingle the blood of the covenant parties in a cup of wine and both parties drink from it. Drinking or eating blood was strictly forbidden in the Torah (Lev. 17:12). The ancient concept was that through this act the two parties become one by partaking of the same blood. Blood was very important in every covenant ritual of the Hebrew nation. When publicly sealing God's covenant with Israel, Moses sprinkled the sacrificial blood of a chosen animal on the altar, the Book of the Covenant, and the people (Exod. 24:6–8).

Blood was also sprinkled on the sacred tabernacle furniture, including once a year on the lid of the ark of the covenant. The ark was a large, gold-covered, rectangular box housing three sacred items: a golden pot of the manna (bread) that fell from heaven, the tables of the law written on stone, and Aaron's rod (Heb. 9:4). Yearly on Israel's sixth festival, the Day of Atonement, the high priest entered the holy of holies in the tabernacle (later the temple), sprinkling blood seven times on the east end of the lid of the ark, called the mercy seat (Exod. 25:10–22; Lev. 16:14). The manna in the ark symbolized God's covenant of provision, the tablets pictured God's covenant of blessing for the Levites and the people, and the rod was God's covenant of authority given to the high priest.

The first covenant meal was eaten when the first king and priest of Jerusalem, Melchizedek, provided a meal of bread and wine for Abraham after Abraham's war victory over five kings (Gen. 14). Isaac had Esau prepare a last meal prior to receiving his father's blessing. Rebekah, Jacob and Esau's mother, realized this was a covenant of blessing meal and intervened to have Jacob pose as Esau to receive Esau's blessing (Gen. 27:6–41). Jacob and his father-in-law, Laban, sealed their Mizpah covenant by eating a meal on a pile of rocks, which would serve as a visible memorial for future generations (Gen. 31:49–54).

For the Hebrew nation, the most important covenant meal was celebrated after God revealed His commandments on Mount Sinai. Moses sprinkled half of the sacrificial blood on the altar, representing God's part of the agreement, and half of the blood on the people, representing their half of the agreement (Exod. 24:6–8). The people sealed their part of the agreement by saying, "All the words which the LORD has said we will do" (Exod. 24:3). Afterward, Moses, Aaron, his sons, and seventy chief elders were invited to the top of the mountain where they "…saw the God of Israel. And there was under His feet as it were a paved work of sapphire stone.…So they saw God, and they ate and drank" (Exod. 24:10–11). This meal *sealed the deal* between God and Israel. In Christian tradition, the Lord's Supper, or Communion Meal, represents the blood and body of the Messiah and forms a spiritual bond between Christ and the believer, sealing our faith and confidence in the new covenant. Therefore Communion is the covenant meal.

After the special meal with Melchizedek, Abraham reconfirmed his covenant (Gen. 15:1–4) and presented a tithe (the tenth) of all goods to Melchizedek (Gen. 14:18–20). This act was significant and is mentioned by Paul:

> Even Levi, who receives tithes, paid tithes through Abraham, so to speak, for he was still in the loins of his father when Melchizedek met him.
> —HEBREWS 7:9–10

Abraham was carrying the original *Levi's genes*. Levi was a future great-grandson of Abraham, who would be born many years after Abraham met

Melchizedek. The sons of Levi would become the priests in the tabernacle of Moses and in both Jewish temples, receiving tithes, offerings, and sacrifices from the Hebrew people. Both Moses and Aaron were from the tribe of Levi (Exod. 2:1; 4:14). Abraham set the pattern for future generations to present the tithe (the tenth) of their animals, agricultural increase, and finances to the Lord in appreciation for His blessings on them individually and nationally.

COVENANT BLESSINGS AND CONDITIONS

Scholars note that there are various agreements (covenants) that God established throughout the Old Testament. Below are several central to the Jewish people.

The Covenant Party	The Promise	Conditional/ Unconditional	The Sign of the Covenant
The covenant with Noah	The earth would never be destroyed by water again.	Unconditional	A rainbow in the sky
The covenant with Abraham	A new nation, new land, new people	Unconditional	Circumcision
The covenant with David	An everlasting kingdom in Israel	Unconditional	Jerusalem will endure.
The covenant of the Sabbath	Blessing for keeping the Sabbath	Conditional	The Sabbath day
The covenant with Israel	Blessing for keeping the commandments	Conditional	The commandments
The covenant of the presence	God's presence going before and dwelling with Israel	Conditional	The ark of the covenant

All covenants involve three major features:

1. Agreements between both parties
2. Conditions between both parties
3. Promises between both parties

Covenant agreements

All contracts and covenants begin with an agreement of mutual understanding between the parties. The agreements reveal the actions and expectations of both parties. A covenant is never one-sided, just as a marriage covenant cannot succeed with just one person. God's agreements are based upon His laws, statutes, and commandments in His written Word. When entering a redemptive covenant with God through Christ, believers *agree* to follow the teachings established in the New Testament.

Covenant conditions

The conditions are the expected requirements to fulfill the agreements. God continually said, "If you will...then I will." God instructed Israel, "If you will hear My word...if you will walk with Me...if you obey My voice." The conjunction *if* when related to a covenant promise is also a condition. When God says *if*, it indicates that the person being addressed must first move to obey the given instructions.

When my wife and I were united in marriage, we stood before a church full of witnesses and agreed to enter into a marriage covenant. The minister gave conditions—"for better for worse, for richer for poorer, in sickness and health, poverty and wealth"—under which we would remain loyal to one another. We sealed the agreement publicly with a kiss and consummated the marriage during our honeymoon.

Abraham's conditions of the covenant were, "Circumcise your sons on the eighth day" and "Teach your children to follow Me." God revealed confidence in Abraham and knew he would follow through in keeping the covenant.

> For I have known him, in order that he may command his children and his household after him, that they keep the way of the LORD, to do righteousness and justice, that the LORD may bring to Abraham what He has spoken to him.
>
> —GENESIS 18:19

Covenant promises

If Abraham's descendants followed the agreement made by Abraham and God to mark their sons with the cut of circumcision, then God would bless them with land, prosper the works of their hands, and make them great in the earth. If they failed to follow the commandment, they would experience great difficulties and lose their natural and spiritual blessings (Gen. 17:14).

Several prominent books have been written forging opinions as to why many Jewish people are gifted with high IQs, creative genius, financial skills, and the ability to survive against the odds. Many authors omit the one feature that has separated the devout Jews from all other nations—their belief that as an ethnic group they have a special, unique covenant with God. Some have interpreted this confidence as arrogance. However, Scripture marked them four times as God's "peculiar people" and His treasure on earth.[15] There is nothing arrogant about being confident about what God has said about you!

What *God* Knew

To fulfill the promise of Genesis 3:15 of a coming Messiah who would defeat evil and redeem mankind, God raised up a new nation with a new spiritual DNA through Abraham. Abraham's seed would become Israel and would receive from heaven God's blueprint for living, build God a dwelling place on Earth through the tabernacle, reveal the plan of redemption through blood sacrifices, and eventually bless the world with the Scriptures and the Messiah.

What Devout *Jews* Know

While many Orthodox Jews and devout religious Jews may not understand Christian teaching and New Testament redemptive revelation, they are aware of the Abrahamic covenant, the commandments through the Torah, the Sabbaths, festivals and celebrations that honor God, and the mighty works He has done for Israel. Many have zealously followed after the instruction in the Torah and Jewish Talmud, seeking to obey their regulations and instructions. They understand they are a unique people manifested through God's divine eternal plan.

What *Christians* Should Know

Believers have received forgiveness of sins through the new covenant sealed by the blood of Christ (Heb. 8:8–13). However, Gentile believers can receive amazing insight and practical knowledge by examining the roots of the Christian faith, which begin in the Torah Code. The first basic step is to understand the meaning of covenant and the Hebrew language, considered by some as the *language of God*.

Chapter 3

SECRETS OF THE HEBREW ALPHABET AND WORDS

CODE 3:
The Hebrew language is the language of God.

The twenty-two sacred letters are the profound, primal spiritual forces. They are, in effect, the raw material of creation.
—RABBI MICHAEL MUNK

IN 1768, THE REV. JOHN PARKHURST PRODUCED THE FIRST HEBREW-English lexicon. In the introduction, he stated that he believed that six thousand years ago, Hebrew was the first language spoken on Earth between Adam and God.[1] If this is correct, you might speak Hebrew when you get to heaven! There is a Jewish tradition that the first man, Adam, spoke an ancient form of the Hebrew language in the Garden of Eden. We know Adam had knowledge of a language, as he named the animals (Gen. 2:19–20). Both Adam and his wife, Eve, *heard* the voice of God in the garden (Gen. 3:8). God entered Eden in the "cool of the day" (Gen. 3:8). The Hebrew word for cool is *ruach*, and it alludes to the "wind, breath, or the air." We would say that God rode into the garden on the wind. This agrees with the scripture that says, "He [God] rode upon a cherub, and flew;

and He was seen upon the wings of the wind" (2 Sam. 22:11). The language Adam spoke was passed on from Adam to Noah, the first ten generations of men (Gen. 5:3–32).

There are also written traditions concerning Adam's ability to communicate with the animal kingdom prior to his eating from the tree of knowledge of good and evil. The temptation to sin was initiated by a subtle, talking serpent (Gen. 3:1–4). Skeptics rightfully point out that snakes don't talk. Yet, the Jewish historian Josephus answered this criticism when he wrote concerning man's early history in the garden:

> But while all the living creatures had one language, at that time the serpent, which then lived together with Adam and his wife Eve, shewed an envious disposition, at his supposal of their living happily, and in obedience to the commands of God...[2]

Any ability to communicate with the animal kingdom was severed following Adam's sin. However, men continued communicating with men, as stated earlier when Josephus recorded how the sons of Seth etched a prophecy of future calamities coming to the earth on brick and stone for all men to see and be warned. These stone monuments have never been discovered, and the language or word pictures inscribed on them are unknown.

At approximately 2344–2342 b.c., the floodwaters swept over the earth, bringing global destruction. There were eight survivors: Noah and his wife, their three sons, and their wives (1 Pet. 3:20). It is likely Noah would have continued to speak the original language of Adam. Three generations later, Nimrod, Noah's great grandson, constructed the first megastructure, called the Tower of Babel, in the plains of Shinar (Gen. 11). Nimrod's goal was to escape any future flood:

> He also said he would be revenged on God, if He should have a mind to drown the world again; for that he would build a tower too high for the waters to be able to reach! And that he would avenge himself on God for destroying their forefathers.[3]

During the tower's construction, all the earth's inhabitants spoke one language.

And the LORD said, "Indeed the people are one and they all have one language, and this is what they begin to do; now nothing that they propose to do will be withheld from them. Come, let Us go down and there confuse their language, that they may not understand one another's speech."

—GENESIS 11:6–7

God saw that man's unbridled knowledge could again cause evil inclinations to spread. In a sudden moment, He struck the tower to the ground and scattered the people by confusing their languages. Nimrod's kingdom was called Babel, whose Akkadian meaning is "gate of God," but the Hebrew meaning is from the verb *balal*, meaning, "confuse or confound." It was at Babel that various world languages were birthed (vv. 7–9).

Hundreds of years later, in the Torah Moses wrote of God dividing the nations at the tower:

When the Most High divided their inheritance to the nations,
When He separated the sons of Adam,
He set the boundaries of the peoples
According to the number of the children of Israel.
For the Lord's portion is His people;
Jacob is the place of His inheritance.

—DEUTERONOMY 32:8–9

Even the early church father Origen reflected on the early language of mankind when he wrote:

All the people upon the earth are to be regarded as having used one divine language, and so long as they lived harmoniously together were preserved in the use of this divine language, and they remained from moving from the east so long as they were imbued with the sentiments of the "light," and the "reflection" of the eternal light.[4]

The original language was a *divine language*, originating with Adam in the garden. According to Origen, there was one group that did not travel to the plains of Shinar with Nimrod, and they alone retained the pure language, spoken from the beginning of time:

> Those who preserved their original language continued, by reason of their not having migrated from the east, in possession of the east, and of their eastern language. And let him notice, that these alone became the portion of the Lord, and His people who were called Jacob, and Israel the cord of his inheritance.[5]

Since the Hebrew tongue became the language of God's chosen people, it is assumed that Adam spoke some early form of the Hebrew dialect. Jewish writings such as the *Mishna* (Genesis Rabbah 38) teaches that Adam spoke in the Hebrew language. The *Mishna* comments that Adam called Eve "woman" (*'ishah*), the Hebrew term for a woman or a female (Gen. 2:23). He later named her Eve (Gen. 3:20), or *Chavah* (meaning "life giver") in the Hebrew language. Of course, the word *Hebrew* was unknown in the time of Adam, and his language would simply be the language of Adam. However, he was speaking the language God gave him. Being created a full-grown man without systematic training from infancy to adulthood, his teaching came directly from God. The name *Hebrew* originated out of Shem's great-grandson's name *Eber* (Gen. 10:21). It comes from the verb *'abar*, meaning to "pass through, or region beyond." Abraham was the first Hebrew (Gen. 14:13), because he passed over from his native land to the Promised Land. The Abrahamic covenant was sealed when God *passed through* the sacrifices, and in Egypt God passed over the Israelite homes that were protected by the lamb's blood (Exod. 12:13). Joshua and Israel passed over Jordan, possessing their inheritance (Josh. 1:2). The sojourning, or wandering, of the Jewish people has fulfilled the meaning of the name Hebrew.

The apostle Paul was a former Jewish rabbi, trained as a Pharisee under noted rabbi Gamaliel. Paul was educated in numerous languages of his time. Paul mentions God speaking to him in Hebrew when he was converted:

> And when we all had fallen to the ground, I heard a voice speaking to me and saying in the Hebrew language, "Saul, Saul, why are you persecuting Me? It is hard for you to kick against the goads." So I said, "Who are You, Lord?" And He said, "I am Jesus, whom you are persecuting. But rise and stand on your feet; for I have appeared to you for this

purpose, to make you a minister and a witness both of the things which you have seen and of the things which I will yet reveal to you."

—Acts 26:14–16

God could have addressed Paul in Greek, Latin, Aramaic, or Hebrew, since all four languages were spoken in Israel. God, however, used the *sacred tongue* from which the Torah and Prophets are written—the Hebrew language.[6] America's early founders were keenly aware of the significance of the Hebrew language. William Bradford (1590–1657), governor of the Plymouth Colony, stated that he studied Hebrew so when he died he might be able to speak in the "most ancient language, the Holy Tongue in which God and the angels spoke."[7] In 1777, Ezra Stiles, president of Yale, stated that studying Hebrew was essential to a gentleman's education. He said, "Isn't it [Hebrew] the language I am sure to hear in heaven?"[8] Even Martin Luther, not known for his kind remarks toward the Jews, commented about the Hebrew language, "The Hebrew language is the best language of all, with the richest vocabulary."[9]

From the time of Moses, Hebrew was the language of the Torah and the Jewish people. The original written form of the Hebrew letters dates back to the eleventh or tenth century B.C., commonly termed *Old Hebrew*. By the sixth century B.C., the old script was limited to religious writing, and a different form, the Aramaic script, called a *square script*, was developed. This Aramaic script is used today when scribes pen a Torah scroll.[10] While written script developed over the centuries, and Hebrew is believed to be a form of an early Phoenician script, I personally believe that the original language Adam spoke was somehow linked to what we today know as the Hebrew language. There is a divine connection as seen when studying the mysteries of the Hebrew alphabet.

THE AMAZING HEBREW ALPHABET

Called the *alef-bet*, there is a sacred mystique shrouding the Hebrew alphabet. The alphabet consists of twenty-two letters that are all consonants. There are no vowels among the twenty-two letters. The vowel marks, consisting of a combination of dots and dashes (called *nikkudim*) placed either above or below the individual letters, were added around between the seventh and tenth centuries A.D. by a group called the Masoretes, who placed these marks under and above the letters to indicate how the text was to be chanted in the synagogue.

The original form of the Hebrew alphabet was actually word pictures. The older text, called the Proto-Canaanite script, consisted of twenty-two forms that represented common images. For example, the first Hebrew letter is *alef*, and the last (twenty-second letter) is *tav*. The word picture for *alef* is the head of an ox, and the word picture of the *tav* is a cross or a plus sign. These first and last letters of the Hebrew alphabet cryptically reveal an early imagery of the redemption plan, which began with animal sacrifices and concluded at the cross of Christ! In the New Testament, Jesus said, "I am the Alpha and the Omega" (Rev. 1:8), which are the first and last letters of the Greek alphabet. In Hebrew, He would have said, "I am the *alef* and the *tav*."

Another significant picture is the twenty-first letter of the Hebrew alphabet, called the letter *shin*. From its earliest inception, its form is similar to our letter *w*, although it is an *s* or *sh* sound and not a *w* sound. In Moses's time, the high priest was commanded to bless the people with what is called the priestly blessing and recorded in Numbers 6:25–27. Jewish tradition teaches that the priest recited the blessing placing both hands, palms outward, with his thumbs touching and the four fingers of his hands split. His hands created the form of the letter *shin* and represented the name *Shaddai*, the name revealing God as the most powerful one (Gen. 17:1).[11]

HEBREW ALPHABET

Value	Name	Letter
1	Alef	א
2	Bet	ב
3	Gimel	ג
4	Dalet	ד
5	Hei	ה
6	Vav	ו
7	Zayin	ז
8	Chet	ח
9	Tet	ט
10	Yod	י
20	Kaf	כ ך
30	Lamed	ל
40	Mem	מ ם
50	Nun	נ ן
60	Samech	ס
70	Ayin	ע
80	Peh/Feh	פ ף
90	Tzadi	צ ץ
100	Kuf	ק
200	Resh	ר
300	Shin/Sin	ש שׂ
400	Tav	ת

Each letter of the Hebrew alphabet has a symbol and a numerical value.

Moses taught that God would bring His people to a place marked by His name (Deut. 12:11, 21; 14:23–24). That place was Jerusalem, where three mountains—Ophel, Zion, and Moriah—merge to form the area of the ancient city of David.[12] When examining the topography of these three areas, the hills merge together, forming a shape similar to the letter *shin*. Since *shin* represents *Shaddai*, a name for God (translated as *Almighty* in Gen. 17:1), then the features of these three mountains in Jerusalem visibly reveal the place where God "placed His name."

The Hebrew text of the Torah has other unique features. When examining Genesis 1:1, in Hebrew there are seven Hebrew words. The English reads, "In the beginning God created the heavens and the earth." In Hebrew it reads:

> Bereshit bara Elohim et hashamayim ve'et ha'arets—*In the beginning God created heaven and earth.*[13]

In the middle of the phrase (the word *et*) are the first and last letters of the Hebrew alphabet, the *alef* and *tav* (pronounced *et*). This nontranslatable word is used in Hebrew grammar to mark a point, identifying the word that follows it as being the direct definite object.[14] Some have suggested (while some rabbis would disagree) that God was saying that in the beginning He created the *Alef-Tav*, or the Messiah. Since Christ was the source of man's redemption, "from the foundation of the world," and called Himself the "Alpha and Omega" (Rev. 13:8; 1:8), it is suggested this verse cryptically reveals that the Messiah preexisted with God at the time of Creation. By Hebraic interpretation, this is not the meaning of this passage. However, Christ said, "Before Abraham was I am," alluding to His preexistence (John 8:58).

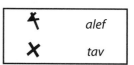

The early Hebrew letter *alef* was the symbol of an ox, and the letter *tav* was a cross.

In Hebrew, the word for *truth* is *emet*.[15] When spelling *truth* in Hebrew, the first letter is *alef*, and the last letter is *tav*. Christ said, "I am the way, the truth, and the life" (John 14:6). Thus, He is the beginning and the end of all truth!

Another uniqueness of the Hebrew alphabet is that all twenty-two letters also have a numerical value. This concept, which seeks to identify the relationship of the letters with numbers, is considered the twenty-ninth rule of the thirty-two rules of hermeneutics taught by Rabbi Eliazar ben Yosi HaGalili. Both the Hebrew and Greek alphabets interchange the individual letters with numbers. This method is employed in Psalm 119, the longest chapter in the Bible, consisting of 176 verses. The chapter is divided into sections of eight verses each, with each of the twenty-two Hebrew letters over the heading of each section, creating twenty-two sections.

THE SACREDNESS OF THE TORAH

Your personal Bible may have a black, brown, blue, or red leather or imitation leather cover. The words may be a fine-print, red-letter edition distinguishing Christ's words. Your translation may be the popular 1611 King James Version, New King James Version, Amplified, or New American Standard. It may have a red ribbon inserted to mark selective passages. Your Bible might be a translation from a language other than English. In the Jewish synagogue, the Torah is in the form of a scroll and not a leather-bound book.

The Jewish Scriptures read by the rabbi in a Jewish synagogue are penned by scribes on a large scroll. The scroll is rolled together on two wooden spindles, and the script is handwritten with special ink on a kosher, animal-skin parchment. The primary scroll in every synagogue is the Torah—Genesis through Deuteronomy. The other books in the synagogue consist of the Prophets (called the *Haftorah*), the writings, and the wisdom literature.

COPYING THE SACRED TEXT

Often critics will claim that the words (English translation) of our Bible cannot be trusted. They allege that throughout the centuries, copyists have made critical errors when scribing the individual letters and have added some words and omitted others. Those who make such statements are perhaps ignorant of the laws that were established by ancient scribes who were given the duty of copying the Scriptures.

1. *The parchment:* The parchment is made from the skin of a "clean" (kosher) animal. A Torah scroll consists of eighty skins. There are 248 columns on each scroll, and each section

holds 3 to 4 columns. There must be three inches across the top and two inches between the columns.

2. *The ink:* The ink consists of a special mixture made of gall-nuts, copper sulfate crystals, gum Arabic, and water. The ink is prepared in small amounts to prevent it from drying up while the scribe is meticulously penning the letters on the scroll. The ink must be very dark for the letters to be seen, and they must remain equal in color throughout the scroll.

3. *The pen:* A quill pen is used to write the letters. It must come from a clean animal. A goose feather is the choice of many scribes. The most important aspect is that the end of the quill must be cut precisely to ensure the letters are formed properly. Many pens are used when writing a scroll.[16]

Some have asked, How could a scribe ensure that there are no mistakes made when copying the individual letters? The scribes followed strict guidelines when preparing a new Torah scroll. These include:

- The new scroll had to be copied directly from another scroll. Nothing was copied from memory.

- The scribe must repeat every word out loud before writing the word down.

- If a Torah was written incorrectly, it could not be kept more than thirty days without being corrected or hidden.

- Every word and letter must be individually counted when it was completed.

- The script was written without vowels—just as they were in ancient times.

Every Hebrew letter and each line is individually examined to ensure that the form of each letter and line is correct. If a mistake is made, that section of the scroll is not permitted to be sewn together with the other parchments.

If there is a letter mistake, a scribe is permitted to scrape off that letter and remake it. It is, however, forbidden to erase the sacred name of God once that name has been penned on the parchment. If a mistake is made related to God's name, that section of the parchment must be buried in a special place for scrolls, and the process must begin again. There are three other trained persons who each examine the individual sections of the parchments before they are approved.

Once the parchments are completed, the scribe will take threads from the sinews of kosher animals (a cow, ox, or a sheep) and sew the back of the scroll in a special manner so the threads are not visible from the front. The large scroll is then placed on the two rollers, called in Hebrew *Etz Chayim*, or the "tree of life."

Writing God's name was so sacred that if a scribe was copying God's name on the parchment and a king walked in, the scribe was not permitted to look up until the name of God was completely written. It is reported that before and after writing God's name, the scribe's pen was wiped clean, and in ancient times scribes would leave the table and wash in honor of writing God's holy name on His holy Word. Each scroll was copied from a previous scroll, using the above guidelines and regulations when copying the Torah.

Is Today's Bible Correct?

Believers are often confronted by skeptics who bark out their opposition to our present translation of Scriptures, charging that the translation is not the same as the original Word God gave to Moses, the prophets, and the apostles. However, an event in 1948 helped settle the controversy of the authenticity of the 1611 translation of the English Scriptures as it relates to the Old Testament.

In 1947, a Bedouin shepherd boy was watching goats in the Judean wilderness near the western edge of the Dead Sea. Exploring several caves, he discovered a group of large clay jars. Inside were pieces of rolled, leather-like parchments. In 1948, the Bedouin sold seven parchments to Mr. Kando, a cobbler and antiquities dealer from Bethlehem, who eventually sold the scrolls. The most famous of the scrolls, it was discovered, was an ancient copy of the Book of Isaiah.

This valuable scroll was examined by scholars and purchased by the Hebrew University, who placed it on display at the Shrine of the Book Museum in Jerusalem. The scroll begins with the sixteenth chapter of

Isaiah and continues through Isaiah 66. To the amazement of scholars, when this two-thousand-year-old scroll was compared to the English translation of Isaiah from the 1611 King James translation of the Bible, they were both parallel, with the only exceptions being a few minor spelling differences and tense-oriented scribal errors. This discovery was good news to believers in the inspiration of the Bible and sad news to skeptics of divine inspiration.

Some Western Hebrew scholars occasionally point out that there are misspelled words in certain sections of the Old Testament. These are usually identified as mistakes by the copyist. Thus the inspiration of the Scriptures is minimized by alleged human mistakes. The Jewish rabbis, however, have discovered that these so-called mistakes actually reveal a deeper meaning or a cryptic prophetic secret, indicating future events.

MYSTERIES OF THE MISTAKES

When studying the Scriptures, Christian ministers often employ one of these methods to interpret or prepare a message:

1. The primary meaning—reading the story as a past or future event

2. The practical meaning—how the story or verse can be personally applied to us today

3. The prophetic meaning—how the prophetic symbols and layers reveal mysteries of the future

Jewish rabbis are taught to analyze the Torah by using four different methods. They are:

1. *Peshat*—understanding the *simple* meaning of the text

2. *Remez*—an *allusion*, or an *allegorical* and *philosophical* level of study

3. *Drash*—the *regal* level, the Bible is understood using *riddles* and *parables*

4. *Sod*—the *hidden* meaning or the *mystical* level[17]

Christ was a master at teaching on all four levels. He taught the simple and practical life truths through the Beatitudes, yet He also revealed the riddles using parables and privately revealed the mysteries of the kingdom to His disciples (Matt. 13:11).

The Jewish mystics spend abundant time searching the mystery level of the Torah and Hebrew alphabet. One such mystery has been called the *Esther code*. I first learned of this code in 1987 while visiting Israel. This code demonstrated that a biblical story can have both a literal (*Peshat*) and a hidden (*Sod*) prophetic application.

The theme of Esther is of a young Jewish orphan girl, named Hadassah, who won a national Persian beauty contest and became the wife of the Persian king. An evil governmental leader, Haman, conspired in secret to have the Jews killed but was himself exposed and hung with his ten sons on the very gallows he had prepared for the Jews. Years ago, a Jewish scholar working at the Qumran caves in Israel pointed out to me the amazing *double reference* found in the Hebrew text of Esther. Two important verses read:

> The ten sons of Haman the son of Hammedatha, the enemy of the Jews—they killed; but they did not lay a hand on the plunder.
>
> —ESTHER 9:10

> Then Esther said, "If it pleases the king, let it be granted to the Jews who are in Shushan to do again tomorrow according to today's decree, and let Haman's ten sons be hanged on the gallows."
>
> —ESTHER 9:13

Esther 9:10 said the Jews slew Haman's ten sons. Three verses later it says his ten sons were "hanged upon the gallows." Were they initially slain (v. 10), and their bodies then placed on the gallows (v. 13)? Why is the death of the ten sons mentioned twice? Or is this a double reference: to a *literal* and a *future* event? In the Esther story, Haman is a prophetic picture of the future Antichrist of prophecy, and Haman's ten sons are a prophetic preview of the ten kings of the Apocalypse who will arise and give their kingdom to the Antichrist (Rev. 17:12–17). This is a *prophetic layer* hidden in the story. If, however, we dig deeper into the actual Hebrew text, there is another message within the text.

Below is a list of Haman's ten sons:

1. Parshandatha
2. Dalphon
3. Aspatha
4. Poratha
5. Adalia
6. Aridatha
7. Parmashta
8. Arisai
9. Aridai
10. Vajezatha

In the Hebrew text, the first, seventh, and tenth names of Haman's sons have one Hebrew letter in each name that is one-half the size of the other Hebrew letters in the ten names. The three Hebrew letters are *tav, shin,* and *zayin.* When adding up the number value of these three letters, they total 5,706, which on the Jewish calendar becomes the Gregorian calendar year of 1946. On October 16, 1946, there were eleven Nazis scheduled to be hung for their war crimes against the Jews. Prior to the hanging, one Nazi, Herman Goring, committed suicide, leaving ten. When these ten Nazis were hung, their deaths fell on Purim, the celebration where Jews remember the defeat of Haman in Persia by Queen Esther! The Nazis' hanging fell on the Hebrew calendar on the twenty-first of Tishri, which is the seventh day of the Feast of Tabernacles, also called Hosanna Rabbah, the "Day of the Final Verdict."

The three smaller Hebrew letters in the Hebrew scroll of Esther were not formed in modern times but existed in that form and were copied in that manner for centuries. Yet, what some thought was a copyist's mistake was actually a prophetic clue of a future event that would one day repeat the same events recorded in the story of Esther.

יב בַּיּוֹם אֶחָד בְּכָל־מְדִינוֹת הַמֶּלֶךְ אֲחַשְׁוֵרוֹשׁ בִּשְׁלוֹשָׁה עָשָׂר לְחֹדֶשׁ שְׁנֵים־

יג עָשָׂר הוּא־חֹדֶשׁ אֲדָר: פַּתְשֶׁגֶן הַכְּתָב לְהִנָּתֵן דָּת בְּכָל־מְדִינָה וּמְדִינָה גָּלוּי לְכָל־הָעַמִּים וְלִהְיוֹת °הַיְּהוּדִיים עתודים [°הַיְּהוּדִים עֲתִידִים ק] לַיּוֹם

יד הַזֶּה לְהִנָּקֵם מֵאֹיְבֵיהֶם: הָרָצִים רֹכְבֵי הָרֶכֶשׁ הָאֲחַשְׁתְּרָנִים יָצְאוּ מְבֹהָלִים

טו וּדְחוּפִים בִּדְבַר הַמֶּלֶךְ וְהַדָּת נִתְּנָה בְּשׁוּשַׁן הַבִּירָה: וּמָרְדֳּכַי יָצָא מִלִּפְנֵי הַמֶּלֶךְ בִּלְבוּשׁ מַלְכוּת תְּכֵלֶת וָחוּר וַעֲטֶרֶת זָהָב גְּדוֹלָה

טז וְתַכְרִיךְ בּוּץ וְאַרְגָּמָן וְהָעִיר שׁוּשָׁן צָהֲלָה וְשָׂמֵחָה: לַיְּהוּדִים הָיְתָה אוֹרָה

יז וְשִׂמְחָה וְשָׂשֹׂן וִיקָר: וּבְכָל־מְדִינָה וּמְדִינָה וּבְכָל־עִיר וָעִיר מְקוֹם אֲשֶׁר דְּבַר־הַמֶּלֶךְ וְדָתוֹ מַגִּיעַ שִׂמְחָה וְשָׂשֹׂן לַיְּהוּדִים מִשְׁתֶּה וְיוֹם טוֹב וְרַבִּים

א מֵעַמֵּי הָאָרֶץ מִתְיַהֲדִים כִּי־נָפַל פַּחַד־הַיְּהוּדִים עֲלֵיהֶם: וּבִשְׁנֵים עָשָׂר חֹדֶשׁ הוּא־חֹדֶשׁ אֲדָר בִּשְׁלוֹשָׁה עָשָׂר יוֹם בּוֹ אֲשֶׁר הִגִּיעַ דְּבַר־הַמֶּלֶךְ וְדָתוֹ לְהֵעָשׂוֹת בַּיּוֹם אֲשֶׁר שִׂבְּרוּ אֹיְבֵי הַיְּהוּדִים לִשְׁלוֹט בָּהֶם וְנַהֲפוֹךְ

ב הוּא אֲשֶׁר יִשְׁלְטוּ הַיְּהוּדִים הֵמָּה בְּשֹׂנְאֵיהֶם: נִקְהֲלוּ הַיְּהוּדִים בְּעָרֵיהֶם בְּכָל־מְדִינוֹת הַמֶּלֶךְ אֲחַשְׁוֵרוֹשׁ לִשְׁלֹחַ יָד בִּמְבַקְשֵׁי רָעָתָם וְאִישׁ לֹא־

ג עָמַד לִפְנֵיהֶם כִּי־נָפַל פַּחְדָּם עַל־כָּל־הָעַמִּים: וְכָל־שָׂרֵי הַמְּדִינוֹת וְהָאֲחַשְׁדַּרְפְּנִים וְהַפַּחוֹת וְעֹשֵׂי הַמְּלָאכָה אֲשֶׁר לַמֶּלֶךְ מְנַשְּׂאִים אֶת־

ד הַיְּהוּדִים כִּי־נָפַל פַּחַד־מָרְדֳּכַי עֲלֵיהֶם: כִּי־גָדוֹל מָרְדֳּכַי בְּבֵית הַמֶּלֶךְ

ה וְשָׁמְעוֹ הוֹלֵךְ בְּכָל־הַמְּדִינוֹת כִּי־הָאִישׁ מָרְדֳּכַי הוֹלֵךְ וְגָדוֹל: וַיַּכּוּ הַיְּהוּדִים בְּכָל־אֹיְבֵיהֶם מַכַּת־חֶרֶב וְהֶרֶג וְאַבְדָן וַיַּעֲשׂוּ בְשֹׂנְאֵיהֶם כִּרְצוֹנָם:

טז וּבְשׁוּשַׁן הַבִּירָה הָרְגוּ הַיְּהוּדִים וְאַבֵּד חֲמֵשׁ מֵאוֹת אִישׁ:   וְאֵת ׀

פַּרְשַׁנְדָּתָא ◄   וְאֵת ׀

דַּלְפוֹן   וְאֵת ׀

ח אַסְפָּתָא: וְאֵת ׀

פּוֹרָתָא   וְאֵת ׀

אֲדַלְיָא   וְאֵת ׀

ט אֲרִידָתָא: וְאֵת ׀

פַּרְמַשְׁתָּא ◄   וְאֵת ׀

אֲרִיסַי   וְאֵת ׀

אֲרִדַי   וְאֵת ׀

וַיְזָתָא: ◄   עֲשֶׂרֶת

י בְּנֵי הָמָן בֶּן־הַמְּדָתָא צֹרֵר הַיְּהוּדִים הָרָגוּ וּבַבִּזָּה לֹא שָׁלְחוּ אֶת־יָדָם:

יא־יב בַּיּוֹם הַהוּא בָּא מִסְפַּר הַהֲרוּגִים בְּשׁוּשַׁן הַבִּירָה לִפְנֵי הַמֶּלֶךְ: וַיֹּאמֶר הַמֶּלֶךְ לְאֶסְתֵּר הַמַּלְכָּה בְּשׁוּשַׁן הַבִּירָה הָרְגוּ הַיְּהוּדִים וְאַבֵּד חֲמֵשׁ מֵאוֹת אִישׁ וְאֵת עֲשֶׂרֶת בְּנֵי־הָמָן בִּשְׁאָר מְדִינוֹת הַמֶּלֶךְ מֶה עָשׂוּ וּמַה־שְּׁאֵלָתֵךְ

In the Hebrew text, notice the three smaller letters in the names of Haman's sons.

THE NUMBER VALUE OF CERTAIN WORDS

While most Christian theologians reject this method of discovering *deeper truth* in the Scriptures, this method is used at various levels of rabbinical Judaism to discover a mystery within the words or the text. Two such examples are as follows.

The sacred name of God consists of four Hebrew letters, and each letter has a numerical equivalent.

The total number value of God's sacred name (*YHVH*) is twenty-six. I was informed in Israel that original acreage of the Temple Mountain consists of about twenty-six acres, matching God's name. This mountain is called the *mountain of the Lord* and the place God said He would put His name!

A second example is the name *Satan* in Hebrew. In 1 Kings 11:14, the English Bible mentions that God stirred up "an adversary against Solomon." The word *adversary* in Hebrew is *satan*. The phrase "the Satan" (*ha satan*) consists of four Hebrew letters, each letter with a number equivalent.

Yod	י	=	10
Hei	ה	=	5
Vav	ו	=	6
Hei	ה	=	5
			26

The sacred name of God, called the *tetragrammaton*, is spelled with four Hebrew letters.

Rabbis teach that there are 365 days in a solar year, and the phrase *the satan* totals 364. When subtracting 364 from 365, it leaves the number 1. The rabbinic teaching says that there is one day each year when Satan is bound and cannot touch a person, and that is the Day of Atonement, when the priest intercedes and God removes the sins of Israel.

There are numerous biblical Hebrew words that have various values and combinations revealing special meanings. Some Christians, who believe this system should

Hei	ה	=	5
Shin	ש	=	300
Tet	ט	=	9
Nun	ן	=	50
			364

The Hebrew phrase "The Satan" has four Hebrew letters totaling 364.

not be employed, may not be aware that it is used in the New Testament in the Book of Revelation, where John reveals the name and number of the future beast, the Antichrist:

He causes all, both small and great, rich and poor, free and slave, to receive a mark on their right hand or on their foreheads, and that no one may buy or sell except one who has the mark or the name of the beast, or the number of his name. Here is wisdom. Let him who has understanding calculate the number of the beast, for it is the number of a man: His number is 666.

—REVELATION 13:16–18

John was using a system familiar to Jewish rabbis called *gematria*, which exchanges the Hebrew or Greek letters of a person's name and gives them a preassigned numerical value. This system was also employed by several early fathers of Christianity when they attempted to interpret John's enigma of the mark of the beast. John had a student named Polycarp, and Irenaeus (A.D. 140–203) sat under Polycarp. Irenaeus recorded one example of *gematria* when he discovered that the word *lateinos* had a numerical total of 666.

L	A	T	E	I	N	O	S
30	1	300	5	10	50	70	200
TOTAL NUMERICAL VALUE—666							

Irenaeus said, "It seems to me very probable: for this is a name of the last of Daniel's four kingdoms; they being the Latins that now reign." Since the fourth empire of Bible prophecy was Rome, and Rome ruled in the days of most early fathers, it was commonly accepted that the Roman Empire would rule as the final empire prior to Christ's return. Eventually, political Rome faded into history and was replaced by the Roman Church, whose influence in Europe and portions of the Middle East controlled the rise and fall of empires for centuries. The Latin language was accepted and used in the church, thus the interpretation of the phrase *lateinos*, alluding to the number 666, maintained a strong following although this method of interpretation is not accepted by most contemporary scholars.

Counting the Letters and the Hebrew Calendar

A Torah scroll has no chapters or verses on the parchment. In a Bible, chapters were added to the translation in A.D. 1227 by Stephen Langton, archbishop of Canterbury. The Wycliffe Bible was the first to use chapter and verse headings. The Hebrew Bible was divided into chapters and verses in 1448 by Rabbi Nathan. Although the chapters and verses were placed by men in the Scripture, a strange and amazing pattern emerges when counting the verses in Deuteronomy and comparing the verses to the actual Jewish year. This is the concept that each verse in the Torah corresponds with a date on the Jewish calendar. The number of verses in the Torah are:

Among the mystics, there is a belief that each verse in the Torah corresponds to a year on the Jewish calendar. According to several rabbinical sources (depending on the count), beginning in Genesis 1:1 and counting to the 5,708th verse in the Torah, we come to Deuteronomy 30:3:

Genesis	1,533 verses
Exodus	1,213 verses
Leviticus	859 verses
Numbers	1,288 verses
Deuteronomy	959 verses
	5,852 total verses

> That the LORD your God will bring you back from captivity, and have compassion on you, and gather you again from all the nations where the LORD your God has scattered you.

This is an ancient promise that the Jews will return from their captivity in other nations and be regathered back to the land of Israel. This 5,708th verse in the Torah corresponds to the secular year 1948. In 1948 the world had compassion on the Jews, and Israel was rebirthed as a nation! God gathered the Jews from the lands where they were scattered. The Jewish year matches the Torah prediction. Is this a coincidence, or is this rabbinical level of interpretation called *Sod* the mystery level of interpreting the Torah?

Meanings in the Years

Since each letter of the Hebrew alphabet holds a number value, numbers can also be translated back to letters of the alphabet. For example, the number one represents *alef*, the first letter of the Hebrew alphabet. The number two is *beit*, the second letter, while the number three is the value of *gimel*, the third letter, and so on. This numbering system concludes with *tav*, the twenty-second letter, whose value is four hundred. Rabbis began to notice that when Jewish years are translated back to letters of the alphabet, at times they contain a *code* revealing a prophetic event or theme that occurred on that particular year. I will share one example.

The year 1997–1998 on the Gregorian calendar was the Jewish year 5758. (The years overlap, as the Jewish new year begins in the fall, and our new year begins January 1.) When translating the Jewish year 5758 to the value of the Hebrew letters, the last two numbers, 58, are the Hebrew letter *nun*, whose value is 50, and *chet*, whose value is 8. These two letters, *nun* and *chet*, spell *Noach*, the Hebrew name for Noah, whose name means "rest."[18] How does 1997–1998 relate to Noah? In 1997–1998 a great comet named Hale-Bopp, fifty thousand times brighter than Halley's Comet, swept through the universe. According to Christian astronomers, the last time it was seen on Earth was at the same time Noah was preparing the ark. Hebrew teacher Bill Cloud states that an ancient Jewish tradition holds that Noah saw a huge comet that warned him of the soon destruction of the earth.[19] Thus, the Jewish year translated to the Hebrew alphabet contains the name of Noah, and the same year a cosmic sign was seen in the heavens, which was linked to the days of Noah. This reminds believers that, "as the days of Noah were, so also will the coming of the Son of Man be" (Matt. 24:37).

Are these many examples coincidences? Are they the product of an over-imaginative Hebraic mind or a rabbi's fantasy, attempting to demonstrate the inspiration of the Torah? I believe they are simply proof of the divine inspiration of the Scripture.

THE RABIN CODE

Yitzhak Rabin was prime minister in Israel until he was suddenly assassinated after a peace rally in Tel Aviv on November 4, 1995, by Yigal Amir, a Jewish radical. After Rabin's death, Jewish rabbis pointed out a rather bizarre *coincidence*. The day before the assassination was the Jewish Sabbath. In the synagogues, the verses being read were from the story of God passing between the sacrificial offering, confirming Abraham's covenant for the land. Rabbis saw the verse in the Hebrew text and noticed that if you simply change the spacing between the letters, a message would be formed that is known today as the *Rabin code*. The passage reads: "...fire which passed between these pieces" (Gen. 15:17, The Chumash). When the spaces are changed between the Hebrew words in the Genesis 15:17 phrase, it reads, *esh esh ra' b'rabin*, or, "fire, evil fire against Rabin." The prime minister was shot twice, an allusion to the firing of two bullets. Some suggest this *code* was already known, and the Jewish man who killed Rabin was attempting to fulfill the prediction, but there is no evidence of such. It does, however, reveal the amazing *layers* of prophetic revelation in the Torah and how future events can be encoded in the text.

אש אשר עבר בין

"...fire that passed between..." Gen. 15:17

אש אש רע ברבין

"Fire, evil fire against Rabin."

This scripture was being read the day that former
Israeli Prime Minister Rabin was assassinated.

PROTECTING THE WORD OF GOD

Torah-observant Jews are extremely respectful of the Torah scroll. In each synagogue, the Torah scroll is placed in a special case called an ark. The scroll is rolled up, and a beautiful, embroidered cover is placed over the scroll to keep dust from collecting on it. When the time comes to remove the scroll for reading, a man is appointed to carefully remove the scroll from the ark and uncover it, placing it on the platform for the speaker. The speaker actually never places his finger on the scroll itself but will use a metal or wooden instrument about eight inches long, called a *yad*, which resembles a small hand with a single index finger pointing upward. Called *the finger of God*, this object is used by the reader and speaker to follow the lines of the text. This serves a dual purpose: it preserves the sanctity of the scroll, and it prevents oily, human fingers from eventually erasing the black-inked letters on the parchment.

It should be pointed out that the Torah is dressed to imitate the high priest's garments. In Exodus 28, the outfit of the priests included a tunic, a belt, a crown, and a breastplate. These four items are a part of the Torah's decoration in the synagogue.

The *tunic* is the beautiful embroidered covering for the scroll, similar to the blue garment of the high priest. Just as the high priest had a crown placed on his head, each Torah scroll has a beautiful *crown* of silver that sits atop the handle of the roller. The priest's garment had a special belt fitting around the waist. Likewise, a *sash* ties the scroll together before placing the adorning cover over it. The high priest also was given a unique breastplate of gold with twelve embedded gemstones engraved with the names of the twelve tribes. A *silver plate*, similar to the priest's breastplate, is hung over the top of the wooden rollers.

The Torah is so holy that it is considered on the same level as a human being. Heroic stories are told of Jewish men who risked their lives through the smoke and the flames to rescue a Torah scroll from its ark when synagogues were burned in Europe in years past. This should come as no surprise, since the apostle Paul wrote: "For the word of God is quick, and powerful, and sharper than any twoedged sword" (Heb. 4:12, kjv). The Greek word *quick* means "alive"! I have in my personal possession a three-hundred-year-old nonkosher (meaning the ink has faded) Torah scroll given as a gift from a Jewish family from a Russian synagogue. It is encased in a wooden case. I still can sense a special awe when I see it.

After a scroll is used for many years, the ink on the parchment can begin to fade. Once the Hebrew text becomes unreadable, the scroll is not destroyed but is removed from its place and is buried in a Jewish cemetery just like a person. This is because the Torah gives life to the believer and must be respected in burial in the same manner of a righteous person.

How Do You Treat Your Bible?

Compare the detailed and careful treatment of the Torah to the manner in which some Christians treat their Bibles. Most Christians have many Bibles and translations available that are often strewed randomly throughout the house, buried under piles of magazines, or accumulating dust on a shelf, undisturbed for days on end. Other Bibles are permanent fixtures in the pew racks of local churches and are opened briefly each Sunday morning when the pastor reads his sermon text.

When you consider the high price paid to translate and print the Bible, you will experience fresh gratitude for God's Word. In the 1380s, Oxford scholar Wycliffe, opposing the organized religions of his day, handwrote a manuscript of the Bible. His followers, called the *Loddards*, translated and copied by hand hundreds of Bibles. Forty-four years later, the pope dug up the bones of Wycliffe and had them scattered. John Hus, a follower of Wycliffe, continued the work of copying God's Word. He was burned alive, with pages from a Wycliffe Bible used for kindling the fire.[20] For some, the price of translating the Scripture was martyrdom.

Today in some Islamic countries, a believer could be beheaded or arrested for reading or preaching from a Bible. In Communist nations such as China, believers have been incarcerated and tortured if found reading or studying a Bible. In 1990, I met a minister from Bulgaria who, while under Communism, possessed only one page from a Bible, which was John 11. For years he preached to his small, secret group of twelve believers, reading the same message each week—the resurrection of Lazarus. To him this one page was priceless.

Christians must take a lesson from our Jewish friends and treat our Bibles with dignity and respect as we would a living person. After all, Paul proclaimed that the "Word of God is living and powerful..." (Heb. 4:12).

THE SACRED NAME OF GOD

The same admonition can be given regarding verbal usage of the name of God. The revelation of God's name was considered so sacred that God Himself established the third commandment: "You shall not take the name of the LORD your God in vain" (Exod. 20:7). This law was so serious that if a Hebrew was caught abusing or speaking evil of God's name, he was labeled a *blasphemer* and was stoned for his disrespect (Lev. 24:11–14).

Today, we often carelessly say things like, "Dear God...O God...My Lord..." Although these phrases are repeated as a casual *comment* or a sudden reaction to some negative situation, we must guard against accidentally misusing the name of God.

In Hebrew, the sacred, divine name of God is spelled with four Hebrew letters: *yod, hei, vav,* and *hei,* or, in English, *YHVH.* This four-lettered name is called the *tetragrammaton,* which means "four letters." This name, *YHVH,* is found 6,823 times in the Hebrew Bible. Hebrew scholars and rabbis all agree that the exact pronunciation of these four letters has been lost throughout the centuries. Some suggest the name is pronounced *Yehovah* or *Yahweh,* while westerners say *Jehovah,* replacing the first letter Y (*yud* in Hebrew) with the English letter J, which does not exist in the Hebrew alphabet. It is Jewish practice never to write this sacred name, but to replace it with the name *Adonai,* meaning, "the Lord." There is also a rabbinical tradition of saying God's name simply as *Ha-Shem,* meaning "the Name."[21]

The Jewish *Mishna* teaches that the high priest would pronounce the tetragrammaton when pronouncing the priestly blessing (Num. 6:24–27). However, outside of the temple, the name was replaced with *Adonai.* The *Mishna* also teaches that on the Day of Atonement (*Yom Kippur*), the sacred name was spoken, causing the people to fall upon their faces and begin blessing the name of the Lord.[22]

If you have ever read a Jewish religious book, you will notice something that appears odd to non-Jewish readers. When writing the name *GOD,* the Jewish writer will leave out the O and write it *G-D.* One reason is because if the paper gets lost, erased, or placed in the garbage, God's name has not been fully written; therefore, it is not defiled. The same is true if it were written fully on paper; they do not wish to erase or defile God's name.

THE PURPOSE OF THE NAME

In the Old Testament God revealed Himself, His nature, and His character by His names. In fact, there are sixteen important names for God revealed throughout the Old Testament. Below is a list of those titles or special names, which reveal the nature of God.[23]

The Compound Names	The Meaning of the Names	The Scripture Reference
Jehovah Elohim	The eternal creator	Genesis 2:4–25
Adonai Jehovah	The Lord our master	Genesis 15:2

The Compound Names	The Meaning of the Names	The Scripture Reference
Jehovah Jireh	The Lord the provider	Genesis 22:8–14
Jehovah Nissi	The Lord our banner	Exodus 17:15
Jehovah Ropheka	The Lord our healer	Exodus 15:26
Jehovah Shalom	The Lord our peace	Judges 6:24
Jehovah Tsidkeenu	The Lord our righteousness	Jeremiah 23:6
Jehovah Mekaddishkem	The Lord our sanctifier	Exodus 31:13
Jehovah Sabaoth	The Lord of hosts	1 Samuel 1:11
Jehovah Shammah	The Lord is present	Ezekiel 48:35
Jehovah Elyon	The Lord Most High	Psalm 7:17
Jehovah Rohi	The Lord my shepherd	Psalm 23:1
Jehovah Hoseenu	The Lord our maker	Psalm 95:6
Jehovah Eloheenu	The Lord our God	Psalm 99:5
Jehovah Eloheka	The Lord thy God	Exodus 20:2
Jehovah Elohay	The Lord my God	Zechariah 14:5

I am using the English transliteration of God's sacred name for the purposes of our English readers. The actual Hebrew name for Jehovah is Yahweh or Yehovah.

Ancient Hebrews would often approach God saying, "In the name of the God of Abraham, Isaac, and Jacob" (Exod. 3:6, 15–16). Christians approach the heavenly throne through the name of Christ, as the New Testament says: "Whatever you ask the Father in My name He will give you" (John 16:23). "Therefore God also has highly exalted Him and given Him the name which is above every name" (Phil. 2:9).

Whether we approach God using *Ha Shem, Adonai,* Lord, Father, or, as Christians, approach the Creator using the name of Christ, we must always remember the sacredness and holiness attached to His name. It is a commandment to do so.

There are many unique aspects and layers of prophetic mysteries linked to the Hebrew alphabet. Since it originated in heaven, we may one day speak it in heaven.

■ ■ ■ ✡ ■ ■ ■

WHAT *God* KNEW

When God revealed His heavenly mysteries and spiritual code to Moses and the prophets, it was heard and written in an early form of the Hebrew language. The Hebrew letters and words hold many levels of mysteries and possible combinations that reveal this language is sacred and important to God.

WHAT DEVOUT *Jews* KNOW

Jews treat the Torah as a living person and the Hebrew language as the sacred tongue spoken in heaven. The Jewish people have preserved the Torah and the Scriptures for each succeeding generation to read and live by. The fact that devout Jews have honored the written Word of God and the Torah scroll and preserved the holiness of God's name has marked them as a special people above all other nations on the earth.

WHAT *Christians* SHOULD KNOW

Christians must view the Scriptures as more than a Bible translation published by a particular publishing company. The printed book is the written revelation of God for mankind and has cost the blood, sweat, tears, and lives of countless numbers of believers who have been willing to give their lives to protect the integrity of the Scriptures.

Not only must the Bible be treated with the highest respect and honor, but the name of God must also never be spoken in vain.

Chapter 4

GOD'S FEASTS, SABBATHS, AND SPECIAL FAMILY CELEBRATIONS

CODE 4:
The Hebrew God loves to have a celebration.

Sing aloud to God our strength;
Make a joyful shout to the God of Jacob.
Raise a song and strike the timbrel,
The pleasant harp with the lute.
Blow the trumpet at the time of the New Moon,
At the full moon, on our solemn feast day.

—PSALM 81:1–3

THE LITTLE GIRL ASKED, "DADDY, WHY IS THAT MAN DRESSED SO strange?" He was an Orthodox Jew dressed in traditional Hassidic black clothing with dark curls bouncing from his temples off his cheeks. He was placing a white prayer shawl over his head, and a small black box looked like it was glued to the upper part of his head. To those outside his religion, he looked rather peculiar.

I knew the feeling of *looking peculiar* while I was growing up. My father was the pastor of a traditional full gospel church. Our denominational *practical teachings* forbade members to wear shorts in public, and women were not permitted to wear slacks (pants)—only dresses. No jewelry, including wedding rings, was to be donned, and wearing makeup was a no-no. Most women never cut their hair but wore it towering high on their head. We did this because of our interpretation of certain scriptures in the New Testament and also from traditions handed down from our spiritual fathers. Just like our Jewish friends, we were tagged very *peculiar* and *odd* by nonbelievers living in the community.

I do not regret being raised in this conservative manner, as my ancestors were very godly, God-fearing, praying believers. However, growing up I tended to perceive that God was very strict and rigid, mostly angry at His Creation and only *really* loved us when we attended church, revivals, or camp meetings. After studying the many celebrations God established in the Torah, I am excited to discover that God really loves to join in with His children and have a good time. In fact, He loves to celebrate! I came to the conclusion that God requires His people to live a holy life, but He despises man-made legalism that requires more than what He does. Although He hates sin, He loves sinners.

I have also learned that once we enter the covenant of redemption, we join a new spiritual nation (1 Pet. 2:9) and should enjoy our families, our jobs, and the fellowship of fellow believers. We should experience seasons of refreshing and celebration, just as God established yearly seasons of rejoicing for the Hebrew nation.

THE CELEBRATIONS

In the American culture there are basically two *religious* and *personal* celebrations recognized each year. Traditional American Christians celebrate what the West calls Easter and Christmas, recalling the birth and resurrection of Christ. Each year most Americans recognize birthdays and anniversaries of friends and family. With three hundred sixty-five days in a year, Americans set aside four days for some form of "celebration" (not counting July 4 or Thanksgiving).

Torah-observant Jews recognize seven God-appointed celebrations called the feasts, which are recorded in Leviticus 23. These appointed times, called *moedim* in Hebrew, are designated yearly convocations. In Leviticus 23:6, the Hebrew word *feast* is *chag*, whose root word is *chagag*, meaning, "to move in a circle" or "to dance." The implication is that a time of *rejoicing* was set aside by God for His people. Each feast includes specific instructions, special meals (except fasting on the Day of Atonement), and freedom from work. Many feasts involve the entire family. Beginning in the spring (usually March or April) and continuing into the fall (usually September and October), these seven festivals are as shown below.

The English Name	The Hebrew Name	The Jewish Time of Celebration
Passover	*Pesach*	First month, fourteenth day
Unleavened Bread	*Chag Ha Matzot*	First month, fifteenth to twenty-first days
Firstfruits	*Bikkurim*	First month, day after the Sabbath of Unleavened Bread
Pentecost	*Shavuot*	Fifty days from Firstfruits
Trumpets	*Yom Teruah*	Seventh month, first day
Atonement	*Yom Kippur*	Seventh month, tenth day
Tabernacles	*Sukkot*	Seventh month, fifteenth to twenty-first days

In addition to the feasts listed above, a special celebration called *Rejoicing in the Torah* is held in the seventh month, twenty-second day (or the eighth day of Tabernacles).

The amazing feature of these festivals is their threefold application: practical, spiritual, and prophetic. The practical application is that they are timed around Israel's seed planting, rain, and harvest cycles. The firstfruits of barley were harvested and presented to the priest at the temple just after Passover (Lev. 23:4–11). The wheat was presented at Pentecost, and the final ingathering of fruit was during the Feast of Tabernacles (Exod. 34:22). The grain and fruit harvests centered on the two rain cycles in Israel called the *former* and *latter* rain (Joel 2:23). The Feast of Tabernacles had special rituals at the temple calling for the winter rains to appear.

These celebrations also marked significant spiritual events linked to Israel:

- *Passover*—reminded the Israelites of their deliverance from Egypt when death passed over their homes.

- *Unleavened Bread*—reminded the Israelites of their quick departure from Egypt, (bread without leaven).

- *Firstfruits*—was to celebrate the first visible ripening of the barley harvest.

- *Pentecost*—was a reminder of God revealing the Law to Moses on Mount Sinai.

- *Trumpets*—was a memorial of blowing trumpets.

- *Atonement*—was marked as the day, once a year, when the high priest would atone for Israel's sins.

- *Tabernacles*—was to remember the forty years of Israel wandering in the wilderness.

These festivals also hold a prophetic application. They are a preview of major prophetic events that will occur in the future, linked to the Messiah's appearing and His kingdom.

The Feast	The Past or Future Prophetic Fulfillment
Passover	Christ was crucified the evening before Passover.
Unleavened Bread	Christ, the sinless sacrifice (without leaven), was in the tomb.
Firstfruits	Christ was alive and seen as the firstfruits of the resurrection of the dead.
Pentecost	The birth of the Christian church occurred in Jerusalem on Pentecost.
Trumpets	This feast carries the imagery of the return of Christ and the first resurrection.
Atonement	This yearly event is a picture of the coming judgments of God, called the Tribulation.
Tabernacles	This feast is a picture of the future reign of Messiah in Jerusalem.

Concerning the Jewish feasts, Paul wrote that they were a shadow of "things to come" (Col. 2:17). He was alluding to the fact that Christ and the church had fulfilled several prophetic applications of certain Jewish festivals, as stated above.

FREEDOM FROM WORK

God required all men over twenty years of age to make a pilgrimage to Jerusalem during three festivals: Passover, Pentecost, and Tabernacles (Exod. 23:14–17). Remembering and honoring all seven festivals meant exemption from work.

The Celebration	The Reference	Freedom From Work
Passover, Unleavened Bread	Leviticus 23:5	You shall do no work.
Firstfruits	Leviticus 23:8	You shall do not work on the seventh day.
Pentecost	Leviticus 23:16–21	You shall do no work.
Trumpets	Leviticus 23:24–25	You shall do no servile work.
Atonement	Leviticus 23:27–28	You shall do no work.
Tabernacles	Leviticus 23:34–35	You shall do no servile work.

Imagine all men over age twenty coming together three times a year at one location for spiritual renewal, celebrating in God's presence, eating special meals, and bonding with their fellow brethren. Being a fourth-generation minister, I can tell you there is nothing quite like a time of extended fellowship with other believers. Each year we conduct three to six major conferences, which continue for five days with nine services. They carry the feeling of a giant family reunion and are becoming highlights each year for our close friends and ministry partners.

PURIM AND HANUKKAH

Although Purim and Hanukkah are not required festivals in the Torah, they developed into minor celebrations due to the amazing, significant events they represent. Purim, which means "lots," is a yearly reminder of how an orphaned Jewish girl named Hadassah won a beauty contest, married Ahasuerus the king of Persia, and became the famed Queen Esther. By finding favor with the king, she intervened, saving the Jews in the Persian Empire from perishing. (See the Book of Esther.)

Today, in Jewish communities, Purim is a yearly reminder honoring Esther's defeat of an enemy named Haman and God's deliverance and perseverance of the Jews living in 120 provinces of the Persian Empire. Today Purim is preceded by the *Fast of Esther*. On Purim, Jews read the *Megillah* (Scroll of Esther) in the synagogue, distribute charity to the poor, including gifts of food, and enjoy a festive meal. Jewish children dress up in costumes reminding them of the great deliverance God performed through the Jewish queen of Persia.[1]

Christians are taught that there were four centuries of *silence* between the Testaments. Malachi, the last book of the Christian Old Testament, is identified as the last Hebrew prophet before John the Baptist appeared four hundred years later. The alleged *silent years* were actually broken by an event occurring about 167 years before Christ at the temple in Jerusalem.

THE OIL AND THE LIGHT

In the year of 167 B.C., the Jews were facing extreme persecution from a notorious leader named Antiochus Epiphanes. Nicknamed "the mad man," Antiochus replaced Jewish priests with Greek priests, offered forbidden sacrifices to idol gods on the temple altar, and stopped Jewish Sabbath worship. He forbade Jewish circumcision and prevented Jews from celebrating the feasts. On the twenty-fifth of Kislev (December) 167 B.C., the temple altar was defiled when Antiochus offered a swine to his god Zeus. An observant priest, Matthias, and his five sons (the Maccabees) initiated a revolt against the Greek occupiers that continued for three years, ending on Kislev 25.

The Jews purified the temple, prepared new sacred vessels, hung a new veil, and placed fresh bread on the table of showbread (1 Macc. 4:50–51). The real miracle, however, involved the gold seven-branched candlestick, called the *menorah*. In the temple the Jewish victors found only one jar of oil with the priestly seal, which could provide light for only one day. The menorah was to burn and be replenished with fresh oil daily (Exod. 27:20).

It would take one week for olive oil to be found and prepared for the menorah. However, the jug of oil continued to provide light for eight days.[2] This miracle birthed a yearly winter celebration called Hanukkah, also known as the Feast of Lights.[3] The temple candelabra holds seven branches, while a Hanukkah menorah has nine. During Hanukkah, observant Jews light one branch each day for eight days as the intriguing story of the temple rededication is retold. The ninth branch is called a *shamash* (servant) lamp and is lit each night also.

JESUS CELEBRATED HANUKKAH

Some Christians are surprised to discover that Jesus (remember He was Jewish) went to Jerusalem to celebrate Hanukkah.

> Now it was the Feast of Dedication in Jerusalem, and it was winter.
> —John 10:22

In Christ's day, this celebration was called *the Feast of Dedication*. Since Hanukkah is celebrated on the twenty-fifth of Kislev, and Kislev falls around the winter months (often in December), Jesus was at Jerusalem during winter. At that time, four large menorahs were placed outside the temple's outer court. Priests would ascend large ladders and pour fresh oil in the branches to keep the temple compound bright. It was said that a person could stand upon the Mount of Olives and read a scroll at night because of the brightness of the lights.

It was also during this setting when Christ announced He was the "light of the world" and then proceeded to cure a blind man. Just as Hanukkah was a celebration of oil and light, Jesus was the light of the world, using the *oil of the Spirit* (anointing) to bring light to a blind man (John 9).

HANUKKAH TODAY

Today in a Jewish home, Hanukkah is a highly anticipated celebration involving the entire family, especially children. One Jewish friend explained this yearly tradition to Christians, saying, "The food, traditions, and gift giving are like a 'Jewish Christmas.'"

During the eight days of Hanukkah, meals are fried or baked with oil.

The mother prepares *latkes*, Yiddish for potato pancakes, with applesauce, and, in many communities, fruit-filled doughnuts grace the tables. Gifts are exchanged over an eight-day period. The children play games with a *dreidel*, a top with four sides, marked with four Hebrew letters. The letters are:

- *Nun*
- *Gimel*
- *Hei*
- *Shin*

These four letters are an acronym for the Hebrew phrase, *Nes Gadol Haya Sham*, meaning, "A great miracle happened there," referring to the miracle of the temple oil and menorah.[4] As the candles are lit, children play the game, starting with fifteen coins, or candy and nuts. Each player begins, placing something in the pot on the table. The player will spin the *dreidel*, landing on one of four Hebrew letters, which determines the action they take. The following is based on the Yiddish version:

- Landing on *Nun, nothing*—the next player spins.

- Landing on *Gimel, all*—the player takes the entire pot.

- Landing on *Hei, half*—the player takes half the pot, rounding up if there is an odd number.

- Landing on *Shin, put in*—the player puts one or two objects (coins, nuts, etc.), in the pot.

The game continues until one player wins everything in the pot. Some Jews teach that the four Hebrew letters also allude to the four kingdoms Israel was subjected to—Babylon, Persia, Greece, and Rome. Yet, like the *dreidel*, these empires eventually quit spinning and came crashing to an end.

As stated earlier, the traditional Christian Christmas falls on December 25 and lasts for one day. Hanukkah, however, is celebrated for eight days. During one Hanukkah, some close friends staying in our home brought their Hanukkah menorah. My little girl loves stories, so each night I told the story as the candle was lit. I was very amused when our small daughter said, "Dad, I like Hanukkah. I like the story, and I get a gift every day!"

It is clear that God loves celebrations, and observant Jews know how to celebrate.

REASONS FOR CELEBRATING

I believe there are other reasons why these appointed times are significant.

Application 1—Reminders of God's blessings

In his book *In Those Days, at This Time*, author Gideon Weitzman writes:

> The yearly celebrations of the seven Jewish festivals are not just to remind the Jews of their past. Rather, each of the seven has a theme from the past that continues to impact the future. Passover is linked to freedom, while Tabernacles reveals Divine Protection. The Day of Atonement, *Rosh HaShanah*, is a reminder of God's forgiveness and His power to renew the people. During the festivals, particular prayers are offered by the Jews giving God thanks for delivering, protecting, and directing their ancestors. They then ask God to continue to perform the same miracles for them today and for their children tomorrow.[5]

Just as Western holidays are reminders of past events, the Jewish festivals are yearly reminders of God's goodness to His people, delivering, protecting, and restoring them to Israel, the land of their covenant.

Application 2—Rest from their labors (the Sabbath)

God created everything in six days, and He rested on the seventh day (Gen. 2:2). This initiated a set time each week called the Sabbath, or *Shabbat* in Hebrew, which means "to rest or to lay aside labor." There are Hebrew words translated *rest* in the English translation of the Torah. They include: *shabath*, which alludes to letting go (Exod. 23:11); *shamat*, alluding to letting alone; and *nuwach*, to settle down (Isa. 23:12). They all carry the same connotation. A *shabbat* was a personal letting go and resting. God commanded that the land and animals rest and be "let alone" in order to fulfill the commandment.

The theme of resting from labor was so important that God hallowed the seventh day each week as a Sabbath of rest. Every seventh year was a Sabbatical rest year (called *Shemitah* in Hebrew). Every seven cycles of seven years—forty-nine years—was designated a Jubilee cycle of complete rest. During these three Sabbatical cycles, people, animals, and the land enjoyed exemption from work (Exod. 23:10–12; Lev. 25:4–55). With each of the seven feasts, God commanded the people to refrain from work. The Sabbath was created for man's enjoyment:

> And He said to them, "The Sabbath was made for man, and not man for the Sabbath."
>
> —MARK 2:27

The physical body needs rest, and the heart rate slows down every seventh day (this may be why people tend to take a *nap* on the Sabbath).[6] During every seventh year, a Sabbatical year, when the land and animals were to rest, no plowing, planting, reaping, or harvesting took place. The practical reason was that this method allowed the fruit to drop to the ground and rot back into the soil, providing minerals back to the topsoil every seven years.

Israel was taken into Babylon captivity for seventy years because they broke the law of the Jubilee cycle (Lev. 25–26), which required the land to rest. God punished the Jews, sending them into Babylon for seventy years so the land could enjoy her Sabbaths (2 Chron. 36:20–21).

The Jewish Sabbath begins at 6:00 p.m. on Friday evening and concludes at 6:00 p.m. on Saturday evening, a period of twenty-four hours. For devout Jews, this is a complete time of rest from work and includes three meals and family time. A normal Jewish Sabbath proceeds as follows:

1. The woman lights two candles to welcome the Sabbath, done, in some communities, together as a family.

2. A blessing is recited over the candles.[7]

3. The family arrives and sits down for the meal, perhaps singing a song, "Peace to You."

4. The father then lays hands on his children and blesses them or embraces them. (See the next chapter.)

5. The husband honors his wife by reading to her of the virtuous woman from Proverbs 31.

6. The blessing over the wine or grape juice, called the *Shabbat Kiddush*, is said (Sabbath sanctification).

7. There is a blessing said over the bread.

8. Once the sun has set, from 6:00 p.m. Friday to 6:00 p.m. Saturday, it is common to greet one another with *Shabbat Shalom*, or Sabbath peace.[8]

When I was a child, there were no stores, gas stations, or restaurants open on Sunday. This gave owners, staff, and workers time to worship in a local church of their choice and spend quality time with family. During the week, our family often ate hamburgers, spaghetti, and sandwiches, but we knew that Sunday was coming, and Mom would cook a *real* Sunday dinner—the best roast beef in the neighborhood always accompanied by mashed potatoes. Throughout the entire day, people spoke about the Lord and the Bible, edifying one another in the faith. Later, at six o'clock in the evening, we went back to church for the evening service.

With today's fast-food restaurants and busy schedules, home cooking is becoming a lost art. Now on the average Sabbath, Mom and Dad exit the front door, the kids head out the back door, and the neighbors pop in to say hello through the side door. In America, the Sabbath day has become just another day of the week to work, clean house, shop, and perform routine activities. Perhaps this is why Americans remain tired, guzzling energy drinks and experiencing stress-related illnesses—we are breaking God's commandment to rest on the seventh day. We are working seven days a week. The feasts provided special seasons to cease from work, but the Sabbath provides one day a week to just *chill out* and enjoy a word from the Lord in His house.

Application 3—Bringing men together for bonding and fellowship

In Jewish thought, the man is not just the head of the home but also the spiritual *priest* of the family. Since the oldest male son carried on the family name and secured the family inheritance, it was important to God that the male child would understand the significance of his responsibility and position. In Exodus 13, Moses said that if a male child was the firstborn in his mother's womb, that child was set apart and holy. When my wife became pregnant in 1989, a friend who was familiar with the Torah said to me, "Your first child will be a boy, because a minister of God must have a male child first." (He was basing his statement on the passage from Exodus 13:12–14.)

Young boys often have a special bond with their mothers, and young girls with their fathers. When all males over twenty journeyed to Jerusalem three times a year, an important male bonding occurred, bringing the men together in one location for spiritual renewal and fellowship.

Application 4—Encountering God's presence at the temple

In ancient Israel the synagogue was the local weekly gathering place, and the Jerusalem temple housed the presence of God. Each Sabbath the community gathered at the synagogue, and, during the special feasts, the men made pilgrimage to the sacred temple, presenting lambs, firstfruits, tithes, and offerings or seeking renewal and repentance. The temple was the dwelling place for God's presence.

While I was growing up, my father pastored in Virginia. We attended church on Sunday mornings, Sunday nights, and Wednesday nights, never missing a revival or special service unless we were sick. Each month the district hosted youth rallies, followed by a meal (usually "fast food"). These monthly youth meetings created relationships we cherished.

Today the average American Christian spends two hours in church once a week. It is virtually impossible to establish relationships and fellowship with believers in such a brief encounter, not to mention that two hours in a worship service leaves one hundred sixty-six remaining hours to work, sleep, eat, and fulfill our personal desires.[9] The weekly encounters and yearly feasts provided time in God's Word with God's people in God's presence—something we could all use a lot more of.

■ ■ ■ ✡ ■ ■ ■

WHAT *God* KNEW

Israel, being an agrarian society, centered its work on farming and raising livestock. Work was long and difficult at times. God used the rain and harvest cycles to formulate a series of appointed times in which the people could rejoice over their harvests and celebrate the goodness of God. These feasts were accompanied by great joy, festive meals, and special activities that renewed the spirits of the laborers. God established seasons of rest to enjoy family and community. God rested on the seventh day and told man to do the same.

WHAT DEVOUT *Jews* KNOW

Although these feasts had practical and spiritual applications, each identifying a specific event in Israel's history, the Jews knew that each generation must be reminded of God's redemptive power and the covenant with His people. These yearly feasts have distinguished the Jews from all other nations and ethnic groups. God loves a celebration, and the Jews enjoy being asked to participate.

WHAT *Christians* SHOULD KNOW

God enjoys a celebration, and we too should celebrate the redemptive covenant through Christ. All seven feasts have a prophetic application. Christ fulfilled the first three at His first coming. The church was born at Pentecost (Acts 2:1–4), and future prophetic events will fall in line with the three fall feasts. God has never *done away with the feasts*, but He allows each feast to be a spiritual preview of a major prophetic event linked to the Messiah. Each feast should remind Christians of the event that occurred and the events that will occur.

CHRISTIANS HONORING THE *Feasts*

Christians recognize that Christ fulfilled three of the first feasts—Passover, Unleavened Bread, and Firstfruits. The church was birthed in Jerusalem during the Feast of Pentecost. Instead of a traditional Easter service, why not incorporate a special *customized* celebration commemorating these festivals?

At Passover

- Invite a Jewish rabbi or a messianic rabbi to perform the Passover Seder as part of the service.

- Partake of the Lord's Supper (Communion) as a visible illustration and meaning of the Passover.

- Conduct a drama illustrating the ancient Passover, and show the spiritual meaning.

- Do an entire Passion Week with each day revealing what occurred at that time during the Passion.

- Have the church present a firstfruits offering for the poor, the widows, and the needy in your community.

- Incorporate a testimony service involving testimonies from several people who came to Christ during the past year.

- Plan a drama centered on the redemptive work of Christ, and invite friends and family.

At Pentecost

- Pentecost should be a joyous occasion. It is the birthday of the church.

- Allow your youth and teens to perform a drama, dressed in biblical clothes.

- Preach an illustrated message showing the first Pentecost (Mount Sinai) and the Day of Pentecost (Jerusalem).

- Have a celebration (just like a birthday party) with the entire church to celebrate Pentecost.

- Have a *Homecoming* meal, inviting all former church members back home for a Pentecost celebration.

- Use banners and costumes to host a processional honoring the coming of the Holy Spirit.

During God's appointed times—Christ's death and resurrection and the birth of the church (the coming of the Holy Spirit)—it should not be *church as usual*. These are momentous and historical celebrations for the Jews and for the Christians. Since God loves to celebrate, why not plan a celebration?

Chapter 5

THE MEANINGS AND PURPOSES OF JEWISH LIFE CYCLES

Train up a child in the way he should go,
And when he is old he will not depart from it.

—PROVERBS 22:6

I T WAS A CHILLY NOVEMBER NIGHT WHEN OUR SMALL GROUP OF FIVE men, led by my guide, Gideon Shor, walked briskly toward the upstairs office of Rabbi Yehudah Getz. It was Hanukkah, and nine large lamps burning with fire and fastened on top of the main building set a mystical glow against the weatherworn, limestone ashlars of the Western Wall. Entering the small office, I was greeted with a smile and warm handshake by a man about five feet five inches tall. He had a long, flowing white beard that lay like cotton candy on the front of his black orthodox coat. His ruddy cheeks, hearty spirit, and big smile reminded me of a Jewish Saint Nicholas.

As our discussion ensued, each question we asked was answered through our Jewish interpreter. At times the mystical rabbi would turn and pull a book from a shelf of seemingly endless Jewish commentaries, quoting from the Oral Tradition, the Talmud, or other rabbinical sources. After a cordial meeting, I inquired about this idea of the Oral Tradition. I discovered the Jews have not only the Torah but also numerous other *spiritual and religious* books. Over the centuries of contemporary societies, at times it was unclear about how to enact certain laws in the Torah, so rabbis compiled a series of writings called the Talmud. One called the *Jerusalem Talmud* was produced in Israel around A.D. 400, and the other, the *Babylonian Talmud*, was completed in A.D. 499. Both accepted the writings of Jewish law compiled by Rabbi Judah ha-Nasi (president of the Sanhedrin) from the second and third century.

As rabbis discussed each Mishna (oral tradition), adding their legends, anecdotes, and theological opinions, a work called the *Gemara* was compiled. The Mishna and Gemara together make up the Talmud. The *Midrash* (meaning study) is an additional commentary on the Scriptures. Devout Jews spend their lives in the study of the Torah and the Oral Tradition, gleaning from all of the above books by reading, asking questions, commenting, and reading again.[1] Is it any wonder that the Jewish mind is centered on education? Many Jews are so studious that while many youth in the West are being entertained for an average of seven hours a day by television, their Jewish counterparts are studying these ancient texts.

LOOK WHO'S RAISING CAIN

After being expelled from Eden, Eve conceived two sons, Cain and Abel. On one occasion, both offered a sacrifice to God. Abel presented a firstling from the flock, and Cain presented grain. God favored Abel's offering, angering Cain, who rose up against his brother and slew him. Cain became a *vagabond*, a word meaning, "a waverer or a wanderer."[2] This vagabond spirit describes many of the youth in America and parts of Europe. The Cain generation is a wandering group, seeking approval, affirmation, and care, looking for love in all the wrong places. Someone other than Mom and Dad—including gangs—are raising Cain. In America many of the younger generation are being raised and influenced by everyone but their parents.

- ■ The television has become the babysitter in many homes.

- ■ Computer games take hours of valuable time away from conversations among family members.

- ■ Cell phones and unnecessary text messaging are consuming large amounts of time.

- ■ Movies, the Internet, and other technologies are creating distractions from family time.

Among Gentile families, parents typically work two jobs, reducing quality family time. In fact, statistics reveal that the average father spends 2.5 hours a day with his child during the week, including watching television.[3] Early in life a cycle begins where a child is under the influence of other people more than his or her parents. For working parents, the cycle starts at age five. The youngster is driven to a day-care center while Mom works helping to "make ends meet." After day care is kindergarten, followed by twelve years of public school, totaling about thirteen years of direct influence from male and female teachers, each attempting to impart knowledge that, hopefully, results in good grades and a graduation certificate. During these thirteen important years, each child will view thousands of hours of crime, violence, sex, and profanity through television, movies, and DVDs. Internet access will add thousands more graphic images and information, including a dark world of perversion and chat rooms. By the time your child reaches the mature age of twenty-two, public schools and colleges have imparted knowledge to them for about seventeen consecutive years.

THE EIGHT STAGES OF GROWTH

There are eight different Hebrew words found in Scripture used to depict a new stage of life.[4]

The Hebrew Word	Scripture Reference	The Growth Level
1. *Yeled*	Exodus 2:3, 6, 8	A newborn
2. *Yanaq*	Isaiah 11:8	A suckling

The Hebrew Word	Scripture Reference	The Growth Level
3. `Owlel	Lamentations 4:4	Asks for bread and not milk
4. Gamul	Isaiah 28:9	Weaned one (the end of 2 years)
5. Taph	Ezekiel 9:6	Clings to its mother
6. Elem (almah)	Isaiah 7:14	Becoming strong and firm
7. Na'ar	Isaiah 40:30	Shaking himself free
8. Bachur	Isaiah 31:8	Ripened and growing (a warrior)

In the Mishnah (Aboth. v. 21), Rabbi Yehuda, the son of Tema, lists the cycles of life beginning at age five up to age one hundred:[5]

The Life Cycle	The Emphasis of Each Life Cycle
Age 5	Read the Bible
Age 10	Begin studying the Mishnah
Age 13	Bound to the commandments
Age 15	Begin studying the Talmud
Age 18	The age of marriage
Age 20	The pursuit of trade and business
Age 30	Full of vigor
Age 40	Maturity of reason
Age 50	A counselor
Age 60	The commencement of age
Age 70	The gray age
Age 80	Advanced old age
Age 90	Bowed down
Age 100	As he were dead and gone

Instructing children must begin at home. The Hebrew word for *parents* is *horim*. The Hebrew word for *teachers* is *morim*. Both words bear the meaning to teach and to instruct. Jewish parents realize they are the main instructors and teachers for their children. This responsibility is revealed in the Torah:

> Therefore you shall lay up these words of mine in your heart and in your soul, and bind them as a sign on your hand, and they shall be as frontlets between your eyes. You shall teach them to your children, speaking of them when you sit in your house, when you walk by the way, when you lie down, and when you rise up. And you shall write them on the doorposts of your house and on your gates, that your days and the days of your children may be multiplied in the land of which the LORD swore to your fathers to give them, like the days of the heavens above the earth.
>
> —Deuteronomy 11:18–21

Instruction must begin in the preschool years. During the first five years, parents can see the child's personality developing. The teen years develop the child's value system, and the twenties develop that person's work ethic. Physical growth and maturity eventually merge over time, but the foundation for a child's spiritual inclination must be laid early. Children learn *values* from home, *knowledge* from school, and *habits* from friends. The early training in a religious Jewish home begins by teaching the child certain prayers, especially the *Shema* and the *Berachot*.

The first learned prayer, *Shema Yisrael*, means, "Hear (O) Israel." It is a kind of *creed*, with the main verse in this prayer being Deuteronomy 6:4: "Hear, O Israel: The LORD our God, the LORD is one!" In Hebrew it reads: "*Shema Yisrael Adonai Eloheinu Adonai Echad.*" The prayer also includes Deuteronomy 11:13–21 and Numbers 15:37–41. The Shema is repeated twice a day and is the central part of the morning and evening Jewish prayers.

Learning to pray is the heart of Judaism. There are eighteen parts of the prayer prayed in a Jewish liturgy, called *shmoneh esre* (which means, "eighteen"). These prayers are prayed three times a day each week. Later the *curse of the heretics* was added, making nineteen themes:

1. A reminder of God's covenant with the patriarchs
2. A description of God's almighty power
3. A contemplation of the divine name
4. Prayer for divine insight
5. Prayer for repentance
6. Prayer for forgiveness of sins
7. Prayer for redemption through Israel's Redeemer
8. Prayer for healing—also for the people of Israel
9. Prayer for a fruitful and productive year
10. Prayer for acquittal in the messianic Last Judgment
11. Prayer that slanderers and blasphemers would be destroyed
12. Prayer for the devout and for true proselytes
13. Prayer that Jerusalem will be rebuilt
14. Prayer for the coming of the Messiah
15. A request that the whole of this prayer may be heard from God
16. Prayer that the glory (*Shekinah*) will return to Zion
17. Thanksgiving for the mercies of God
18. Prayer that the peace of God will rest upon his people Israel[6]

After learning the Shema, a child learns to bless. This prayer, called the *Berachot* (blessings), is offered in front of the child. Once children learn to speak, they are encouraged to pray over their food and to thank God for the little things such as their fruit, candy, or juice. It is said that any act performed for twenty-one consecutive days can become a habit. Therefore, praying should not be random but steady and consistent—in fact, daily. I saw this in my youngest child, Amanda, who even at two and three years of age always requested to bless the food. If eating in a restaurant, she still reminds people to give thanks! The normal Jewish prayer over food is:

Blessed are You, O Lord, King of the universe who brings forth bread from the earth.

The prayer can include:

Blessed are You, O Lord, King of the universe who creates the fruit of the vine...who creates various types of fruit...who has created everything.

At an early age parents will read special storybooks to their children. This was a practice followed by my wife, Pam, with both of our children. Pam would end the day by reading a chapter from a book while lying on the bed with the children, and we concluded the day by having our children pray a prayer for good sleep and blessing on the family, the house, and even the cat. (God does include healthy animals in your blessing portfolio!)

Children of all faiths love toys and games. The American culture empha-sizes dolls for girls and various toys for boys. Western toys are seldom developed for religious education. In the Jewish culture many toys are created with religious themes in mind. There are stuffed Torah scrolls, Hebrew alphabet building blocks, toy charity boxes to teach giving of charity to the needy, Purim noisemakers, Passover (Seder) props, and numerous toys linked to Hanukah.[7] As the child reaches maturity, he or she is presented a *tallit* (a Jewish prayer shawl) and taught the history and spiritual significance of the *shofar* (the horn made from an animal horn).

As children grow, they are taught to hold the elderly in high respect. In Orthodox communities, the older men are the elders and are looked upon for their experiences in life and their wisdom. In early Jewish families, members of the families were so close knit that at death, deep mourning lasted for seven days, followed by a lighter mourning for thirty days. Children were taught to mourn for their parents for twelve months, and the anniversary of the day of the death was to be observed.

THE FIVE STAGES IN LIFE

The life cycles in a Jewish family can be summed up in one word: celebration! This concept of celebrating life is manifested through the seven yearly feasts and the Sabbath cycles and begins at birth and continues to the moment of marriage. This life celebration progresses through five stages, with each stage initiating a new religious ritual or experience that introduces and commemorates each stage.

Stage 1: The celebration of circumcision

According to God's commandment, a Jewish male child was to be circumcised on the eighth day after his birth. This act of physical circumcision is more of a spiritual ceremony than a surgery and was initiated by God as a token (visible sign) of a Jewish son becoming a part of the covenant with God. Circumcision was commanded in the law, and any Hebrew male child not circumcised was "cut off" from the people:

> And the uncircumcised male child, who is not circumcised in the flesh of his foreskin, that person shall be cut off from his people; he has broken My covenant.
>
> —GENESIS 17:14

Abraham's circumcision is mentioned thirteen times in the Torah. In Israel, the act of circumcision, called *Bris* in the Hebrew, is performed by a *Mohel* (a circumciser) who is especially trained for the procedure. The most honored person is the *Sandak* or godfather who holds the infant on his knees for the circumcision. At times two chairs are used, one for the Sandak and the other chair for Elijah. The infant is placed in the chair while the Sandak prays that the spirit of Elijah will stand over him as he performs the ceremony.

Another interesting detail is that the infant son's name is not given or revealed at birth. It has been discussed in secret among the parents and closest friends or relatives. It remains a secret until the eighth day at the ceremony of circumcision. At a designated moment, the father whispers the son's name into the ear of the grandfather or godfather. The name is then publicly announced to those gathered, accompanying great anticipation and excitement. The greatest honor is to name a son after a father, a grandfather, a great biblical character, or a famous Jewish person. The naming of the son is a highlight during the event and is celebrated since every Hebrew name carries a unique meaning.

Other blessings over the infant include prayers for his success in life, his future marriage, and a prayer that he will grow up to know the Torah.

Following the ceremony, a festive meal is enjoyed by the family and closest friends.

The purchase price and dedicating a child

Shortly after a child's birth, most Christian parents will arrange for a baby dedication at their local church. Accompanying the proud parents are siblings, grandparents, godparents (spiritual guardians), close relatives, and special friends. The ceremony is emotionally moving as the presiding minister cuddles the newborn, speaking a blessing or prayer, and charges the parents to raise the child in the knowledge of the Lord. Afterward the worship service continues on schedule.

As a Christian, I believe each child should be celebrated in the church where the family attends. The traditional baby dedication is also an opportunity to invite relatives to a worship service that they may not have attended in years. However, parents may choose to follow an example from Jewish families who center their firstborn son's *dedication* in the home.

This ceremony for a son is called the *Pidyon HaBen* (Redemption of the Son). This ancient commandment is written in Numbers 18:15–16:

> Everything that first opens the womb of all flesh, which they bring to the LORD, whether man or beast, shall be yours; nevertheless the firstborn of man you shall surely redeem, and the firstborn of unclean animals you shall redeem. And those redeemed of the devoted things you shall redeem when one month old, according to your valuation, for five shekels of silver, according to the shekel of the sanctuary, which is twenty gerahs.

There are rabbinical explanations given as to why five shekels were selected. First, Joseph, Rachel's firstborn son, was sold by his brothers for twenty pieces of silver, the equivalent of five shekels. Therefore, five shekels are given to the priest to redeem the son back. The fifth letter of the Hebrew alphabet is *hei* and was the letter God inserted into Abram's name when He changed it to Abraham. In Christian theology, five is a number alluding to the grace of God.

The Jewish custom begins when the infant is at least thirty-one days old. God wanted all men in Israel to be a nation of priests. After Israel sinned with the golden calf, God selected Levi as the single priestly tribe. By providing the five shekels to the priest, the father redeemed the son from entering the priesthood. It also reminds the Jews of God preserving the firstborn sons of the Hebrews on the night the destroying angel entered Egypt (Exod. 12).

The silver tray, jewelry, and coins

Normally, ten men are present for the ceremony. The priest asks the father if he would prefer the child or the five shekels he must pay. The father chooses the child, recites a blessing, and hands the silver coins to the priest.

Holding the coins over the infant, the priest declares the redemption is paid. He blesses the child and then returns him to the parents. The coins are usually returned to the child as a gift.

At times the child is placed on a blanket on a silver tray, surrounded by jewelry borrowed for the ceremony from women in attendance. This could allude to the Hebrews borrowing the jewelry from their neighbors when departing from Egypt. A festive meal follows, and some will hand out cubes of sugar and garlic cloves.

Girls are not omitted from experiencing their own naming ceremony, called *Zeved habat* among the Sephardic Jews and *Simchat bat* among the Ashkenazi sect. These ceremonies often occur within the first month of a girl's birth and can be celebrated privately in the synagogue or in a party at home. A rabbi and a cantor often participate.

The varied traditions and customs are too numerous to elaborate on. However, some customs include lighting seven candles, representing the seven days of Creation, while holding the infant or wrapping the child in the four corners of a tallit (Jewish prayer shawl). Other customs are lifting the baby and touching her hands to the Torah scroll.

The Christian dedication celebration

How can such beautiful customs be applied to Gentile believers?

There is no set manner in Scripture on how to dedicate an infant, other than the examples of Hannah (1 Sam. 1:23–28) and Mary and Joseph (Luke 2:21–27). Every parent should perform a dedication in God's house, but they may also consider a special ceremony at home. This enables more family and friends to be invited in a comfortable family setting. It also prevents time restraints often associated with Sunday morning dedication services. A special meal can also be prepared to celebrate the arrival of a new life.

Here are several suggestions for incorporating these wonderful Jewish traditions into a Christian infant's dedication in the parents' home:

- Prepare the time of dedication after the child has reached his or her thirtieth day (Num. 18:15–16).

- For traditional Christians, Sunday is a good day, since those attending are normally not working.

- Prepare five shekels of silver (silver dollars if possible) as a token of redemption (Num. 18:15–16).

- Have your pastor, priest, or minister participate to pray the special blessing on the infant.

- As the prayer is being offered, you may choose to wrap a tallit (prayer shawl) around the infant, indicating God's Word and His commandments.

- A family meal should follow the ceremony.

- You may wish to affix a small child's mezuzah to the right door frame of the infant's room.

If you choose a home celebration, be sure to inform all parties involved of their importance and duties during the dedication. The birth of both a son and a daughter should be celebrated and confirmed by a public or private dedication ceremony. This is the first stage of life.

Stage 2: The celebration of adulthood

The next celebration occurs when a Jewish boy (or girl) reaches the age of thirteen. The young boy experiences a ceremony called *bar mitzvah*, and the girls, *bat mitzvah*. The word *mitzvah* means, "commandment." Since *bar* in Hebrew means "son," and *bat* in Hebrew means "daughter," the phrase *bar mitzvah* means a son to whom the commandments apply. In the Bible, all of God's commandments are called *mitzvoth*. These ceremonies are a celebration recognizing the coming of age for sons and daughters when reaching the significant age of thirteen.

Several times in Israel I have watched the bar mitzvah ceremonies at the famed Western Wall (called by some the Wailing Wall). The female family members and friends stand behind a large stone partition, separating them from the men's section of the plaza. Eventually, the male relatives exit from a side tunnel on the left, parallel to the historical Western Wall. At times the young candidate for bar mitzvah rides atop the back of his father or the nearest kin, shrouded in his *tallit* (prayer shawl) and wearing a *yarmulke* (head covering).

The men enter the stone-slab plaza clapping, singing, and skipping as a rabbi leads the procession holding a large Torah scroll above his head. Suddenly, the women send their resounding sound of approval with shouting and begin throwing handfuls of candy toward the group.

Prior to this moment, the father bore the responsibility for the actions of his children. At a bar and bat mitzvah the young adult will now accept responsibility for his or her actions. While Gentiles often dread their children becoming teenagers, the religious Jews commemorate the occasion, which not only transfers moral and spiritual responsibility to the boy and girl but also affirms them through this family celebration involving parents, relatives, and close friends.

In Western culture, a girl recognizes the age of sixteen as *sweet sixteen*, and a teenage boy feels he has entered manhood when he becomes eighteen, leaving home released from parental guardianship and family influence. If, however, we delay in spiritually and morally instructing our children until the ages of sixteen and eighteen, then the train has already left the station. In Judaism, the bar or bat mitzvah initiates a *rite of passage* into the Jewish adult community. Christians often debate, "What is the age of moral and spiritual accountability for a child?" Numerous suggestions are made, from the age at which they can pray and repent to the age of knowing right from wrong. Christ at age twelve was in the temple with the scribes and doctors of the law. Joseph found Him, and Christ said, "I must be about My Father's business" (Luke 2:49). Christ was nearing His thirteenth year.

I personally believe the true age of moral and spiritual accountability begins between ages twelve to thirteen. There are physical and hormonal changes that begin, called *puberty*. The bar mitzvah is the *commandment age* and the *age of majority* in Judaism. I recall when my friend Bill Cloud's son turned thirteen. We gathered at a local restaurant for a special meal, prayers, and blessings, affirming him in the faith and celebrating a new entry into the community of adulthood. Instead of waiting until graduation when a teen leaves home to recognize personal and spiritual accountability, why not celebrate the age thirteen, the beginning of the teen years?

Stage 3: The celebration of maturity

The age of eighteen is a mile marker in North American culture. Most teens have graduated from high school and are preparing for college or a trade, or they are training for a career. It is also the age when the four branches of the U.S. military recruit men and women for jobs or careers in the armed services. It may come as a surprise that God began His recruiting for the Israeli military at age twenty and not age eighteen.

So what is the difference with two years?

Any parents raising children (especially boys) know that ages sixteen to nineteen are the most challenging for the average teenager. They are attempting to discover themselves, attempting to ignore parental influence. There is peer pressure to experiment with alcohol, sex, and illegal drugs. My wife and I have questioned why most parents have a rebellion story about their teenage children and why numerous parents tell us, "It seemed everything changed for the good after they turned twenty." Some have stated, "When my kids turned twenty, it was like the light came on, and I wondered, 'Is this same defiant child that was resisting my instructions?'"

God knew that something biological occurs at age twenty, which medical sources have recently discovered. When numbering the Hebrew men, God began at age twenty up to age sixty, requiring a half shekel of redemption for every male over twenty (Lev. 27:3–5). All men over twenty (not eighteen) were prepared for war if needed:

> Take a census of all the congregation of the children of Israel, by their families, by their fathers' houses, according to the number of names, every male individually, from twenty years old and above—all who are able to go to war in Israel. You and Aaron shall number them by their armies.
> —Numbers 1:2–3

The United States recruits future soldiers at age eighteen when most are exiting high school and entering the college or career cycle. What did God know about age twenty that we don't? In *For Parents Only*, the authors report why teenagers seeking their freedom often make foolish and dangerous decisions, ignoring obvious warnings. The authors write:

> Our teens are not only addicted; they are also brain deficient. Science demonstrates that the frontal lobe of the brain—the area that allows judgment for consequences and control of impulses—doesn't fully develop until after the teen years. So in the absence of a fully functioning frontal lobe, teenage brains rely more on the centers that control emotion—which in effect means they give in much more easily to impulses.[8]

Society places heavy responsibilities on teens to make major decisions about career, college, and the military at age eighteen, when in reality the mental judgment for such major decisions is better developed after the teen years. Obviously, the Creator knew that at age twenty and beyond, the judgment and reasoning lobe of the brain was fully developed, allowing for better decision making and mental judgments. God permitted young men to fight in battles at age twenty.

When the leadership of ancient Israel conducted a census, numbering the men from age twenty and above, a silver half-shekel was collected from each man, symbolizing the price of redemption. The coins were presented to the priests and used to repair the tabernacle and the temple (Exod. 30:13–15). Thus, age twenty was the introduction into a level of mental and emotional maturity among the men of Israel, with confidence that good mental decisions could be made. At age thirteen boys were affirmed into adulthood, but at age twenty they became an adult.

Stage 4: The celebration of spiritual development

In the Torah, age thirty introduced another life cycle of spiritual maturity. A Levite could not officiate in the temple priesthood until he was thirty years of age (Num. 4:3, 23, 30). Christ was baptized and entered the public ministry at about the age of thirty (Luke 3:23). While spiritual maturity does not always match a person's chronological age, there appears to be significance to the age thirty.

According to rabbinical thought, age thirty is when we reach the peak of our strength. This was especially true in ancient Israel, when the average life span of a person was about forty-five to fifty years. In ancient times people married in their mid to late teen years. God exempted the newlyweds from work for an entire year to bond with each other. In earlier times, by the time a father had a son who was turning age thirteen, the average father was nearing or slightly past thirty years of age. By this time there is a spiritual inclination and focus that a father has that may have been absent in his twenties when he was concentrating on his education, business, wife, or early career. However, once the children begin arriving and maturing, some parents who lacked spiritual direction become concerned for moral attitudes and spiritual development of their children.

Everyone knows that moving from age twenty-nine to thirty becomes a milestone in life in the same manner that turning forty, fifty, and seventy holds important symbolism. Each of these four ages indicates important life cycles, carrying a new spiritual level of growth and development.

Stage 5: The celebration of marriage

To Orthodox Jews and dedicated Christians, it is important to marry in the faith. When a Jewish man marries a Jewish woman, it helps preserve the Jewish identity, traditions, and culture. Abraham refused to allow Isaac to marry a Canaanite (Gen. 24:3), and Rebekah did not want Jacob to marry a daughter of Heth, also a Canaanite sect (Gen. 27:46). Christians marrying other Christians helps create more peace in the home, as there will not be a division over religion or questions about what faith to raise the child in. Christians and Jews understand that faith and belief are generational and can be passed on to the children.

The original purpose of marriage was for procreation. Out of 613 commandments in the Torah, the first is, "Be fruitful, and multiply, and replenish the earth" (Gen. 1:28, kjv). To the ancient Hebrew, marriage was more of a lifelong commitment than an emotional feeling of, "I am in love." In fact, the ancient form of engagement was more like a business proposition than a contemporary engagement. Love was to blossom and mature as you spent your lives weaving the fabric of a home.

Selecting a life mate and entering marriage is one of the highest expectations in life. In Western culture we are very familiar with preparations for a marriage ceremony. Many Christians, however, know very little about the customs and traditions of the ancient Jewish wedding process.

Years ago I researched the ancient Jewish wedding customs, which were a preview of the Messiah's appearing. When a young man selected his future bride, he would meet with the woman's father to initiate the process. During this meeting, several important events occurred. First, the young man produced a marriage contract outlining the details of what he expected from his future wife and what she could expect from him as a husband. Once the contract, called a *ketubah*, was agreed upon, the couple drank from a glass of wine as a token of their covenant agreement. The father of the groom then provided a special price for the woman. It might have been camels, goats, or a piece of property.

After these procedures were completed, the groom returned to his father's house, and the woman remained at her parents' home. From that moment forward the couple did not date or visit one another. Two individuals, called the friend of the bride and the friend of the bridegroom, relayed messages between the bride and groom. The woman remained faithful to her future husband, publicly wearing a veil covering her face, which indicated she was spoken for. The man worked at his father's house preparing a special room for the couple for consummating their marriage.

Upon completion of the room, the groom's father permitted his son to take his bride. At times a group of men would be sent secretly to the bride's house and would stand at her window and announce, "The bridegroom is coming. Make yourself ready." The woman would prepare herself, and often several young virgins would be present with her during this exciting moment. She would be whisked from her house and brought to the groom's prepared chamber. If the event occurred at night, torches on long poles were lit and led the way through the dark night to the waiting groom.

Upon arrival, the waiting groom would bring his new bride into the special room called a *chuppah*. There, the couple would consummate their marriage.

This ancient procedure parallels the new covenant a believer enters when receiving Christ. First we are invited to receive Him. We seal our agreement through the cup of Communion (the Lord's Supper). Christ has gone to prepare a place for us at His Father's house (John 14:1–2). While He is away, we are to keep our lamp trimmed and burning (Matt. 25:7) and keep our garments white (Rev. 16:15). The heavenly Father will determine when the heavenly wedding chamber is completed for the bride's arrival. Christ will secretly and unexpectedly return with a "shout, with the voice of the archangel, and with the trumpet of God" (1 Thess. 4:16–18). When we arrive in heaven, we will be treated to a marriage supper (Rev. 19:7–9).

The marriage covenant—the sign

As stated, the word *covenant* is the word *b'rit*, which means, "to cut." The early biblical covenants were sealed with sacrificial offerings. God gave every woman a physical sign of her marriage covenant. When a bride who is a virgin consummates her marriage, she sheds a portion of blood. In the Torah, this blood was considered a token (sign) of her entering into the marriage covenant with one man. The law required proof of her virginity; therefore, the following morning the sheets from the bed were presented to the city elders, who looked for blood on the sheets as proof of the woman's virginity. If she had lied, and the blood evidence was absent from the sheets, she could be executed (Deut. 22:15–20).

Sadly, in Western culture, youth often pride themselves on losing their virginity. Marriage is viewed as obsolete, replaced by living together and new sexual freedom. We should begin teaching young, unmarried women that marriage is a covenant. If a young woman remains sexually pure, she will have a token of her marriage covenant with her husband on her honeymoon night. Perhaps this emphasis would encourage young women to remain pure until the moment of consummating their marriage.

The lifeblood of each marriage flows from a spiritual covenant sealed by the redemptive blood of our heavenly Bridegroom. In the beginning there was one man, Adam. God performed the first surgery and created a counterpart for Adam, a woman. God took a rib from Adam, creating Eve. The Hebrew word *rib* is also used in Scripture to indicate pillars and beams that hold up a building. In Genesis 2:23, the Hebrew word for man is *'iysh*, and the word for woman is *ishah*. In Hebrew, the words *man* and *woman* share two identical Hebrew letters—the letters *alef* and *shin*. Man's name has an additional *yod* and woman's name an additional letter, *hei*. Together they spell *YAH*, an abbreviation of the name of God. However, if you remove the *yod* and *hei* (God's name) from man and woman's name, all that is left are two letters that spell *'esh*, the Hebrew word for fire! The rabbinical interpretation is that this fire can produce passion, but without God there is passion without common spiritual beliefs and values, leading to the destruction of the union.[9]

These five cycles—age eight (circumcision), thirteen (coming of age), twenty (emotional and mental maturity), thirty (new spiritual maturity), and marriage are the five major Jewish life cycles. It is the fifth cycle of marriage where a couple begins dreaming of children whose entry into the world will birth a new family. Children will bring a new level of responsibility of raising, teaching, and instruction.

PRAYING BLESSINGS UPON YOUR CHILDREN AND GRANDCHILDREN

The Torah reveals the importance of verbally blessing your children. Isaac spoke blessings over Jacob and Esau (Gen. 27), and Jacob blessed the two sons of Joseph (Gen. 48), later passing blessings to his sons (Gen. 49). Before Moses's death, he pronounced a prophetic blessing on the tribes of Israel (Deut. 33). Devout Jewish parents and grandparents continually offer blessings over their children and grandchildren, believing in God's ability to transfer His favor through their prayers.

Blessings are performed on Sabbath days, feast days, and various special occasions. It is important to begin the prayers of blessing when the children are young, tenderhearted, and more receptive, as they tend to feel more awkward as they enter their late teens.

The pattern for blessing children is narrated in Genesis 48:2, when Jacob blessed Ephraim and Manasseh. Jacob sat on the edge of his bed when blessing his grandsons. The writer to the Hebrews wrote that Jacob blessed his own sons, "…leaning on the top of his staff" (Heb. 11:21). Today, those performing the blessing on their children prefer to stand up in respect to approaching God's throne. When preparing for a blessing, ask the children to bow their heads, teaching them reverence to God, and tell them the blessing was practiced by their ancestors as in Genesis 24:48 and in Exodus 12:17, when Israel was departing from Egypt.

In Hebrew, the word *smicha* means, "laying on of hands." In the temple, the priests would lay hands upon animals, symbolizing the transfer of sins. On the Day of Atonement, a goat was used, which became the scapegoat. Jacob blessed the sons of Joseph, Ephraim and Manasseh, by laying hands upon their heads (Gen. 48:14). Before his death, Moses transferred his wisdom and authority to Joshua by the laying on of hands (Deut. 34:9).

Prior to the blessing, lay both hands upon the head of the child or one hand on the head of each child if there are two children. A general Jewish blessing that is prayed every Sabbath by the father over his son is: "May God make you as Ephraim and Manassah." A general blessing spoken over a daughter is: "May God make you as Sarah, Leah, Rebekah, and Rachel." A favorite blessing that can be pronounced are the same words Jacob spoke over Ephraim and Manasseh:

> The Angel who has redeemed me from all evil,
> Bless the lads;
> Let my name be named upon them,
> And the name of my fathers Abraham and Isaac;
> And let them grow into a multitude in the midst of the earth.
>
> —GENESIS 48:16

One ancient blessing that was prayed over the people by the high priest is the special blessing the priest prayed over the people in the time of Moses and at both Jewish temples.

> The LORD bless you and keep you,
> The LORD make His face shine upon you,
> And be gracious to you;
> The LORD lift up His countenance upon you,
> And give you peace.
>
> —NUMBERS 6:24–26

FATHER KNOWS BEST

Remember the popular television program *The Waltons?* They were a large American family living in the mountains of Virginia, farming, working, eating meals together, and bonding with the future generation. Had they been Jewish, their names may have been the "Walsteins"! In early America, the father was the *breadwinner,* and divorce or separation was not an option. In the religious Jewish community, the father is central to the stability and success of a growing healthy family. In a strongly religious Jewish family, the father is directly involved in the spiritual and religious training of his children:

- Directing the celebration of circumcision for his son and presenting the silver shekel

- Planning and overseeing the bar- or bat-mitzvah ceremonies for his sons and daughters

- Participating in the feasts, especially the three that all males over twenty are to attend

- Participating in Hanukkah, telling the story, providing the gifts, and lighting the candles

- Leading the family to the synagogue each Sabbath

- Teaching the children the Torah and Scriptures and relating stories to them

- Participating as the head of the home during the weekly Sabbath meal

In the devout Jewish home, there is an emphasis on the family meal. The *Se'uda* is the Jewish meal. Each meal should be sanctified by a blessing prayed over the food. The meal is special; since the destruction of the temple, the Jewish table is said to be the atoning altar (The Talmud, Berachoth 55a). Salt should appear on each table since salt was used for the temple sacrifices. Since Abraham served the three guests (Gen. 18:7) and Moses served the elders (Exod. 24), if guests are present the father is to serve the meal, especially if the poor are present. The special meals to be prepared are three Sabbath (Shabbat) meals, the Passover Seder, Pentecost, and the Tabernacles meals. Other special meals are prepared on Purim, Hanukkah, and the *Simchat Torah* (Rejoicing in the Torah). There is a special meal before the fast begins on the Day of Atonement, the wedding breakfast, and the *brit milah* (circumcision) and bar mitzvah. It is also common to prepare a special meal for a person who has recovered from sickness or been rescued from danger. When a father is absent in the life of his children, there are often negative emotional and social effects that follow.[10]

AMERICA AND THE "I" GENERATION

America is experiencing a father shortage as many dads have simply gone AWOL, deserting their position as head of the home. The Bible gives an example of a son who was left without his father. You've heard of the "boomers" and "generation X." Have you heard of the "I generation"? The letter "I" does not refer to being self-centered but alludes to the first letter in the name Ishmael. He was a son of Abraham born through Sarah's Egyptian handmaiden, Hagar (Gen. 16:15).

After Abraham's wife, Sarah, birthed Isaac, she demanded that Abraham excommunicate Hagar and her son, Ishmael, from the house. Ishmael was a teenager when he and his mother were expelled from Abraham, departing toward the wilderness on their own (Gen. 21:14). Ishmael was a teenager between the ages of fifteen and sixteen when he was permanently separated from his biological father, Abraham.

Young men need a father or father figure in their life to affirm them. The teen years are most important for forming the value system in a child. God made a prediction about Ishmael's future when He said:

> He shall be a wild man;
> His hand shall be against every man,
> And every man's hand against him.
> And he shall dwell in the presence of all his brethren.
> —Genesis 16:12

Ishmael would be a wild man. The Hebrew word for *wild* here alludes to a *wild donkey*. The same word is used in Job 24:5 and 39:5. In seven other Old Testament references, it is translated "wild ass." Wild donkeys live in the wilderness and mountains and are difficult to tame. The idea is that Ishmael would dwell in the wilderness and would tend to be continually fighting, with his "hand against every man."

> The rod and rebuke give wisdom,
> But a child left to himself brings shame to his mother.
> —Proverbs 29:15

The traditional mother-father family system established in the Bible has been challenged by the frequency of divorce and the increased emphasis on alternative lifestyle structures, thus depriving children of their God-ordained role models. America has become an "I" (Ishmael) generation, a one-parent society without dads. Between 1960 and 1990, the percentage of children living apart from their biological father more than doubled, from

17 percent to 36 percent.[11] That number is headed toward 50 percent. A fatherless generation creates a void in children and in the nation.

World War I continued from 1914 to 1918, causing over eighteen million military and civilian deaths and leaving millions of homes fatherless.[12] Under Joseph Stalin, Communism became the new "father" of the Russian people. The leadership void in homes was replaced by a political system, promoted as the answer to the nation's ills. The same occurred in World War II. Germany had ten million soldiers, counting Austrians, involved in World War II. The separation of the sons and fathers from their families created a vast emotional void. Hitler granted to himself the title the *Fuhrer*, meaning "leader or guide" in the German language. The German cry was, *Ein volk, ein reich, ein fuhrer*—"one people, one state, one leader." Hitler was Germany's new "father." To demonstrate this, in 1922 the Hitler Youth Movement was established. It went underground for a season, but in 1930 it recruited twenty-five thousand boys fourteen and upward, adding a junior branch for boys ten to fourteen. One German poster read, "Youth serves the leader. All ten-year-olds into the Hitler Youth."[13] These blond-haired, blue-eyed youth were viewed as a future super-Aryan race and were indoctrinated in Hitler's anti-Semitic message. By 1936 all German young men were to join Hitler's movement. By the end of 1933, 2.3 million youth had joined the movement, and by 1935 over 5 million were members. By 1940, the extermination of the Jews had begun, and 8 million youth were under Hitler's control! These world wars killed many future fathers and husbands, causing both Communism and Nazism to become the "god" or the new father for the fatherless sons and daughters.[14]

The lack of fathers in American culture is cracking an opening for sons (and daughters) to slip through the cracks of their homes seeking affirmation elsewhere. Gangs are filling the void in major cities as, like Ishmael, the youth wander in the back alley wilderness without fatherly guidance. Former gangbangers have told me they joined gangs seeking power, respect, affirmation, protection, and attention that were absent from their broken home or dysfunctional family. In most cases there were no fathers or male role models in their lives.

I also believe the fatherless spirit may attribute to the gay lifestyle. Some homosexuals reveal they were abused or molested as a child, pulling them into the lifestyle. In other examples I have known of former homosexual men who felt that the root cause of their struggles was having no male role model to affirm them as men. Obviously, this is only one cause of this lifestyle choice. However, a young fatherless son with no caring male influence can be pushed into seeking affirmation from older males who may take advantage of them through misdirected affections.

ISHMAEL, THE WILD
CHILD TO OIL TYCOON

Ishmael and his mother, Hagar, dwelt in a remote desert. He became an archer. Ishmael had to learn to hunt for food and defend himself since his father (Abraham), his trained servants (Gen. 14:14), and his closest friends were no longer in his life. It was a matter of self-survival by self-defense. Ishmael was the wild child who no doubt held resentment for the treatment of his mother and himself.

I have driven through numerous inner cities observing teenage boys prowling the streets with their pants hanging down to their knees and their gold and silver *bling-bling* swaying from their necks. Like zombies seeking a resurrection, they look for any cheap thrill and thrive on self-inflicted trouble. If I ask, "Where is your dad?" many of them answer, "I don't know," or "He's doing time," or "He's running around with some woman." The *death* of a father is different from the *disappearance* of a dad. Death is a natural process of life, but dads gone AWOL become silent signals to children: "I'm gone, and it's all about me and not about you."

Although Ishmael was alone with Mom, God planned a great future for Ishmael's children. God promised Ishmael He would bless him, making him fruitful and multiplying him from one man to twelve sons who would be princes over great nations (Gen. 17:20; 25). The sons of Ishmael produced twelve nations, whose descendants settled throughout the Arabian Peninsula and the Persian Gulf. Ishmael's kids ended up with the oil in the Middle East. Not too bad for a rejected son! Ishmael's blessings followed his descendants because his natural dad was Abraham, and Abraham had a covenant with God.

WHAT CAN A SINGLE MOTHER DO?

With so many one-parent families, especially single mothers, what spiritual provision does a single mom have in affirming and blessing her children when a father is absent from the home? First, a believing mother has a true friend in God, in Christ, and in the Holy Spirit. When Christ was preparing for His departure back to heaven, He said, "I will not leave you comfortless...I will send you another Comforter." (See John 14:16–18.) The word *comfortless* is the Greek word *orphanos*, from which we derive the word *orphan*. Paraphrased, He was saying, "I will not leave you like a fatherless child." Christ promised to send the Holy Spirit who is the "Comforter," or in the Greek a *paraklētos*, meaning "one who is called to aid another."[15]

God has stated distinct provisions and promises for the fatherless. Today, not only does death snatch away Dad, but also there are other forms of being fatherless: when a divorce occurs and the dad moves out of state, or when a father rejects the mom for another woman, leaving her to raise the children. Just as the Holy Spirit promises to stand by and aid you, God becomes more than your Creator, as it is written:

> For your Maker is your husband,
> The LORD of hosts is His name.
>
> —ISAIAH 54:5

> He administers justice for the fatherless and the widow, and loves the stranger, giving him food and clothing. Therefore love the stranger, for you were strangers in the land of Egypt.
>
> —DEUTERONOMY 10:18–19

> But You have seen, for You observe trouble and grief,
> To repay it by Your hand.
> The helpless commits himself to You;
> You are the helper of the fatherless.
>
> —PSALM 10:14

> A father of the fatherless, a defender of widows,
> Is God in His holy habitation.
>
> —PSALM 68:5

Widows and single mothers

Just as the phrase *fatherless* implies several different applications, the word *widow* has several possible applications. The primary meaning is, "a woman whose husband has died and she has not remarried." I personally believe there are three types of women who can be classified as widows.

- Widows indeed—women whose husbands have passed away and they remain unmarried

- Spiritual widows—women whose unbelieving husbands never attend church and hinder the family spiritually

- Single mothers—women who are divorced, have AWOL husbands, or perhaps a husband incarcerated for life

Church memberships include these three types of women with children who are often balancing on a tightrope of working a secular job, being a homemaker, and being the spiritual priest of the family. Widows in the Bible received special favor from God. There is the woman from Zarephath whom God prevented from starving (1 Kings 17:9–16), the widow whose family was spared from bankruptcy through the miracle of oil in her house (2 Kings 4:1–7), and the widow who gave all her offering at the temple, capturing the attention of Christ (Mark 12:42). An aged prophetess, Anna, who served in full-time ministry at the temple, recognized Christ as the Messiah when He was an infant (Luke 2:37). Christ interrupted a funeral to raise a widow's son from the dead (Luke 7:12–14). Another widow pressed a judge for vindication and got what she wanted by persistence (Luke 18:1–5). Each widow received a unique blessing.

It is a comfort for a single mother to know that the fatherless and widows are especially favored by God. In the Torah, God forbade mistreatment of the stranger, fatherless, and widow (Exod. 22:21–22; Deut. 10:18). As a single mom or a widow with children, it is important to find a local assembly that emphasizes ministry for children and youth, where your kids can sit under biblical teaching, fellowship with other believers their age, and experience the love of a spiritual community of believers.

A mother can also pronounce blessings if the father is absent! After learning she was pregnant, Mary traveled to visit her cousin Elizabeth.

Elizabeth spontaneously spoke a blessing over Mary concerning her unborn child (Luke 1:41–45). At the time of Christ's death, Joseph was not present. (Some believe he died before Christ's ministry began.) Mary, however, was at the Crucifixion, the Resurrection, and in the Upper Room (Acts 1:13–14). In the first-century church, both men and women hosted churches in their homes (1 Cor. 16:19; Philem. 2). Mom, step in and perform the prayer and blessings over your children. Your redemptive covenant gives you spiritual authority to approach the eternal throne of God and make your petitions known.

IMPORTANT LIFE TRUTHS FOR CHILDREN

Torah-adherent Jewish parents take time to teach their children prayers, study the Torah and the Talmud, and speak blessings for their future. As a Bible believer, you can follow the same biblical examples and customs of our Jewish counterparts by making operational these seven important life truths for your children.

1. Teach your children.

Parents know that there is an inbred tendency in all children to eventually rebel against instruction. There is a Hebrew word, *yetzer*, which means, "tendency or inclination." Judaism teaches that man is created with two opposing tendencies: to do good (*yetzer ha'tov*), and to do evil (*yetzer ha'ra*). Each human is created with a free will to choose either good or evil. Before the Flood, God said of mankind: "…every intent [*yetzer*] of the thoughts of his heart was only evil continually" (Gen. 6:5). The Talmud teaches that God gave the Torah to accompany man on his journey in life, that by studying God's Word, man can control the *yetzer* and dissuade his evil inclination.[16]

Children love learning by example, not just words. Scripture says, "Train up a child in the way he should go, and when he is old he will not depart from it" (Prov. 22:6). Many parents are not as concerned about the way their child *should* go, but more concerned about the way their child should *not* go!

Orthodox Jewish fathers living in Jerusalem relate various stories of sons from the Bible to teach their own sons how to act responsibly. For example, in Jerusalem's Kidron Valley there are a series of ancient tombs carved out of the limestone rock. These hewn tombs, like stone towers, are a silent reminder of men who once had influence in the Holy City. One tomb is traditionally identified as the tomb of Absalom, the son of David. Absalom secretly revolted against his father and attempted to hijack the kingdom. His stubbornness and rebellion led to his demise and early death. (See 2 Samuel 18 and 19.)

Orthodox Jews bring their sons to the tomb of Absalom, located near the edge of a Jewish cemetery, and recall the tragic story of Absalom's rebellion against his father. Their purpose is to paint a vivid mental image of the dangers of disobedience and the high price a son pays when not following wise counsel.

A similar method was employed by a youth minister who took his entire youth group to a local cemetery and had them sit down on the grass. Near him was a tombstone with the name of a young man who had once served the Lord but had died in a sinful condition. He began telling about this young man's life and revealed how his life was cut short by his rebellion. He said the image painted by his message and the setting of the graveyard impressed the minds of the youth, and he noticed an immediate change in the attitude of the entire group for many months, especially after they discovered it was the grave of the youth leader's own brother. Visual learning helps stimulate recall. Our weekly telecast, *Manna-fest*, uses large props and graphics to form visual images of the message. Parents of young children often tell me, "My kids love your program. They love to see what props you use."

2. Teach your children how to pray.

Christ's disciples said, "Teach us to pray" (Luke 11:1). They knew Christ engaged in early morning prayer (Mark 1:35) and witnessed miracles resulting from His prayer life. The best way of teaching your children how to pray is to be an example and pray yourself!

As a child in the 1960s, I can recall my father praying in his upstairs church office with the windows opened. I just knew they could hear him across the river at the county jail. Many times in the evening I could hear Dad's prayers filtering up through the air vents in my bedroom floor as he interceded in the basement of our house. When I was sick or in difficulty, I believed God would hear Dad's prayers. His prayer life was an example and a pattern for me to understand *how* to pray. Let your children see and hear you pray at home and not just in church.

The simplest *beginner* prayers are praying at bedtime. In bedtime prayer,

Orthodox Jews mention four archangels, two of whom are mentioned in the Bible (Michael and Gabriel) and two found in Apocryphal (nonbiblical) sources. They pray, "In the name of the Lord, the God of Israel: Michael on my right, Gabriel on my left, Uriel before me, Raphael behind me, and above my head the Shekinah [presence] of God." Raphael was traditionally an angel of healing, and Uriel was believed to be the guiding light of the Holy Scriptures.[17] Children should learn a bedtime prayer as soon as they can speak.

Before sending a child off to school, a parent should pray with them. Using the scripture, "So Abraham rose early in the morning" (Gen. 22:3), the *Shacharit*, meaning "early morning hour," prayers were the first of three daily prayers. The moment a devout Jew awakes, he prays, "I gratefully thank You, O living and eternal King, for You have returned my soul within me with compassion—abundant is your faithfulness."[18] We know Christ prayed a great while before sunrise (Mark 1:35), and at the temple, morning prayers were offered as the sun rose, beginning a new day. As a parent, speak a protective prayer over your children before they depart from the security of your dwelling.

3. Involve your children in a local assembly.

Most churches in North America have a children's ministry. Growing up, our church's children's ministry was more of a babysitting service where kids went to *kill time* while their parents worshiped in the main sanctuary. Today, some of the most progressive church programs are found in a local children's ministry, especially among the larger congregations.

Traveling with us until he was eleven, my son Jonathan was a connoisseur of children's ministries. After a service he would inform me where that ministry's strengths and weaknesses were as well as their communication skills at reaching the kids. If you attend a church without a children's ministry, consider getting with the leadership and initiating a ministry for the children.

4. Speak blessing over your children.

Words are arrows that can cut or a balm that can heal. As it is written, "Death and life are in the power of the tongue, and those who love it will eat its fruit" (Prov. 18:21). Parents and grandparents should never speak down to their children in a condescending manner. A child should never hear, "You're dumb…You're stupid…You're never going to amount to anything…" Throughout their life, children remember wounding words.

The patriarchs are examples of how to speak over your children. They knew when it was time to rebuke their sons when they did wrong (Gen. 34:30), but they also knew how to commend them when they did right. Speaking blessing is not an exemption from discipline but is an affirmation to the child for choosing the right path.

5. Pray for their spiritual growth and protection.

There is never a day that passes without me petitioning God to bless my children and family in the morning and evening. I find myself praying the same prayer my father prayed over his four children: "Lord, protect them, keeping them from harm, danger, and any disabling accident." Do not assume that just because the Scriptures give promises of protection, these promises operate automatically without any effort of the believer to claim the promises personally. In the same manner Christ did in Matthew 4:1–11, we must read, believe, and verbally speak (confess) the Scriptures for them to be activated and effective.

6. Lay hands upon them and bless them (Matt. 19:13).

> Then they also brought infants to Him that He might touch them; but when the disciples saw it, they rebuked them. But Jesus called them to Him and said, "Let the little children come to Me, and do not forbid them; for of such is the kingdom of God."
>
> —LUKE 18:15–16

The Jewish tradition of having a righteous person bless a child was repeated by Christ throughout His ministry. In the Jewish faith, the Sabbath begins on Friday at sunset (about 6:00 p.m.). Every Friday night, the devout father will lay hands upon his children to bless them. This custom comes from Jacob's blessing on Ephraim and Manasseh (Gen. 48). As a Christian, you can follow the role model of Jacob and bless your children each week during the Jewish Sabbath or the traditional Christian Sabbath.

7. Have men and women of God bless your children.

When I was a child, many great men and women of God ministered at my dad's churches. I was always in awe of their amazing testimonies and faith-building stories. I also sat under large tents and witnessed men of God praying for those in need and can recall the excitement charging the atmosphere. When these individuals would pray over us, I experienced a spiritual and emotional *charge*, which I still remember. There is heavenly reaction through prayer, and spiritual authority is released through the power of the blessing. When you are in the presence of great servants of God and those carrying God's presence in their life, ask them to pray over your children as Christ did the children He encountered.

JEWISH SECRETS TO TRAINING CHILDREN

Most Christians know the verse, "Train up a child in the way he should go, and when he is old he will not depart from it" (Prov. 22:6). The Western notion of training a child includes verbal instruction and education mixed with correction when necessary. The Hebrew verb translated "train" is *chanak* and has become part of contemporary Hebrew terminology for learning. Today *chinuch* means "education," and *mekhanekh* alludes to an educator. The Hebrew word *child* is *na`ar* and can refer to the age between childhood and maturity.[19]

The Torah instructs parents to teach the words of God to their children and their children after them (Deut. 4:9; 6:7). The Talmud reveals the father's significance in teaching his son by saying: "The father is bound in respect of his son, to circumcise…teach him Torah, take a wife for him, and teach him a craft" (The Talmud, Kiddushin 29a). In ancient Israel, the men were the spiritual leaders at home and providers for their families. The priests were the spiritual leaders at the temple who daily practiced the *sacrificial* and *ceremonial* aspects of the law for and on behalf of the people. The prophets taught the revealed instructions of God, pronounced blessings for obedience, and warned of impending judgment if the nation rejected the moral, social, and judicial commandments. Jewish fathers from the twelve tribes raised their families to follow all aspects of God's commandments to ensure God's continual favor. Teaching began at an early age.

From a Hebraic perspective, *training* a child is more than consistently instructing a child in right and wrong. Every child is born with a distinct personality, certain inner gifts, and abilities that are as unique as that child's individual fingerprints. As children grow from infant to child, child to teen, and teen to young adult, the parents are to discern the *inclinations* and possible *gifts* within the child's personality, tapping into the possibilities of how God can and will use the child to fulfill his or her appointed destiny.

Scripture tells us: "Delight yourself also in the LORD, and He shall give you the desires of your heart" (Ps. 37:4). Traditionally, this has been interpreted as, "Whatever we desire, God will give it to us." We know God answers prayer and grants petitions (John 14:13; 16:23). However, another way of interpreting Psalm 37:4 is that God gives, or places in our hearts, certain desires that He will help us to fulfill. Christian teenagers often request prayer for God's will to be done in their lives. I reply, "What do you feel deep in your spirit that you want to do?" After they answer the question, I respond, "Then make preparations to do it."

Their concern is, "What if it is not what God wants?"

The answer is, "Who do you think gave you the *desire* that is in your heart and the inclination toward that particular gift or career? God gave you those desires, and God will help you fulfill them." These inclinations begin early in life, and directing them must begin early.

IT'S AS SWEET AS HONEY

God called the Promised Land a land of milk and honey, which is both an allusion to the richness of the land and a Hebrew idiom for prosperity. The Mishna Rabba says that the study of Torah is compared to milk and honey, since the Word is sweeter than honey (Ps. 19:10). John the Baptist ate "wild honey" (Mark 1:6). It was an Arab custom to rub the roof of an infant's mouth with date juice. The famous sixteenth-century Protestant reformer John Calvin mentions a custom where the Jews would take honey and smear it on the palates of newborn children.[20] According to rabbinical tradition, on the first day of school a child is shown a slate containing two verses of Scripture—Leviticus 1:1 and Deuteronomy 33:4—along with letters of the alphabet and the sentence: "The Law will be my calling." The teacher reads the words, and the child repeats them back. Afterward the slate is coated with honey, and the teacher licks the honey in front of the children (Ezek.

3:3). Following this, each child is given sweet cakes with scriptures written on them.[21] There are 613 commandments in the Torah that devout Jews are to follow, and rabbis do not want children to view the law of God as filled with negative warnings and commandments. They want the children's tender minds to perceive the law as being sweet. This illustrated "sermon" makes a lasting impression on the young minds.

JEWISH METHODS OF TEACHING

There are several methods developed in the Jewish teaching process that, in my opinion, are effective in helping a child or young person retain knowledge. I divide these methods into four categories, each influencing a different part of the person. They are:

1. *Visual*—knowledge received through visual illustrations
2. *Repetitive*—knowledge received through repeating information
3. *Chanting*—knowledge received through the repetitive musical tones
4. *Musical*—knowledge received through singing songs

Visual teaching

Judaism is a religion that uses visual religious objects to illustrate the Jews' faith. The doorposts of a religious Jewish home are marked by a mezuzah. (See chapter 8.) Thus, a Jew cannot enter or exit his home without being reminded of his commitment to obey God's Word and raise his family in the knowledge of the Torah. Jewish men pray at the Western Wall in Israel and in synagogues throughout the world, wearing a specially designed prayer shawl called a *tallit*. The tallit has a remarkable history, rich in symbolism. The blue color, the fringes (called *tzitziot*), and the number of knots on the four corners all hold spiritual significance. A tallit is often presented to a son at age thirteen or a son-in-law at his wedding; at times a student receives one from his teacher. Jewish men also wear *tefillin*, also called *phylacteries*. These are a pair of black leather boxes with small parchments inserted, connected to a long leather strap that is wrapped around the right arm, beginning with the fingers and hand. The box is placed above the forehead and is to be worn in the morning during weekly prayers. This concept is based upon the command to bind the Word: "You shall bind them as a sign on your hand, and they shall be as frontlets between your eyes" (Deut. 6:8).

These religious items are strictly Jewish and set them apart as the "chosen people" (Deut. 7:6). The yearly feasts are also *illustrated messages*. During Passover, a *Seder* plate and four cups of wine are set on the table. The *matzot* (unleavened bread) is a reminder of the Hebrew nation's quick departure from Egypt. The *maror*, or bitter herbs, recall the bitterness of their slavery. A special mixture of nut, apples, cinnamon, and wine, called *horoset*, symbolizes the mortar used to make bricks in Egypt. The shank bone is a visual reminder of the sacrificial lamb eaten the night before their departure. Passover is an illustrated message. During Hanukkah, a nine-branched candlestick (menorah) is lit for eight consecutive nights. Each night the amazing story of the cleansing of the temple is retold and gifts are given. Children play games, and the mother prepares special food for this season. Again, history is more than told—it is illustrated.

Christ used the visual method in His teaching, much of which was outdoors. As He spoke parables about sheep and goats, wheat and tares, and men sowing the seed of the Word, He was surrounded outdoors by the very things of which He was speaking. When asked a question, He often illustrated the answer. When asked about children, He placed a child in the midst of the people, and when being questioned about taxes, He requested a coin to illustrate the law of paying taxes (Mark 9:36; 12:13–17).

Repetitive teaching

A person can usually retain information if it is repeated seven times. When Jesus taught the multitudes, He would say, "Again I say to you…" (Matt. 19:24). In the Torah, God continually reminded Israel not to forget His law once they entered the Promised Land (Deut. 4:9, 23, 31). My son and daughter both learned the English alphabet by quoting a scripture that began with a letter of the alphabet, such as: A—"All have sinned, and come short of the glory of God" (Rom. 3:23, KJV); B—"Believe on the Lord Jesus Christ, and thou shalt be saved" (Acts 16:31, KJV), and so forth. I was amazed with the speed with which they were able to learn the alphabet and the scripture.

Chanting or singing

When the Torah is read in the synagogue, a cantor (*hazzan* in Hebrew) will sing a melodious prayer and chant in a rhythm from the Torah. Five times a day, Muslims around the world hear prayers from the mosque being said in a chanting song-type fashion. The psalms were originally sung and not simply read. I can take a ten-line poem, give it to a hundred people, and ask them to learn it and repeat it back in ten minutes. Some can, and others will stumble. If the same poem is set to music, most can sing it back in ten minutes. Remember the little alphabet song in kindergarten, "A, B, C, D, E, F, G…"? Knowledge is easier to remember when set to music and singing. I believe this is because knowledge passes through the mind first, afterward becoming part of the spirit. Music, however, moves us from the inside out. Music moves the inner part of a person, the spirit, as seen when David played his harp and Saul was delivered from an evil spirit (1 Sam. 16:23).

Music and singing are important parts of Jewish worship today, just as they were in ancient Jewish worship. The Torah records the victorious song of Moses (Exod. 15) and a prophetic hymn at the conclusion of Moses's ministry (Deut. 32). The Scriptures indicate that Deborah and Barak sang at the defeat of the Canaanites (Judg. 5). David was an expert harp player and was often called *the sweet psalmist of Israel* (1 Sam. 16:16–17). Solomon wrote thousands of proverbs and penned one thousand five songs (1 Kings 4:32). The tabernacle of David was a tent where continual worship went up to God (1 Chron. 15:1), and the temple of Solomon was filled with music and singing, including one hundred twenty trumpet players (2 Chron. 5:12). Instruments included trumpets, harps, and lyres, blending with the daily rituals of the house of God.

In Israel, I was told that musical repetition was believed to be the method by which the ancient prophets taught their students in the schools of the prophets (2 Kings 2:3–7). The class was divided in half, as one group sang the Scriptures, and the second group repeated the words through chanting or singing.

Three places to sing

In the early days of Israel there were three places where the sound of singing could be heard: in the home, in the synagogue, and in the temple. The home was the place for daily prayers, the synagogue hosted weekly worship, and the temple was the site of yearly gatherings when all men over twenty traveled to Jerusalem three times a year. In the home, hymns were sung, as illustrated by when Christ sung with His disciples after the supper (Mark 14:26). In the synagogue, the cantor led the chanting as the Torah was read, and in the temple, the priests directed the choirs of Levites in praise. After A.D. 70, the Jewish dinner table became the altar of the temple. Once seated, the family sang songs (*zimrot*) replicating the choirs in the ancient temple.

Paul mentions that believers should be "speaking to one another in psalms and hymns and spiritual songs, singing and making melody in your heart to the Lord" (Eph. 5:19). The psalms were words accompanied by musical instruments, hymns are songs of praise to God, and the spiritual songs are songs the Holy Spirit births in our hearts. The New Testament reveals three places where songs can be and will be sung:

1. In the home: In the first century, worship was conducted in the homes of believers (Philem. 2). These were the first churches.

2. In the church: Believers united for weekly gatherings for fellowship, study, and worship (Acts 20:7).

3. In the heavenly temple: In A.D. 70, the Jewish temple in Jerusalem was destroyed. However, John saw a heavenly temple with twenty-four elders and one hundred forty-four thousand Jews from twelve tribes playing harps and singing new songs (Rev. 4:10; 14:1–3).

Hebrew songs focus on God—His power, majesty, mercy, and ability. The songs are based upon the many stories in the Torah and Prophets.

It is noted that Jewish praying is more worship than petitioning God for needs to be met. "The song is critical to a correct understanding of Jewish prayers. As Herschel has observed, 'Let us not misunderstand the nature of prayer, particularly in Jewish tradition. The primary purpose of prayer is not to make request. The primary purpose is to praise, to sing, to chant. Because the essence of prayer is song, and man cannot live without a song.'"[22]

I keep gospel music CDs in our home, in both vehicles, and in my office. Studies have indicated that when children listen to music, they are able to perform certain cognitive computer skills, such as solving computer math puzzles, faster.[23] Other studies have shown that spending just thirty minutes a day listening to music has a beneficial effect on blood pressure.[24] Some studies have even shown that listening to classical music, such as Mozart, can increase IQ scores.[25]

The power of inspired music, such as hymns and spiritual songs, can not only edify and lift up a person's spirit, but it can also relieve emotional and spiritual distress and stress. David proved this when he played a harp and King Saul, who was mentally tormented, was refreshed and made well (1 Sam. 16:23).

FULFILLING YOUR LIFE CYCLES

Psalm 90:12 says, "So teach us to number our days, that we may gain a heart of wisdom." All living things move through cycles. The moon experiences four cycles, which mark one month. The earth circles the sun in 365.25 days, making one year. Just as the earth experiences four distinct seasons of spring, summer, fall, and winter, our lives move from the youth of spring, to the growth of summer, into the maturity of fall, and into the closing days of our life represented by winter.

Each human life cycle has a new level of maturity and spiritual responsibility. Spiritual maturity is not automatically inbred at birth but is taught by example, instruction from the Word, and by prayer. This is why Peter wrote that believers should, "Grow in the grace and knowledge of our Lord and Savior Jesus Christ" (2 Pet. 3:18). Be in prayer that you and your children will fulfill all your days, each of you completing your specific life cycle and destiny.

■ ■ ■ ✡ ■ ■ ■

WHAT *God* KNEW

Being the Creator, God understood the physical, emotional, and spiritual development of each human being, and He initiated specific time frames for special life cycles, giving each person an opportunity to learn, mature, and experience a new level of grace and blessing. God intended that we celebrate these life cycles and affirm each person in the faith and give encouragement.

WHAT DEVOUT *Jews* KNOW

Training a child begins early in life. The main cycles of life for a male child—eight days, thirteen years of age, twenty years of age, thirty years of age, and marriage—are significant seasons that are to be celebrated. Life is a celebration from birth until the day of departure.

WHAT *Christians* SHOULD KNOW

Believers must understand the significance of these major life cycles and center special celebrations and emphasis on these seasons.

1. Eight days after birth

There is no requirement for Gentiles to circumcise their sons other than for possible health reasons. However, eight days after a son's birth should be marked as a special moment, and appreciation should be given to God. A special meal prepared with family and friends present can be enjoyed.

Following the Jewish pattern, a child should be dedicated after about thirty days. By this time, the infant has physically adjusted to being in the world and hearing the voice of others.

2. The age thirteen

It is possible this is the age of accountability, and it is important to honor this time of entering into adulthood and the age of responsibility with celebration—and not with the attitude of, "Now you're on your own…time to grow up…you're not a baby anymore…" Christian parents can customize a special ceremony and a meal at home or book a private room for family and friends to join in a celebration.

- Have friends read letters expressing what your son or daughter means to them.

- Mother and Dad should affirm the child publicly, yet without embarrassing them. (They are teenagers now.)

- Present them a special study Bible honoring their new entrance into adulthood.

- Present them with an item (signed perhaps) from the person whom they admire the most or look up to.

- Have a spiritual leader they love or respect present to pray a blessing for God's favor over them.

- Begin treating them with respect and giving them responsibilities not given before.

3. The age twenty

At age twenty, a new maturity has arrived. They are no longer teenagers but have entered into a new level of mental and emotional judgment and choices.

- Host an all-girls event for a daughter.

- Host an all-guys event for a son.

4. The age thirty

If a person is married, this should be a significant moment of maturity in a man or woman's life. Everyone can remember the emotional feeling of turning thirty. To some, it brings a reality that we are getting older. Instead of being a "depressing time," we should be reminded that Jesus's ministry did not begin—nor could a man be a priest in the temple—until age thirty. Thirty is a good age!

5. The marriage

Most Christian couples preparing for marriage have their own customs and traditions for this beautiful life-changing celebration. Some couples are now asking messianic rabbis to perform a special blessing in Hebrew over them during the ceremony. Others simply request that the priestly blessing in Numbers 6:24–26, which was—and still is—spoken over Israel, be spoken over them:

> The LORD bless you and keep you;
> The LORD make His face shine upon you,
> And be gracious to you;
> The LORD lift up His countenance upon you,
> And give you peace.

Believers must always celebrate life, from the *womb* to the *tomb*, from the conception of a child until we step out into eternity and enter our eternal home. Then it can be said: "Precious in the sight of the LORD is the death of His saints" (Ps. 116:15).

Chapter 6

NAMES ARE PROPHETIC AND CAN REVEAL A CHILD'S DESTINY

CODE 6:
*There is significance in the names
you give your children.*

*And He said, "Your name shall no longer be called Jacob, but
Israel; for you have struggled with God and with men, and
have prevailed."*

—GENESIS 32:28

SINCE ABRAHAM'S TIME, WHEN A HEBREW CHILD WAS BORN, THE
most significant element of the event was the *meaning* of the name
given to the infant by the father or both parents. Circumcision demonstrated inclusion in the Jewish covenant, but the child's birth name often
identified his or her prophetic destiny or God's purpose for that child's life.
Names could be linked to a particular event in the parent's life or an unusual
circumstance in the child's birth. The meaning of the name was very significant to ancient Hebrews, and it still is to Jewish families today.

The Dueling Baby Makers

Jacob had two wives, Rachel and Leah. Rachel was unable to conceive. However, Leah was quite fertile. When Leah wasn't birthing children, her handmaids and Rachel's handmaids filled in the gap! It was like a baby-making contest to see which wife could tally the most children's births. The process concluded with twelve sons, all given specific names that identified them personally and prophetically.

THE SONS OF JACOB

The Birth Order and Name	Meaning of the Name	Statement From the Mother	Reference
The first sons of Leah			
1. Reuben	Behold a son	My husband will love me.	Genesis 29:32
2. Simeon	Hearing	God has heard me again.	Genesis 29:33
3. Levi	Joined	My husband will be joined to me.	Genesis 29:34
4. Judah	Praised	I will praise the Lord.	Genesis 29:35
Rachel's sons through her handmaiden Bilhah			
5. Dan	Judge	God has judged me and heard.	Genesis 30:6
6. Naphtali	Wrestlings	With great wrestling I prayed.	Genesis 30:8
Leah's sons through her handmaiden Zilpah			
7. Gad	A troop	A troop comes.	Genesis 30:11
8. Asher	Happy	The women will call me blessed.	Genesis 30:13
Leah's other sons she birthed			
9. Issachar	Hire	I gave my maiden to my husband.	Genesis 30:18
10. Zebulon	Dwelling	Now will my husband dwell with me.	Genesis 30:20

Rachel's sons she birthed			
11. Joseph	Increase	God take away my reproach.	Genesis 30:24
12. Benoni or Benjamin	Sorrow	She was dying in Ephrath.	Genesis 35:18
	Son of my right hand	Name given by Jacob.	

Each of the twelve sons received a name based upon the circumstances of his birth and the prayers prayed by his mother.

THE POWER OF A NAME

The personality profile of a child is developed through the DNA passed on from both parents and ancestors. However, the value system, self-esteem, and affirmation that mold how a child thinks about himself or herself, and how he or she treats others, grow from the seeds planted over the years by parents and family members. This is understood in the Jewish faith and confirmed throughout Scripture. Parents have three responsibilities in naming and disciplining a child.

1. Selecting a child's name that bears a significant spiritual meaning and of which the child can be proud

2. Consistently encouraging and affirming the child during the parental training process

3. Determining proper actions for discipline based on each child's unique personality

In many cultures, prior to a child's birth the birth parents agree on the selection of a special name. The child is often named after a beloved family member, relative, special friend, or famous person. Christians often select biblical names such as Abigail, Sarah, Martha, and Mary for girls, or names such as Timothy, Peter, Paul, Mark, or Luke for boys. High on the list are biblical names reflecting great feats, famous stories, or high moral character. Seldom if ever are the biblical names Judas, Ichabod, or Bathsheba selected—no doubt because of the negative incidents linked to their lives.

All names have meanings. At times in the Scriptures when God was aligning the future destiny of a person, He would change that person's name. Abram's name was changed to Abraham, and Sarai's name was changed to Sarah (Gen. 17:5, 15). Moses's servant Oshea's name was changed to Joshua (Num. 13:16, KJV). Christ changed the name of Simon to Peter and the name of Saul to Paul (Matt. 16:18; Acts 13:9). One of the most noted name changes was when God changed Jacob's name to Israel. The name Israel means, "One who prevails, or one who rules with God," alluding to how Jacob successfully wrestled the angel (Gen. 32).

These name changes were significant because the new name identified them as a person in covenant with God or revealed a prophetic destiny God had designed for their future.[1]

The Original Name (meaning)	The New Name (meaning)
Abram—many	Abraham—father of many
Sarai—contentious	Sarah—lady or princess
Oshea—salvation	Joshua—God is salvation
Simon—he has heard	Peter—a little stone
Saul—asked for	Paul—small; humble

Genesis 35 illustrates the prophetic significance of a child's name. Jacob's beloved wife, Rachel, died while giving birth to a son. As her spirit was departing, she suggested naming the baby *Ben-oni*, which means, "son of my sorrow." The father rejected the suggestion, instead naming the infant *Benjamin*, meaning, "son of my right hand." Jacob had no desire to identify his last son with the sad death of his mother during his childbirth.

Occasionally, God became directly involved in the naming of a child. In Luke 1, the angel Gabriel told a temple priest, Zacharias, that he would father a son named John. Nine months later the people chose to name the newborn after his father. Zacharias refused and insisted on giving his only son the name revealed by the angel—the name John (Luke 1:59–63). John's name is derived from the Hebrew *Yochanan*, meaning, "God is gracious." At conception, Mary was informed that her son's name would be Jesus, or *Yeshua* in Hebrew (Luke 1:31), meaning, "salvation."

In ancient Israel, children born in times of national disaster or calamity were often named as a reminder of that tragedy. In the days of Eli the high priest, the ark of the covenant was seized, and Eli's two sons, Hophni and Phinehas, were slain in battle (1 Sam. 4:11). Phinehas's wife began travailing in childbirth after hearing the news. She named the son *Ichabod*, meaning the glory of God had departed, because the ark of God was captured (1 Sam. 4:21).[2]

NAMING YOUR CHILDREN

When selecting a name for your child, parents should understand the meaning of the name. After the birth of our son, my wife and I selected the name Jonathan, which means, "Jehovah has given." My son's middle name is Gabriel, commemorating the angel who announced Christ's birth. (We brought him home on Christmas day!) Twelve years before my daughter was born, I saw her in a dream, and she told me her name. It was Amanda, meaning, "she who must be loved." This is the name we gave her twelve years after the dream on August 2, 2001, the day she was born.

I am named after my father, Perry Stone Sr. My father's father gave him the name Perry. His middle name, Fred, was requested by the doctor. Dad said, "When Doctor Hatfield traveled six miles on horseback, through two feet of snow, I was already born. The doctor said, 'For all of my difficulty getting here, I want you to give the boy the middle name of Fred, after a famous actor that I like.'" I once researched the name Perry and found the name in the Hebrew text of the Old Testament. It is spelled *periy*, and it means *fruit* (Prov. 11:30). Since our ministry is worldwide and we are seeing fruit for the kingdom of God, my name fits my destiny!

This concept of receiving a new name is not isolated to biblical history. One of the future blessings of believers in heaven is that all believers will receive "…some of the hidden manna…a white stone, and…a new name" (Rev. 2:17). When Christ returns as the King of kings to rule on Earth, He also will receive "a name written that no one knew except Himself" (Rev. 19:12). We will all enter the thousand-year reign of the Messiah with new names!

Selecting the proper name should be seasoned with prayer and research and be agreed upon by the parents. The biblical evidence is clear that the Jewish people understood the meaning of names and were careful to select names that would apply to the child. In the lists below, I have listed biblical names and their meanings for both sons and daughters. Some are common among Christians, and others among the Jewish community. As you will see, these names all have a positive meaning.

BIBLICAL NAMES FOR BOYS

Hebrew/Biblical Name	Scripture Reference	Meaning
Adam	Genesis 2:19	Man, mankind
Aaron	Exodus 4:14	Exalted one
Abraham	Genesis 17:5	Exalted father
Asher	Genesis 30:13	Happy, blessed
Barak	Judges 4:6	Lightning
Barnabas	Acts 13:43	Son of exhortation
Benjamin	Genesis 35:18	Son of the right hand
Boaz	Ruth 2:1	Swiftness
Dan	Genesis 30:6	God is judge
Daniel	Daniel 1:6	God is my judge
David	Ruth 4:22	Beloved
Eleazar	Exodus 6:25	My God has helped
Elijah	1 Kings 17:1	My God is God
Elisha	1 Kings 19:16	My God is salvation
Enoch	Genesis 5:21	Dedicated
Ephraim	Genesis 41:52	Fruitful
Ezekiel	Ezekiel 1:3	God strengthens
Gabriel	Daniel 8:16	God is my strength
Gideon	Judges 6:11	Feller or hewer
Isaac	Genesis 17:19	Laughter
Isaiah	2 Kings 19:2	God is salvation

Hebrew/Biblical Name	Scripture Reference	Meaning
Jacob	Genesis 25:26	Holder of the heel
Japheth	Genesis 5:32	Enlarged
Jeremiah	Jeremiah 1:1	God has uplifted
Jethro	Exodus 3:1	Abundance
Joel	Joel 1:1	God is God
John	Matthew 3:1	God is gracious
Jonathan	Judges 18:30	God has given
Joseph	Genesis 30:24	He (God) will add
Joshua	Deuteronomy 1:38	God is salvation
Judah	Genesis 29:35	Praised
Levi	Genesis 29:34	Connected, attached
Matthew	Matthew 9:9	Gift of God
Michael	Daniel 12:1	Who is like God
Nathan	2 Samuel 5:14	Gift, giver
Nehemiah	Nehemiah 1:1	Comforted by God
Noah	Genesis 5:29	Rest, comfort
Obadiah	1 Kings 18:3	Servant of God
Philemon	Philemon 1	Affectionate
Philip	Acts 6:5	Friend of horses
Reuben	Genesis 29:32	Behold a son
Samuel	1 Samuel 1:20	God has heard
Seth	Genesis 4:25	Place, appointed
Simeon	Genesis 29:33	He (God) has heard
Solomon	1 Kings 1:30	Peace
Stephen	Acts 6:5	Crown

Hebrew/Biblical Name	Scripture Reference	Meaning
Thomas	John 20:27	Twin
Timothy	1 Timothy 1:2	To honor
Zechariah	Zechariah 1:1	Remembering God

BIBLICAL NAMES FOR GIRLS

Hebrew/Biblical Name	Scripture Reference	Meaning
Abigail	1 Samuel 25:3	My father is joy
Anna	Luke 2:36	Grace
Bernice	Acts 25:13	Bearer of victory
Bethany	Matthew 21:17	House of figs
Beulah	Isaiah 62:4	Married
Deborah	Judges 4:4	Bee
Elizabeth	Luke 1:41	My God is an oath, abundance
Esther	Esther 2:7	Possibly meaning star (Persian)
Eunice	2 Timothy 1:5	Good victory
Eve	Genesis 3:20	To breathe, or to live
Hadassah	Esther 2:7	Myrtle tree
Hannah	1 Samuel 1:2	Gracious, full of mercy
Jemimah	Job 42:14	Dove
Joanna	Luke 8:3	God is gracious
Judith	Genesis 26:34	Jewess
Keturah	Genesis 25:1	Incense
Lydia	Acts 16:14	From Lydia
Martha	Luke 10:38	Mistress of the house
Mary	Matthew 1:20	My beloved, my love

Hebrew/Biblical Name	Scripture Reference	Meaning
Miriam	Exodus 15:20	A form of Mary (above)
Moriah	Genesis 22:2	Seen by God
Naamah	1 Kings 14:31	Pleasant
Naomi	Ruth 1:2	Pleasantness
Ophrah	1 Chronicles 4:14	A fawn
Priscilla	Acts 18:2	Ancient
Rachel	Genesis 29:6	Ewe, the daughter
Rhoda	Acts 12:13	Rose
Rizpah	2 Samuel 3:7	Coal, hot stone
Ruth	Ruth 1:4	Friend
Salome	Mark 16:1	Peace
Sapphira	Acts 5:1	Sapphire
Sarah	Genesis 17:15	Princess, noble
Sharon	Song of Solomon 2:1	A fertile plain
Sheba	1 Kings 10:1	An oath
Shua	1 Chronicles 7:32	Wealth
Susanna	Luke 8:3	A lily, a rose
Tabitha	Acts 9:36–43	Gazelle
Tamar	Genesis 38:6	Palm tree
Zipporah	Exodus 2:21	Bird

THE WORDS WE SPEAK

Affirmation of a child is important to his or her mental and emotional development. Affirmation confirms the child is studying, making good decisions, and properly following instructions. Affirming occurs with your words. According to examples in the Torah, once a verbal blessing left the mouth of a righteous person, the blessing could only be reversed if the people (or nation) went into sin or disobedience to God. For example, when Balak, the king of Moab, hired the seer Balaam to speak a curse upon the nation of Israel, Balaam opened his mouth to curse, but a prophetic blessing of God's favor flowed from his mouth. When Balak demanded that Balaam reverse the blessing, the old prophet said:

> Behold, I have received a command to bless; He has blessed, and I cannot reverse it.
>
> —NUMBERS 23:20

Balaam and others discovered that you can't bless what God has cursed, and you can't curse what God has blessed! Proverbs 18:21 tells us, "Death and life are in the power of the tongue." Solomon mentions the "tongue" nineteen times in Proverbs. He reveals that wholesome words are life and blessing, but negative, lying words cause ruin and affliction to the soul (Prov. 26:28).

In the New Testament we are instructed to "let your 'Yes' be 'Yes,' and your 'No,' 'No,'" or, as we would say today, keep your answers to a simple yes or no (James 5:12). When someone asks for your opinion, it is often easy to tell everything you know about a person or a situation. "Did you hear about…" or "Have you heard the latest on…" or "What have you heard about…" are questions commonly asked among ministers as they *fellowship* over a cup of coffee. I recall years ago hearing about a fellow minister who had fallen in a weak moment to an act of immorality. Because we were ordained in the same denomination, I knew his name would be brought up among groups of ministers. The Holy Spirit spoke to me and said, "I don't want you to say one thing about this man…do not even engage in a conversation about him. He has asked for My forgiveness and is going through a restoration process. Leave the matter between him and Me!" From that moment on, I refused to hear, repeat, or listen to anything regarding this man. My conscience was clear toward him and God.

THE ACTIONS WE TAKE

Noah had three sons: Shem, Ham, and Japheth (Gen. 6:10). As Noah was building the ark to save his family from the coming flood, God gave this promise:

> But I will establish My covenant with you; and you shall go into the ark—you, your sons, your wife, and your sons' wives with you.
>
> —Genesis 6:18

Noah understood that God's will meant the preservation of his entire family and not just himself. The three sons and their wives were predestined to repopulate the earth following the Flood. When the time of the deluge arrived, God instructed, "Come into the ark, you and all your household…" (Gen. 7:1). After spending over one year in this floating zoo, God "remembered Noah, and every living thing" (Gen. 8:1). As they exited from the boat, "God blessed Noah and his sons, and said to them: 'Be fruitful and multiply, and fill the earth'" (Gen. 9:1). This blessing was imparted to Noah and his three sons.

Afterward, Noah planted a vineyard and was drunk with the wine. It is written that Ham "saw the nakedness of his father" (v. 22). However, Shem and Japheth walked backward into the tent to cover their father. Growing up, I heard people teach that God cursed Ham for what he did. There is no place in the biblical record that Ham was cursed. In fact we read:

> Then he said: "Cursed be Canaan; a servant of servants he shall be to his brethren."
>
> —Genesis 9:25

Why was Canaan cursed and not Ham? Canaan was the youngest of Ham's four sons (Gen. 10:6). When Noah cursed Canaan, why didn't he also place a curse on Ham's other three sons? The answer is that Canaan may have actually sinned with Noah while he was drunk. We do know that Canaan settled in the Promised Land prior to Abraham's arrival and was the father of numerous tribes who also lived in that region.

The point is that Ham was never cursed, because Ham was blessed by God! Canaan, however, placed a terrible curse on his descendants because of the sin he committed and the curse he lived under. The actions of parents can have an impact upon future generations.

Preserving Your Name

Proverbs 22:1 says, "A good name is to be chosen rather than great riches, loving favor rather than silver and gold." Solomon wrote, "A good name is better than precious ointment, and the day of death than the day of one's birth" (Eccles. 7:1). Your character, words, actions, work ethic, and treatment of others all impact your name. When I hear the name *Judas*, I think of a traitor. The name *Korah* brings to mind rebellion, and the name *Jezebel* paints an image of a self-serving, controlling woman.

By guarding your words and actions, you can protect a good name. By giving your child a meaningful name, you can help point them to a future destiny filled with expectation and excitement.

WHAT *God* KNEW

The meaning of names is very significant to God, and often the destiny of the person is linked to the meaning of the name. Joseph had two sons in Egypt: Ephraim and Manasseh. The name *Manasseh* was given because God had made Joseph to forget all his toil. *Ephraim* meant, "God has made me fruitful" (Gen. 41:51–52). These sons indicated a new beginning for Joseph. The names of redeemed believers are written in a book in heaven, and God promises a new name for us in heaven (Rev. 2:17). If names are this important to God, then names and their meaning should be important to us.

WHAT DEVOUT *Jews* KNOW

Devout Jews understand the importance of giving a meaningful name to their children. Traditionally, the name of a son is not revealed until the day of his circumcision. The announcement is highly anticipated and often followed by tears and rejoicing when the name of the child is announced before family and friends.

WHAT *Christians* SHOULD KNOW

The Scriptures indicate we should properly name our children, train them in the ways of God, pray over them, and bless them with our words through the laying on of hands. This process is a progression that plants the seeds of spiritual growth in the minds and spirits of our children. When they grow older, they will not depart from what you have planted in them.

Chapter 7

BIBLICAL SECRETS FOR A WOMAN WHO WANTS A CHILD

CODE 7:
God can make the barren womb rejoice.

He maketh the barren woman to keep house, and to be a joyful mother of children. Praise ye the LORD.

—PSALM 113:9, KJV

ORLDWIDE, ONE IN EVERY SIX COUPLES HAS DIFFICULTY IN conceiving.[1] Infertility, defined as the biological inability to conceive a child, has numerous causes—some related to the man and others related to numerous biological causes in the woman's body. For any young couple who strongly desires children, the barren womb is often an unexplainable mystery. Hopeful parents live with, yet continually question, "Why not us, Lord?" According to the Scriptures, there is a promise of children for the barren womb!

The Hebrew nation was birthed out of barrenness. Not only did the barren, empty wilderness blossom like a rose (Isa. 35:1), but also the seed of Israel's family tree was planted by sons whose mothers were barren. The first three male patriarchs were Abraham, Isaac, and Jacob. Abraham's wife, Sarah, was ninety years of age and childless (Gen. 11:30). Abraham's son Isaac was married at age forty (Gen. 25:20), yet his wife Rebekah was barren (v. 21). Isaac's son Jacob was married for many years, and his favorite wife, Rachel, could not conceive (Gen. 29:31). Eventually, a miracle of conception occurred in the wombs of Sarah, Rebekah, and Rachel, and all three matriarchs gave birth to sons of destiny.

Sarah gave birth to Isaac, Rebekah to Jacob, and Rachel's first son was Joseph. These three men—Isaac, Jacob, and Joseph—were the cornerstones for building a new spiritual house called Israel. The matriarchal mothers were *not* the only three women in the Bible whose wombs were closed and who required a special miracle in childbirth.

SUPERNATURAL CHILDBIRTH

During the time of the judges, an angel visited a childless woman from the tribe of Dan and promised her a son who would be set apart as a Nazirite (Judg. 13:2–5). Thus Samson, Israel's mighty judge and deliverer, was born. Years later, another barren woman named Hannah prayed earnestly for a son, and the Lord opened her womb and gave her Samuel (1 Sam. 1:20). Prior to Christ's birth, Elizabeth, a very aged woman and wife of a temple priest named Zacharias, had prayed years for a child. The angel Gabriel visited the father at the golden altar in the temple, announcing that he and his wife would have a son named John, who was a cousin to Christ and a forerunner announcing the appearing of the Messiah (Luke 1:7, 24).

Each son entered the stage at a critical time in Israel's history. Samson was born during a time of Israel's long captivity to the Philistines (Judg. 14). Samuel was exalted as God was debasing the corrupt priesthood of Eli and his sons (1 Sam. 3:11–13). During John's birth, the temple rituals had become formal and somewhat meaningless to the average Jew. John's *church* was in the wilderness, his message was repentance, and his converts were Jews dissatisfied with the religious rituals without righteousness (Matt. 3:1–8). These sons of the barren womb each wrote their own chapter in the book of Israel's destiny:

- Isaac *transferred* the nation's destiny when Esau's blessing was transferred to Jacob.

- Jacob *transported* the nation by moving them out of Canaan to life in Egypt.

- Joseph *transplanted* the nation by relocating them to Egypt during a global famine.

- Samson *transfixed* the nation through his supernatural strength and single-handed victories.

- Samuel *transfused* the nation, bringing new hope and life by his example and by anointing King David.

- John the Baptist *transitioned* the nation from the age of law and prophets to the age of grace and mercy.

Barren women birthed six of the greatest men in Israel's biblical history. Each infant arrived at a crucial time on Israel's clock of destiny and left their mark on time and eternity, saving, delivering, and transitioning their own people to carry out God's will on the earth. Isaac carried on Abraham's vision through Jacob, and Jacob carried on Isaac's promise through his twelve sons. Joseph preserved the nation during famine, and Samson's name is listed in the hall of faith (Heb. 11:32) because of delivering Israel from captivity. All six men were born from mothers who prayed for a child.

THE PERCEPTION OF BARRENNESS

Few women in contemporary society are aware of the stigma that once accompanied infertility, or barrenness. From ancient biblical times until the late 1800s, a barren woman carried a social stigma—she was somehow under a "curse from God." In Roman times, a barren woman was an offense against the state. The ancient Chinese would not allow a barren woman to die at home.

It was an ancient custom for a barren woman to legally offer her handmaid to her husband to procreate, as narrated in Genesis chapters 29 and 30. Biblically, Hebrew women who were sterile would fall under great distress and heartache if they continued to be barren. After the Torah revelation, they knew the many promises and blessings placed upon a firstborn son and desired that their firstborn child would be a son (Num. 18:15–16).

It has always intrigued me that the barren women in the Bible always gave birth to a son, not a daughter. I have wondered if the ancients understood something about the timing of conception that we may not understand today. Were there certain things they did to assist in ensuring the child would be a boy and not a girl?

My wife once told me about a doctor's theory of conceiving a boy. The doctor says the male sperm carrying the Y chromosome (a boy) moves faster than the X chromosome (for a girl). The doctor suggests that to conceive a boy, the couple should have intercourse no more than twenty-four hours before ovulation to no more than twelve hours past ovulation.[2] Some doctors believe having intercourse earlier in your monthly cycle is more likely to produce a son. There is a Chinese legend about an ancient Chinese gender chart found more than seven hundred years ago near a royal tomb in Beijing, which revealed that a woman can conceive a son based on the mother's age and month of conception.[3] Others suggest that potassium in the woman is necessary to conceive a child.[4] I am certain the suggestions are endless. However, from a covenant perspective, prayer and God's favor are the two primary keys for conceiving a child.

There are several dynamic promises in the Torah that women should read and accept. They reveal that God will prevent a miscarriage, and He will make the barren womb conceive. Childbirth is a normal part of the human life cycle for a woman. The Lord has said:

> No one shall suffer miscarriage or be barren in your land; I will fulfill the number of your days.
>
> —EXODUS 23:26

The apostle Paul also revealed a special promise of protection for a woman during childbirth:

> For Adam was formed first, then Eve. And Adam was not deceived, but the woman being deceived, fell into transgression. Nevertheless she will be saved in childbearing if they continue in faith, love, and holiness, with self-control.
>
> —1 TIMOTHY 2:13–15

These scriptures are not man-made opinions on this subject, but they are wonderful promises from the inspired Word of God. Orthodox Jews believe in large families, believing that numerous children are signs of God's blessing, as it is written:

> And He will love you and bless you and multiply you; He will also bless the fruit of your womb.
>
> —DEUTERONOMY 7:13

> Behold, children are a heritage from the LORD,
> The fruit of the womb is a reward.
> Like arrows in the hand of a warrior,
> So are the children of one's youth.
> Happy is the man who has his quiver full of them;
> They shall not be ashamed,
> But shall speak with their enemies in the gate.
>
> —PSALM 127:3–5

Israel was God's plan, Abraham's vision, and Jacob's dream, evolving out of the barren wombs of three matriarchs. Four hundred years after Abraham's vision, one man's seed had produced six hundred thousand Hebrew men of war marching across the Red Sea with their wives and little ones (Exod. 12:37). Today an estimated 15 million Jews live on the earth, with an estimated 5.5 million Jews living in Israel. Not bad for one man whose wife couldn't conceive until she was ninety!

Children, especially sons, were important to the ancients. A man's family name and legacy are carried on through the son. Many couples, however, would be happy just to hear the laughter of one infant—girl or boy—echoing through the halls of their home. The voice of infertility has muted the laughter. The wonderful news is there are promises in the Word of God revealing that God can and will cause the barren to rejoice and give birth.

FOUR PROMISES FOR A BARREN WOMAN

The Jewish faith understands the importance of reading, believing, and praying the Scriptures. Often Christians read a scripture, but we seldom confess aloud and repeat what we have read, and rarely if ever do we sing a promise from God's Word. Yet Isaiah spoke of the barren singing:

Sing, O barren,
You who have not borne!
Break forth into singing, and cry aloud,
You who have not labored with child!

—Isaiah 54:1

Since the Bible reveals God's covenant to mankind, then these four promises for a woman who desires to have children should be viewed as covenant promises and be read, spoken, believed, sung, and confessed!

The first promise: God will open the womb of the barren woman.

And He will love you and bless you and multiply you; He will also bless the fruit of your womb.

—Deuteronomy 7:13

You shall be blessed above all peoples; there shall not be a male or female barren among you or among your livestock.

—Deuteronomy 7:14

He maketh the barren woman to keep house, and to be a joyful mother of children. Praise ye the Lord.

—Psalms 113:9, kjv

Specifically, God promises that there will be no barren womb among those who follow His Word and are in covenant with Him. David wrote that God promises motherhood. So get the room painted and buy a baby crib. Faith without action is dead, so let the Lord see your faith in action.

The second promise: Pregnant women will not miscarry.

Millions of women who love God have experienced a miscarriage. This occurred to my own wife at age thirty-eight. After miscarrying, she said, "Perry, I don't think I can get pregnant again." I saw Exodus 23:26 and began to speak and believe that Pam would not miscarry. Months later she did become pregnant. The doctor informed her that at her age there could be physical or mental damage to the *fetus*. We began confessing and claiming the promises that the barren womb would rejoice and God will bless the fruit of her womb (Deut. 7:13). Today we have a very healthy, intelligent, growing daughter. I was forty-two and Pam was almost forty when our daughter was born. Friends affectionately nicknamed us Abraham and Sarah!

The promise of not miscarrying is not an automatic guarantee just because it is in written in the Scriptures. All biblical promises from God must first be understood, then believed, and verbally confessed for the promise to be activated in your situation (Matt. 18:19). It requires the action of faith. Faith takes hold of the invisible and hangs on until the impossible becomes possible.

Third promise: The woman will be saved in childbirth.

Prior to the revealing in the Torah of the promise of protection during childbearing, Jacob's wife Rachel died in childbirth. This promise was reinforced in the New Testament by Paul's promise that a believing woman would be spared in childbirth (1 Tim. 2:13–15).

When a woman enters heavy labor, certain physical dangers exist. However, believers must again lay hold of this promise, reminding God that the child needs its mother and that He has promised to rebuke death as the woman walks through the seasons of travail to give birth.

Fourth promise: The child will be blessed.

The fourth promise for the parents is that God's will is to bless the child with a good mind, a healthy body, and a spiritual inclination to follow God. The Lord will "give you increase more and more, you and your children" (Ps. 115:14). Of Samson it is written: "The child grew, and the LORD blessed him" (Judg. 13:24). We read of John the Baptist: "So the child grew and became strong in spirit" (Luke 1:80). Of Christ we read, "And the Child grew and became strong in spirit, filled with wisdom; and the grace of God was upon Him" (Luke 2:40).

Because you are a spiritual seed of Abraham, your children too shall be blessed!

THE SECRET OF PRAYING TO HAVE A CHILD

If you carry a strong desire to conceive a child, then Scripture gives a pattern of intercession and prayer used by a barren woman named Hannah who seized God's attention and moved Him to open her womb. We will also examine a lesser-known *secret* that Hannah understood, which motivated divine favor toward her. There was a threefold process Hannah used as she prayed to conceive a child:

1. She prayed a prayer of deep desperation.
2. She vowed a special vow to God.
3. She promised to lend the child unto the Lord.

A prayer of deep desperation

Hannah's desire for a son kindled a burning passion in her spirit that moved her into a prayer of desperation. Her praying moved from the simple request of asking for a child (a petition) to one of weeping and desperation, which is termed as *intercession*. Intercession bumps prayer to another level, because the prayer is not merely words from the head but travail from the human spirit. Hannah was becoming weary with others birthing children and was exasperated with no results. Her unquenchable determination rose like a torrent of floodwater carving out a new riverbed. The Bible records her prayer:

> And she was in bitterness of soul, and prayed to the Lord and wept in anguish.
>
> —1 Samuel 1:10

Believers often pray a general prayer asking God for a special favor. However, the most effective prayers are prayed when combining a petition with a burden of intercession. Paul mentioned that at times when we are burdened, the Holy Spirit makes intercession for us, which comes out in the form of groaning sounds (Rom. 8:26). Hannah tapped into a well of intercession that moved her to tears. We know that tears and brokenness move God toward us, because He says that our prayers are preserved in golden vials in heaven (Rev. 5:8) and our tears are recorded in His heavenly book (Ps. 56:8). God cannot despise or reject a broken and contrite spirit (Ps. 51:17).

Weeping indicates a broken and contrite spirit, which moves God toward that person (Ps. 34:18). The word *contrite* in the Hebrew is *dakka*, which means "to be crushed like a powder." This alludes to a time when you feel totally helpless without God's intervention. Hannah's prayer was filled with desperation and was so intense that when Eli the high priest saw her lips stammering, he thought she was drunk (1 Sam. 1:14–15). A sincere prayer of desperation, accompanied by weeping, will grip the heart of the Almighty. We are promised, "Weeping may endure for a night, but joy comes in the morning" (Ps. 30:5).

A special vow to God

During her intercession, Hannah made a special vow (a vow is a binding promise) to God if He would give her a son.

> Then she made a vow and said, "O LORD of hosts, if You will indeed look on the affliction of Your maidservant and remember me, and not forget Your maidservant, but will give Your maidservant a male child, then I will give him to the LORD all the days of his life, and no razor shall come upon his head."
>
> —1 SAMUEL 1:11

This vow was a part of Hannah's *secret* for getting God's attention. In Hannah's time, the Hebrew priesthood was corrupt. Hophni and Phinehas, the sons of the high priest, were walking in sin (1 Sam. 2:22–24), and God was preparing to remove the Eli priesthood from Israel. Hannah realized God needed a new priesthood, a true man of God to lead Israel away from apostasy and direct a return to the Torah. Hannah vowed that if God gave her a son, she would in return give God a prophet, a dedicated Nazirite. Numbers 6:2–20 records the Nazirite vow she was making for her unborn son. A Nazirite could not drink wine or strong drink, must avoid dead carcasses, and never cut his hair. After vowing that she would set him apart as a Nazirite, she then made an amazing promise for a barren woman—requesting a firstborn child. Hannah vowed that the child would be "…lent…to the LORD; as long as he lives" (1 Sam. 1:28). This meant the boy would be raised around the tabernacle of Moses and never be raised in her own house. This *lending principle* was Hannah's third key for gaining God's attention.

Lending unto the Lord

After making this promise, she became pregnant and gave birth to a male child named Samuel, which by Hebrew definition can mean, "God has heard," or can be a contracted form of *sha'ulme'el*, meaning, "asked of God."

After Samuel was weaned, which took place at about two years, Hannah brought her only child to the tabernacle and presented him for a lifetime ministry to God. This doesn't seem fair. She wanted a son, conceived him, and then lent him back to God, only visiting him once a year. However, the story does not end here. We read:

> And Eli would bless Elkanah and his wife, and say, "The Lord give you descendants from this woman for the loan that was given to the Lord." Then they would go to their own home. And the Lord visited Hannah, so that she conceived and bore three sons and two daughters. Meanwhile the child Samuel grew before the Lord.
>
> —1 Samuel 2:20–21

Hannah, a once barren woman, birthed five other children because she returned her firstborn son, lending him to God for ministry. God took one seed that Hannah planted and multiplied it into five other blessings. She only asked for one son, but instead enjoyed raising five children, three sons and two daughters.

Promises for the Infertile

Hannah's story reveals three truths that are practical for any woman who desires a child but is experiencing infertility.

1. Heartfelt prayer, weeping, and intercession will get the attention of the Lord.

Intercession changes circumstances, circumstances transform people, and people change nations. Abraham interceded for Lot, and his nephew was rescued from the destruction of Sodom (Gen. 18). After Israel worshiped the golden calf, God planned to destroy the Hebrews and allow Moses to father a new nation. Moses interceded, and God changed His mind, preserving Israel in the wilderness (Exod. 32). Aaron stood between the living and the dead making intercession, and God stopped a deadly plague from slaying the Israelites (Num. 16:48). If you desire a child, do not just pray passively, "Lord, help me have a baby." Spend time alone in prayer, and allow your heart to be laid open before God in deep intercession. Your tears of travail will turn into tears of joy when you hear the cries of your newborn.

2. There is power in a vow to dedicate a child completely to the Lord.

The Almighty chose Abraham, knowing he would instruct his children in righteousness (Gen. 18:19). Noah was set apart because God knew that Noah's three sons would follow God and eventually repopulate the earth (Gen. 9:1). At times, God desires a person to "stand in a gap," filling a spiritual void (Ezek. 22:30). Parents' willingness to teach, train, and raise their children in the admonition of the Lord brings great joy to the heavenly Father. God is not preventing the birth of children, as most infertility is considered a biological or medical cause hindering conception. He is, however, moved to open the womb for those who will teach their children that way of righteousness.

3. Hannah discovered what God needed (a prophet) and promised to give God what He needed.

When God needed an ark builder, Noah was born. When He needed a man to save the Hebrews from starvation, Joseph was born. When He needed a deliverer, Moses arrived. When He needed a judge, Deborah was on the earth. Spiritual voids in the kingdom of God give God opportunities to birth future leaders. God told Jeremiah, "Before I formed you…I ordained you a prophet…" (Jer. 1:5).

When Hannah realized that Israel was in spiritual decline and the ministry team at the tabernacle was living in sin, she pledged that her son would change the course of the nation by setting a public example of a Nazirite vow. God needed a voice, and Samuel would speak. God needed a Nazirite, and Samuel would follow a vow. God needed a prophet, and Samuel would be it. God needed an example, and Samuel would live it. God's need became Hannah's passion, and when intercession collided with need, an infant's laugh once again echoed from a tent—as in the days of Abraham and Sarah.

WHAT THIS MEANS TO A BARREN WOMAN

These inspired stories "happened to them as examples" (1 Cor. 10:11). Hannah gives a powerful pattern of prayer for a barren woman to pray. It begins with a strong desire for a child that nothing can quench, such as when

Rachel cried out, "Give me children, or else I die!" (Gen. 30:1). By following Hannah's pattern:

1. A woman must believe and claim the promises that the barren womb will rejoice. Write the biblical promises for childbirth on a card and place them with a magnet on your refrigerator or bedroom mirror, where you can see them morning and evening and confess them aloud.

2. A woman and her husband, together, must commit and vow to instruct and raise the children in a home environment of faith, prayer, and love, teaching children the redemptive covenant at a young age. This instruction must continue until they depart from home to begin their own journeys, and then it begins again with grandchildren.

3. Parents should believe that their child (or children) has a purpose and destiny to fulfill in life. David said God knew him, his bodily features, and even numbered his days before he was born (Ps. 139:13–16). The barren womb will sing because a voice for the future is developing in the belly of a praying woman.

■ ■ ■ ✡ ■ ■ ■

WHAT *God* KNEW

God commanded Adam to replenish the earth (Gen. 1:28) and gave Noah and his sons the same instruction after the Flood (Gen. 9:1). Replenishing can only occur by reproduction. A son can carry on the family name, while sons and daughters continue the family legacy. In the Torah, God desired that a man's name and family heritage would continue from generation to generation (Deut. 25:5–6). This can only be done through procreation. God's family blessing is still intact and commands that we should "be fruitful and multiply" (Gen. 1:22).

WHAT DEVOUT *Jews* KNOW

The Jews know that their entire nation was formed from barren wombs blessed with sons of destiny. The Orthodox communities recognize that children are a heritage from God (Ps. 127:3) and begin planning their families immediately after marriage. The devout Jews also believe that God has promised in the Torah to bless them with children who will carry on the family name from generation to generation. This concept is so important that Orthodox Jews are taught not to marry outside the faith, and never marry a Gentile, in order to preserve their Jewish ethnicity.

WHAT *Christians* SHOULD KNOW

I know the power of faith and prayer related to childbirth. On several occasions we were asked to pray for women who were medically unable to conceive, and in each case, within a year the women were holding infants in their arms, dedicating their children to the Lord. Any husband and wife who have a strong desire for children must first come into total agreement concerning the will of God and the covenant promises of God. While seeking medical assistance is certainly not a lack of faith and can be effective, in Scripture, every barren woman conceived through prayer and faith. Never underestimate the power of prayer and the compassion of God to hear and answer. Hannah sets the example of how to get God's attention.

Chapter 8

LESSONS FROM THE MEZUZAH FOR MARKING YOUR HOUSE FOR GOD

CODE 8:
Every house should be marked by God's Word.

Hear, O Israel: The LORD our God, the LORD is one! You shall love the LORD your God with all your heart, with all your soul, and with all your strength. And these words which I command you today shall be in your heart. You shall teach them diligently to your children, and shall talk of them when you sit in your house, when you walk by the way, when you lie down, and when you rise up. You shall bind them as a sign on your hand, and they shall be as frontlets between your eyes. You shall write them on the doorposts of your house and on your gates.

—DEUTERONOMY 6:4–9

THERE WERE 119 AMERICANS WITH ME AS OUR THREE TOUR buses crossed the Jordan River at the Allenby Bridge, the border between Jordan and Israel. When my feet touched Israeli soil, I was immediately overwhelmed with emotion, which continued for hours, climaxing after arriving in Tiberias for our overnight stay. At the hotel, as I stood outside the door of my room I noticed a strange object that was attached to the right side of the outside door frame. It was a permanently affixed rectangular metal object about four inches long. I later discovered that these religious objects are attached to the outside door frames in Torah-observant Jewish homes and outside the rooms of Jewish-owned hotels in Israel. This mysterious object was called a *mezuzah*.

Since learning its meaning, I have affixed the mezuzah to the door frame of my house. The mezuzah developed from the command in the Torah for the Hebrews to place the Word of God on the posts and gates of their homes. This instruction was to be obeyed when Israel entered their homes in the Promised Land, as we read in Deuteronomy 6:4–9.

How can a person "bind" God's Word on their hands and as frontlets between their eyes and write it on the gates and doorposts of their house? From these commandments, several Jewish customs emerged. The first was the creation of a *tefillin*, also called a *phylactery*. This is a small, square black box with a long flowing leather strap. The box contains four compartments with four scriptures: Deuteronomy 6:4–9; Deuteronomy 11:13–21; Exodus 13:1–10; and Exodus 13:11–16. These verses for the tefillin are written by a scribe on a small kosher parchment with a special black ink.

The tefillin have two boxes, each attached to the black leather straps. One is attached around the biceps about heart level and the other above the forehead, but not lower than the hairline. The straps are then wound around the fingers, palm, wrist, and arm. Two blessings are repeated as the tefillin is placed on the biceps and the forehead. In the time of Christ, the phylacteries were donned by Torah-observant Jews. Jesus, being Jewish, would have worn the phylactery. However, He rebuked certain Pharisees for enlarging the boxes to make themselves appear more spiritual than others and to be seen of men (Matt. 23:5). Most Jewish young men begin wearing the tefillin just prior to their thirteenth birthday.

The second article created from Deuteronomy 6:4–9 was the mezuzah. An actual kosher mezuzah contains the words of the Shema (Deuteronomy 6:4–9) and a passage from Deuteronomy 11:13–21 written by a trained scribe on a small parchment of a kosher animal (cow or sheep). The name of God is written on the backside of the parchment, and the tiny scroll is rolled up and placed in the mezuzah case.

The case is usually a decorated case made of ceramic, stone, copper, silver, glass, wood, or even pewter. The designs vary and are not spiritually significant, but the parchment itself holds the significance of the mezuzah. Most mezuzahs on the outer surface have the Hebrew letter *shin*, the twenty-first letter of the Hebrew alphabet, which represents the first letter in God's name, *Shaddai*. The name *Shaddai* is a name that serves as an acronym for "Guardian of the doorways of Israel." The box is designed to protect the parchment from the weather or other elements that could harm the ink.[1]

THE PURPOSE FOR THE MEZUZAH

The word *mezuzah* is the Hebrew word for *doorposts*. Some have suggested that the purpose for the mezuzah was to remind the Jewish people on a continual basis of the blood of the lamb, which, when applied on the doorposts in Egypt, prevented the destroying angel from entering the home and killing the firstborn. This theory, however, is an opinion and not based on the rabbinical understanding of the purpose of the mezuzah.

Some Jews, identified as *mystics*, tend to see the mezuzah as some form of a charm designed to ward off evil spirits, but this is certainly not the original intent. It is a reminder to those living in the home that the house has been dedicated to God, and those living therein should commit to walk in accordance with God's Word. It is viewed as an object that reminds God to protect the home. The Talmud teaches that a proper mezuzah *can* bring long life and protection to the household. A Talmudic story tells of a king who gave a diamond to a rabbi as a present, and the rabbi, in return, gave the king a mezuzah, which insulted the king. The rabbi commented to the king, "I will have to hire guards to protect my home because of the gift you gave me, but the gift I gave will protect your home."

Affixing a mezuzah

Just as there are very strict laws instructing scribes on writing and preparing sacred parchments, there are strict guidelines on how to affix a mezuzah and the prayers that should be prayed.

First, the mezuzah should be attached on the right side of the door as you are entering a room. In Jewish homes, every door has a mezuzah except the bathroom or unless the door has been boarded up. The mezuzah is placed about shoulder height, underneath the door's lintel. The Ashkenazi Jews place the mezuzah at a slight angle with the top facing toward the room. The Sephardic custom is to place the mezuzah at a vertical angle.

It is also a custom to kiss the right hand and touch the mezuzah when entering the home. It reminds the person entering the house to keep God's Word in their sitting down and in their rising up, in their coming in and their going out (Deut. 11:19).

The prayer

Before placing the mezuzah, a special prayer is prayed:

> *Blessed are You, Adonai, our God, ruler of the universe, who sanctifies us with holy commandments and commands us to affix a mezuzah.*

On a personal note, each time I enter and exit my home I pass by the mezuzah. It is a physical reminder that my home and family are dedicated to God. I am also reminded that I am a representative of the Lord in my calling and work and should endeavor to follow the requirements of His covenant. When I return in the evening, I see the mezuzah, reminding me that our home is a dwelling place for the Lord, and in all I do I must glorify Him, setting the example of faith in my family and teaching my children the Scriptures. Thus, for me, the purpose of the mezuzah is evident—it is a daily reminder of God's covenant with my family and my dwelling place.

Through the mezuzah, a person is marking their doors (or gates) with God's Word. Shortly after being married, we purchased a house. Just for *fun*, I found several stickers with scriptures on them and stuck them to the post of the door that entered our house through the garage. We were often away from home for up to eleven weeks at a time. After several years, I was painting the basement and removed the stickers, thinking, "Those stickers aren't protecting this house." The following week our house was broken into through the very door where the stickers were removed!

I felt like I learned a lesson. They weren't just stickers—printed on them were God's covenant promises of protection. The small sticker could never stop a thief. However, if God saw that I believed His promise by placing His Word on my house, He could be moved to initiate supernatural help or assistance to protect the property. In fact, a few items were stolen, but the new Apple computer I had just purchased, which held the names of my ministry mailing list, was not taken. I remembered the night a small group of friends laid their hands on the computer, dedicating it for the Lord's work. The thieves didn't take the computer, which, at the very least, made me think.

Obviously, we don't need scriptures on stickers glued to the walls for protection, because a fervent prayer forms a hedge of protection. The mezuzah, however, is a tangible tool of faith that marks the house for God.

■ ■ ■ ✡ ■ ■ ■

WHAT *God* KNEW

The Lord knew the Hebrew nation needed a continual reminder of His love for them and their commitment to Him. God continually warned Israel not to forget His words or His covenant (Deut. 4:9, 23, 31). For the Jews, marking their doors and posts with verses from the Torah is a daily reminder of God's covenant with them and their duty to teach their children and grandchildren the commandments of God. It also reminds them of God's willingness to protect the household.

WHAT DEVOUT *Jews* KNOW

Various religious articles, such as the tallit (prayer shawl), the tefillin (phylactery), and the mezuzah, were developed from the commandments in the Torah and distinguish the Jewish people from their Gentile counterparts. Not only does the mezuzah identify a Jewish home, but it also identifies the household as followers of the commandments and believers in the one true God. The tradition of kissing the mezuzah is not required in the Torah, but it reveals deep respect and love for God's Word.

WHAT *Christians* SHOULD KNOW

Paul wrote that our bodies are now the temple of the Holy Spirit (1 Cor. 3:16). The Word of God must dwell in us and be manifest through us by our outward conduct. However, our personal homes are miniature sanctuaries and should be dedicated to the Lord. In the early church, many believers met weekly in their homes (Rom. 16:5). While Gentiles have no New Testament requirement to mark their physical homes with Scripture, nothing prevents a Gentile believer from marking their home with God's Word by following the tradition of affixing a mezuzah to the door frames.

Chapter 9

AMAZING HEALTH SECRETS OF KOSHER DIET FOODS FROM THE HOLY LAND

CODE 9:
Eating from God's restaurant menu keeps you healthy.

For the LORD your God is bringing you into a good land...a land of wheat and barley, of vines and fig trees and pomegranates, a land of olive oil and honey; a land in which you will eat bread without scarcity, in which you will lack nothing.

—DEUTERONOMY 8:7–9

MAY OF 1985 MARKED MY FIRST TRIP TO THE HOLY LAND. Arriving in Ammon, Jordan, my excitement released such adrenaline that I didn't sleep for nearly forty-eight hours! Years later, I began flying direct to Tel Aviv, spending three nights at the Sea of Galilee. Each year I noticed that by the third day of the tour, I felt energized, very alert, and experienced a surprising sense of well-being. I later discovered three important facts that I believe contributed to this sort of *natural high*.

I learned that the Sea of Galilee is about 670 feet below sea level. There are much higher levels of oxygen in the air per cubic foot in the Sea of Galilee. Some suggest it may be 2 percent more than in other areas, with the exception of the Dead Sea, the lowest place on Earth. Breathing the oxygen-enriched air benefits mental alertness and a good night's rest. I heard the suggestion that the students in Galilee score well on tests because the air may assist in their mental awareness, since the brain depends on oxygen more than any other organ in your body.

Second, all of the food at the hotel was prepared fresh after being purchased from local farms throughout the country. This included fresh fruit juices, cereals, olives, sweet peppers, tomatoes, various cheeses, raw veggies, pickled herring—and this was just breakfast! Few meats were fried, and most meat and fish were broiled or baked. Some kitchens also used olive oil in their cooking process.

Third, the majority of the food was prepared *kosher*, a term that's known by Jews but seldom known, spoken, or understood by most Gentiles. Religious Jews and numerous nonreligious Jews often eat from a kosher menu. The word *kosher*, or *kashrut*, means "fit" or "proper." Kosher is not a style of food or a method of cooking, but it is food that meets the requirements of Jewish dietary laws, including laws instructing the types of food that should avoided altogether. These *kosher commandments* were revealed to Moses in the wilderness and can be found in Leviticus 11 and Deuteronomy 14. The basic kosher requirements are:

- Milk, meat, and eggs of certain species are permitted, and others are forbidden.
- Animals must be slaughtered in a certain manner, and only certain parts are to be eaten.
- Milk and meat are never combined, and separate utensils are used for each.
- Most grains and vegetables are kosher, but they must be examined for insects prior to preparation.
- Animals with split hooves and those that chew the cud are kosher, such as cows, sheep, deer, and goats.
- Most domestic birds, chicken, turkey, duck, and geese are kosher.

■ Fish with scales and fins are permissible, such as salmon, tuna, flounder, pike, and herring.[1]

There were six types of foods in Egypt—cucumbers, leeks, onions, garlic, fish, and melons (Num. 11:5). In Deuteronomy 8:8, God provided the Hebrew nation with seven types of food that they would enjoy after possessing the Promised Land. The seven food types were:

■ Wheat
■ Barley
■ Grapes
■ Figs
■ Pomegranates
■ Olives
■ Honey

SEVEN FOODS FROM THE HOLY LAND

It is important to note the health value and the physical health benefits provided when eating in proper portions these seven foods found in the Promised Land.[2]

1. Wheat

Many wheat products today—for example, our cereals—have been processed, removing much of the valuable nutrients. This includes wheat, which has been bleached into white four for bread, noodles, pastas, rolls, and cookies. This human process removes 40 percent of the significant nutrients from the grains. In ancient times, Israel had no processing other than separating the chaff from the wheat and crushing the hard grain into flour. Unprocessed wheat contains both wheat bran and germ, containing needed fiber and manganese. Studies reveal that a high-fiber diet is good for the colon and digestive system and helps to fight certain types of cancer.[3]

2. Barley

In ancient Israel, barley was harvested in the early spring. Barley is used in soups and is a wonderful grain with high nutritional value. The fiber from barley provides good bacteria to the intestines, contains beta glucan (which helps lower cholesterol), and can help prevent blood sugar levels from rising in diabetic patients. Barley also contains selenium (a cancer fighter), tryptophan, copper, manganese, and phosphorus, all vital nutrients for personal health.[4]

3. Grapes

Israel was, and is, a land covered with vineyards. It has been known for many years that grapes contain flavonoids, which are effective in combating heart disease. Drinking grape juice increases nitric oxide, which works with the body to reduce the formation of blood clots. Grape juice is high in antioxidants, which fights free radicals in the body. Grapes contain great vitamin and mineral value, including vitamin B_6, B_1 (thiamin), vitamin C, manganese, and potassium. Grape leaves are also cooked and wrapped with meat, especially in the Greek/Mediterranean diet.[5]

4. Figs

In Israel, figs have been a staple for thousands of years. We know that the fig tree was one of the main trees in the Garden of Eden (Gen. 3:7). Figs are a sweet delight to eat and are high in potassium. Potassium is important in producing energy for our bodies and assisting cell membranes. Research shows figs have been effective in lowering high blood pressure. In the Mediterranean, fig leaves have been used to reduce and lower the insulin levels in diabetic patients and can assist in lowering triglycerides in the bloodstream.[6]

5. Pomegranates

The pomegranate is considered a holy fruit for several reasons. According to rabbis, there are 613 deeds and commandments that are required of the Jews in the Torah. Tradition says there are 613 individual seeds in a mature pomegranate. Thus, the pomegranate is an image of the commandments of God. The top of both pillars at the entrance to Solomon's temple were hand-carved pomegranates. The hem of the high priest's garment was graced with golden bells and small carved pomegranates (1 Kings 7:18; Exod. 28:34).

Recent research has revealed that the pomegranate is extremely rich in antioxidants, and pomegranate juice is excellent in keeping blood platelets from clumping together and forming blood clots. Other research indicates that 8 ounces of pomegranate juice daily for three months increased the oxygen to the heart muscle. Others suggest the fruit may help prevent prostate cancer and reduce breast cancer. It is one of the best fruits provided in a Holy Land diet, with numerous health benefits.[7]

6. Olives

The olive has been the staple in Israel from its beginning. The olive, olive oil, olive leaf, and even the olive wood have all been used for food, cooking, medicine, and carving olive wood figurines for millions of tourists. The health benefits of the olive and olive oil include reduced blood pressure. Olives and olive oil also assist in heart health. Among the Arabs and Bedouins in the Middle East it is common to drink a small amount of olive oil each morning. One Arab friend told me, "It's good for greasing the bones!" It is far healthier to cook in olive oil than it is to use other cooking oils with animal fats.[8]

7. Honey

Forty-six times in the Old Testament we read where the land of Israel is called the *land of milk and honey*. Some suggest this was a term identifying the economic prosperity Israel would experience after possessing the Promised Land. Milk ordinarily comes from cows or goats, and honey from bees. The diet of John the Baptist included honey (Mark 1:6). Honey has been researched and shown to be effective in treating coughs. It contains antioxidants, which help to protect human cells. Honey is also a natural sweetener and provides energy for the human body.[9]

THE OLIVE AND THE OLIVE OIL

In the time of Moses there were 8,580 Levites, age thirty and upward, ministering at the tabernacle (Num. 4:47–48). By the time Solomon built the temple, their population increased to 38,000 (1 Chron. 23:3). The Levites lived near the tabernacle and the temple, serving in full-time ministry. One purpose of the numerous sacrifices and offerings offered at the tabernacle and temple was to provide food for the priests and their families.

When preparing a burnt offering, God instructed Moses to prepare the meat with fine flour mixed with a quarter *hin* (one and one-third gallons) of olive oil. Olive oil is recognized as one of God's greatest natural gifts to mankind. It is the center of the Mediterranean diet. First, olive oil contains monounsaturated fatty acids high in antioxidants. Two spoonfuls of pure olive oil each morning can reduce bad (LDL) cholesterol and raise good (HDL) cholesterol. Extra-virgin olive oil produced by the first pressing of the olives contains vitamin E, DHA, and omega-3 and omega-9 oils, which aid in overall good health.

There are four pressings of olives that bring forth the olive oil:

- *Extra virgin*—this is the first pressing from the olives and considered the best quality.

- *Virgin*—this oil is produced by the second pressing.

- *Pure*—olive oil marked "pure" has undergone some form of processing and filtering.

- *Extra light*—this oil has been heavily processed and has very little olive oil flavor.[10]

In Israel, when cooking with any form of oil, the type used in Jewish restaurants, religious Jewish homes, and in the preparation of kosher food is olive oil. Olive oil has a high smoke point, 410 degrees Fahrenheit, and does not degrade as rapidly as other oils do with repeated heating. This is the only type of oil my wife has used in preparing food for many years. Most of the fast-food restaurants in America use cooking oil that raises the bad cholesterol and reduces the good. The partially hydrogenated vegetable oil contains trans fats that doctors say are not healthy. This unhealthy oil is a combination of vegetable oil and hydrogenated gases. The best choice for cooking is olive oil.

Salted With Salt

Salt contains sodium, and too much salt can raise the blood pressure and cause other complications. However, in Leviticus 2:13, God said that all grain offerings were to be seasoned with salt. The salt produced today contains some form of iodine (potassium iodide or sodium iodide), which has been added to help reduce the iodine deficiency in humans. Prior to this time, many Americans had goiters, a result of a lack of iodine in the body.

Two main sources of salt are rock salt and sea salt. In Israel, the Dead Sea area has a huge content of salt. In the southern part of the sea there are large piles of salt crystals, sitting silently along the shore like crystal monuments. On the western bank of the southern shore of the Dead Sea are several large mountains that, upon closer investigation, are seen to be mountains of salt. Several small mining companies remove the salt from these salt mountains and use it for table salt. The strong salt from the Dead Sea is collected and packaged and used in bathwater for therapeutic purposes. One Web site for Dead Sea salt products states that Josephus wrote: "The Dead Sea cannot be praised too highly…travelers take as much of this salt as they are able to take home with them because it heals the human body and is therefore used in many medicines." Dead Sea salt contains a high concentration of minerals, including magnesium, potassium, bromine, and calcium, and too many chemicals for table salt. Normal sea salt has 90 percent sodium, while the Dead Sea salt has only 10 percent sodium. However, through a modern filtering process, sea salt can be separated from normal seawater and used to season foods. Sea salt contains various trace minerals that the body needs, and is the healthiest form of salt available.

Years ago I would preach up to sixteen consecutive weeks without a break. I perspired easily, and after each service I observed that the back of my dark suit jackets were streaked white, where the salt (and potassium) had remained after my perspiration had evaporated. While ministering on one occasion, I became weak, nearly passing out! Afterward, I discovered my electrolytes, salt, and potassium levels were extremely low. I began taking vitamin and mineral supplements to keep my mineral levels balanced. Ultra-endurance athletes and those who exercise intensely can lose one to two grams of salt each hour, which if not replaced properly can lead to hyponatremia, which is a low concentration of salt in the blood. People who perspire a lot need a proper amount of sodium replacement. Sea salt contains potassium, which is important to maintain an effective energy level. While too much salt is not good, God instructed the meat offerings to be salted with salt.

REMOVING BLOOD FROM THE MEAT

When slaughtering a kosher animal, such as a cow, goat, or a sheep, there is an important process that must be followed, as commanded by God. In Genesis 9:3–4, Noah was instructed, "Every moving thing that lives shall be food for you. I have given you all things, even as the green herbs. But you shall not eat flesh with its life, that is, its blood." The Jewish manner of preparing kosher meat is to use a sharp knife and kill the animal in a quick manner by a deep cut to the throat. In a Jewish kitchen, all of the blood must be drained from the animal, and then the meat is soaked in water for half an hour. Following that, it is sprinkled with salt and left to stand for about one hour. Then it is rinsed and ready to be used in cooking.

The second biblical instruction concerning meat is a requirement to avoid eating the animal fat (Lev. 7:23). Animal fats contain high cholesterol, trans fats, and saturated fats. Eating the fat will most definitely increase a person's chances of heart problems, since the human body has difficulty processing trans fats, which create cholesterol buildup in the arteries. A Jewish butcher also removes the sciatic nerve and the fat that surrounds the liver and vital organs. Scientists have discovered biochemical differences between this fat and the fat permissible for consumption surrounding the muscles and skin.[11] It is clear that two parts of the animal are forbidden to be eaten—the blood and the fat (Lev. 3:17).

There is another unusual requirement, which forbids eating the milk and the meat together (Deut. 14:21). The Jewish mystics explain that milk represents life, and meat, death; thus combining them creates a spiritual clash. Plants contain the right type of nutrients to keep people healthy, whereas the *red* meats can take hours to digest and can remain in the colon for extended time. It is believed that the Egyptians used to boil the animal in the mother's milk; thus God was separating His people from Egyptian customs. As another example of God's separation rules, when the Torah forbids the wearing of wool and linen together, it may be because pagan priests would mix the two fabrics in their garments, wearing them during idol worship. Thus, some regulations make little sense today, but the main purpose was to distinguish and separate God's people from the surrounding heathen nations.

Certain animals are, without a doubt, unhealthy for a person's consumption, yet they are popular, especially in the southern states. One such animal is the pig—the source for all types of pork products. No forms of pork are kosher, and all pork is listed among the *forbidden* animal meats in the Torah. Years ago the *mountain folks* would cook with lard, which was actually the fat, two to six inches thick, that was found under the skin of a pig. No one should be surprised that by age fifty-five so many individuals were experiencing clogged arteries and heart problems. Pigs were eaten by the ancient Egyptians and were associated with the Egyptian god *Seth*, but they were not listed as the six foods the Hebrews ate while living in Egypt. Again, God separated His people from the practices of the Egyptians.

SOME MOUNTAIN CURES

The *old timers* passed down certain *home remedies*—those peculiar mountain cures that oddly enough seemed to work. Because the drinking water was often spring or well water, the moms and dads understood the danger of tapeworms and parasites. They believed *religiously* in the use of castor oil, cod liver oil, and Epsom salts.

Rural families often prepared their own meals from their fresh produce grown in their gardens. At every dinner there was usually some form of pickled food—either pickles, pickled beets, pickled eggs, or even pickled beans or corn. They believed in using vinegar. Research by the Heinz Company now indicates that just a 5 percent solution of vinegar kills 99 percent of bacteria, 82 percent of common mold, and 80 percent of germs and viruses.[12] The folks from the hills may have exercised little wisdom in eating certain types of meats. They did, however, consume many vegetables and understood the benefits of pickled foods.

HEALTH RECOMMENDATIONS BY DR. MOSES

Numerous books and articles have been written confirming the medical and health benefits of eating from God's restaurant menu. Since the early Hebrew nation was a large community of families that lived in the close confines of a hot wilderness for forty years, God also prepared guidelines to prevent transmittable diseases or viruses from spreading throughout the camp. The full meaning and appreciation of these *sanitation and personal hygiene* regulations would not be realized until many centuries later.

The writer S. I. McMillen, in his book *None of These Diseases*, comments on the bizarre remedies used in Moses's time in Egypt:

> Several hundred remedies for diseases are advised in the Papyrus Ebers (written in Egypt). The drugs include "lizard's blood, swine's teeth, putrid meat, stinking fat, moisture from pigs' ears, milk, goose grease, asses' hoofs, animal fats from various sources, excreta from animals, including human beings, donkeys, antelopes, dogs, cats, and even flies."[13]

Being raised for forty years in Egypt, Moses would have known these cures, yet none of these ridiculous remedies are found in the Torah. Instead, God the Creator gave several unique *sanitation codes* that prevented the passage of germs and disease.

One notable feature is that God believed in washing! God instructed the priests to wash their hands and feet before ministering and slaying the sacrifices (Exod. 30:18–21). The innards and inside legs of the sacrifices were to be washed (Lev. 1:9–13). A person touching a dead carcass was to wash his or her clothes and body (Lev. 11:24–28). After touching a scab, a running sore, a possible leper, or anyone with a skin disease or infection, the person making contact with the afflicted individual must wash both himself and his clothes in water—and in some cases, running water (Lev. 15:13).

Unknown in ancient medical circles, certain diseases, infections, and germs could be passed from person to person through physical contact. God commanded water to be used to cleanse and purify a person. The importance of washing was understood in the early twentieth century at the Vienna Medical Center Hospital, when doctors noticed one in six women was dying in childbirth from infections. Previously, doctors had washed their hands in a basin of water. Later it was discovered this was a source of passing infection to the other women. Today, doctors scrub their hands in an alcohol-based soap or hand scrub, washing them in warm running water, thus helping to prevent the passing of infections to their patients. This simple procedure was revealed to Moses thirty-five hundred years ago.[14]

Unknown in early times, diseases, infections, and germs could be passed on by the bacteria on a dead carcass. Throughout the Torah, God emphasized the importance of washing when contacting anyone or anything considered ceremonially unclean, such as when touching the dead carcass of an animal or a dead person. A person was instructed to wash both their clothes and their bodies in running water and was considered unclean until evening. Leviticus 15 lists specific things that caused a person to be unclean, requiring ritual purification:

- Any bodily discharge or sore (Lev. 15:2–3)

- Any bed, chair, or clothes of a person with a discharge (Lev. 15:4–6)

■ Any person who is spit upon is unclean and must wash (Lev. 15:8).

■ Any clay pot must be destroyed and wooden vessel cleansed (Lev. 15:12).

The law of washing prevented the spread of disease during Israel's close confines of living in tents in the wilderness. Washing also prevents passing germs and viruses from person to person in our time.

Don't Forget Your Paddle

While in the wilderness, the Hebrews were instructed to carry a small wooden paddle on the side of their outer garment. When they needed to relieve themselves, they would walk to the outer edges of the camp, dig a small hole, and afterward cover up the excrement with earth (Deut. 23:12–13). This rather strange process was actually a life-saving sanitation code.

In Moses's time, six hundred thousand men, not counting women and children, were camping in a rocky, hot desert. If they allowed open sewage near their tents, in a short time dysentery, typhoid, and other diseases would have spread like wildfire through dry shrubs. In nations like India and Haiti, there are open sewers, which are the main source of numerous diseases and sicknesses that spread among the populace. God established a simple yet healthy way to dispose of human waste, thus preventing the spread of dangerous diseases among His people.

It's All in the Torah

These dietary and sanitation laws are not an outdated code from an ancient nomadic tribe. Modern research indicates that a kosher diet assists in a healthy lifestyle and can help prevent sickness and disease. These facts should demonstrate that the Torah is not some ancient book that has been abolished by the New Testament Scriptures. By following God's kitchen menu and basic health codes, a person will feel better, live longer, and be stronger.

■ ■ ■ ✡ ■ ■ ■

WHAT *God* KNEW

The Creator understood how the human body worked and what foods nourished it or could shorten life. He also was aware of the way germs and diseases were passed through the population, and He set specific regulations for eating and living in a community. These amazing codes were revealed thirty-five hundred years ago in a time when the brightest and wisest men in the ancient nations would not have known the secrets understood to God.

WHAT DEVOUT *Jews* KNOW

Eating God's way will assist the body's natural immune system, strengthen the organs and cells, and can help add years to your life. Following these biblical health regulations will also prevent the passing of sickness from person to person.

WHAT *Christians* SHOULD KNOW

According to Paul, Gentiles can eat what is set before us, but we should avoid meat where the animal was not properly slain and the blood properly drained (Acts 15:20; 1 Cor. 10:27). All foods should be blessed prior to eating. While there are no specific New Testament stipulations as to what a Gentile eats, medical research confirms that eating God's way will produce better long-term health.

Chapter 10

THE SPIRITUAL PRINCIPLES OF WEALTH AND PROSPERITY

CODE 10:
There is a covenant of wealth
God has with His people.

And the LORD will make you the head and not the tail;
you shall be above only, and not be beneath, if you heed the
commandments of the LORD your God, which I command you
today, and are careful to observe them.

—DEUTERONOMY 28:13

JUST MENTION THE PHRASE "JEWISH WEALTH." SOME BELIEVE the term is a preconceived stereotype planted by a few Gentiles, while others visualize a vast, secret Jewish conspiracy planning a new world order. Others suggest a different secret—some unknown X factor or special genius factor encoded in the Jewish DNA that gives this ethnic group the edge in economic investment and planning. Few individuals who recognize Jewish success acknowledge the real source of Jewish success in global business, and that is a covenant of wealth established in the Torah.

For certain, not all Jews are wealthy. Soviet Jews returning to Israel are often poverty stricken, and Jews living in foreign nations have endured persecution, opposition, and anti-Semitism specifically designed to block their economic progress and business influence. Other nations have recognized the creative genius and business expertise of Jews in the fields of religion, finances, the arts, science, and medicine. As an ethnic group, Jews have survived against all odds, and, like the mythological phoenix, they have risen from the ashes of near extinction to rebuild their nation (Israel) and prosper where they are planted. Torah-practicing Jews know there is a covenant of prosperity found in God's covenant for the Hebrew nation:

> Therefore keep the words of this covenant, and do them, that you may prosper in all that you do.
>
> —Deuteronomy 29:9

God's plan for prosperity began with Abraham and was passed to Jacob and Joseph long before the Torah was revealed:

> But he said to me, "The Lord, before whom I walk, will send His angel with you and prosper your way."
>
> —Genesis 24:40

> And his master saw that the Lord was with him and that the Lord made all he did to prosper in his hand.
>
> —Genesis 39:3

During the time of the kings of Israel, God reminded Israel of His covenant of prosperity:

> And keep the charge of the Lord your God: to walk in His ways, to keep His statutes, His commandments, His judgments, and His testimonies, as it is written in the Law of Moses, that you may prosper in all that you do and wherever you turn.
>
> —1 Kings 2:3

> Believe in the Lord your God, and you shall be established; believe His prophets, and you shall prosper.
>
> —2 Chronicles 20:20

The words *prosper* and *prosperity* bring out strong opinions from believers and nonbelievers. Is prosperity the amount of money in your checking and savings accounts? Do the appraised value of your home, the model names and cost of your cars, and the type of clothing in your closet identify you as prosperous? Actually, the definition of the word *prosper* depends upon *whose* definition you are using.

The secular world, the average Christian, and the inspired Scriptures each disclose a different perception of prosperity. To the secular nonbeliever, prosperity is the learned ability that enables one to climb to the top of the business ladder of success and accumulate a massive portfolio of personal wealth. For some Christians, any preaching that includes a prosperity message is an overemphasis of money or things that blurs the vision of a believer, who winds up stressed out with the "cares of this world" (Mark 4:19). Other Christians tend to make prosperity the heartbeat of their ministry, proving it *works* by the *stuff* they accumulate.

The purest meaning of the word *prosper* is found in the Scriptures themselves. The word *prosper* is penned forty-nine times in the English translation of the Bible, while the word *prosperous* is recorded eight times, and *prosperity* is found seventeen times. In the Old Testament, the common Hebrew word for *prosper* is *tsalach* and can mean "to come out, go through, and accomplish success." God prospered Israel when He brought the children of Israel *out* of Egyptian bondage, commanded them to *go over* the Jordan River, and promised them *success* if they would follow Him. Joshua was instructed:

> This Book of the Law shall not depart from your mouth, but you shall meditate in it day and night, that you may observe to do according to all that is written in it. For then you will make your way prosperous, and then you will have good success.
>
> —Joshua 1:8

This is the only passage where the word *success* is found in the King James Version of the Bible. The root word means, "to be intelligent," but it also means, "to act intelligent, instruct, or to be expert." Today, we would say that success alludes to the intellectual ability to make expert decisions that lead to positive results, or prosperity. My complete definition of prosperity is, "the ability to leave the condition you are in, follow the will of God, make good choices, and inspire decisions that pave a road for an abundant life." Prosperity in the true biblical sense is much more than making and saving money or amassing a huge portfolio of stocks, bonds, and mutual funds. Prosperity affects much more than your economical position. Your entire life is a continual journey from one significant moment to another. Your journey must be blessed.

> So they said to him, "Please inquire of God, that we may know whether the journey on which we go will be prosperous."
>
> —Judges 18:5

> Making request, if by any means now at length I might have a prosperous journey by the will of God to come unto you.
>
> —Romans 1:10, kjv

Believers petitioned God for a prosperous (successful) journey, including asking God's favor in times of war. A victory during battle was a sign of God confirming His covenant with Israel for the land He had promised them.

> And he sought God in the days of Zechariah, who had understanding in the visions of God: and as long as he sought the Lord, God made him to prosper. And he went forth and warred against the Philistines, and brake down the wall of Gath, and the wall of Jabneh, and the wall of Ashdod, and built cities about Ashdod, and among the Philistines.
>
> —2 Chronicles 26:5–6, kjv

Success during the journey and victory during wars were just two indications of *prosperity*. A third sign signifying God's favor was success when working with your hands, as indicated when the Hebrew captives who were returning from Babylon appealed to God to prosper them in rebuilding the holy temple:

> Then answered I them, and said unto them, The God of heaven, he will prosper us; therefore we his servants will arise and build.
>
> —Nehemiah 2:20, kjv

God's Word and His will reveal that believers are promised blessing and success through the works of their hands (Ps. 1:3). In ancient Israel, signs of

God's blessings included an abundant yearly harvest, fruitful trees, healthy animals, the winter and spring rains, and the birth of numerous children. Each year these visible benefits were witnessed by surrounding tribes and nations as an indication of the Hebrew God's covenant of prosperity with His chosen people.

> And you shall remember the Lord your God, for it is He who gives you power to get wealth, that He may establish His covenant which He swore to your fathers, as it is this day.
> —Deuteronomy 8:18

The Hebrew word *wealth* in this passage is *chayil* and alludes to resources, goods, and riches. God was guaranteeing the Hebrews abundant resources as a reward for following His covenant. This blessing cycle would repeat each year. For example, the rain caused the grains to grow, producing a plentiful harvest of grains and fruits. The animals produced the milk, cheese, and meat. The food and animal products could be personally enjoyed or sold for profit. Thus a cycle of blessing began with something as common as rain! Without rain, droughts occurred, followed by famines; therefore rain represented prosperity.

God's pledges of prosperity in His Word have been read by believers for centuries, yet the teaching on prosperity has only recently resurfaced. Why did previous generations not emphasize or teach business/blessing principles that devout Jews have known and acknowledged for thirty-five hundred years? Coming from four generations of ministers, I will answer this question based upon my personal experience and observation.

A POVERTY MIND-SET

Both my grandfathers and their fathers were West Virginia coal miners. In the early 1930s, mining was a laborious, backbreaking job, executed with a pick and shovel. My great-grandfather Rexroad and my granddad Bava both worked in the mines and preached in the evenings. At times, their only earnings from ministering would be a handful of old onions and warm cow's milk. When my granddad Bava conducted a revival in the 1930s, the offering was only a nickel. During the 1930s, the common people had little expendable income, but some also felt no need to assist a minister who was already working a job! For many centuries there was a "poverty mind-set" among many Full Gospel believers, based upon their preconceived idea that any accumulation of money was forbidden or spiritually destructive.

The early pioneers of the Full Gospel faith were very godly in morals and character and very simple in their lifestyles. Their income came from farming, factory work, mining, and odd jobs. In the early days, the messages centered on holiness and sanctification; therefore, anyone acquiring wealth was looked upon with suspicion for *loving the things of the world.* (See 1 John 2:15.) However, as time progressed and churches moved from canvas tents and small storefronts into larger sanctuaries, members and ministers recognized that finances were needed to accommodate church growth and reach the masses. Ministry expansion included printing Bibles and gospel literature and building Bible schools, Christian schools, foreign churches, and orphanages, coupled with sending missionaries to evangelize and disciple the masses. Eventually radio, shortwave, and television led to gospel satellites, Christian programs, and live Internet Web casting. Each new avenue of ministry was built on a road paved with the finances of previous generations.

As ministries grew, the need for finances increased. The biblical commandment of tithes and offerings was often ignored or seldom emphasized in early days. When a truth is hidden or ignored, God always brings a season when that truth is restored. The restoration of God's covenant of blessing has been restored. *It is God's will for His people to be blessed in body, soul, and spirit, and to prosper in their personal lives in order to be a blessing to others!* Clearly, both the Torah and the New Testament reveal the promises of prosperity for those believers who will follow the rules of conduct and commitment to God and His Word.

HISTORY'S WEALTHIEST HEBREW

Solomon, the son of David, is noted as one of the wealthiest Hebrew leaders in history and one of the wisest men to ever live. As a young man, Solomon was chosen to replace his father, David, as king (1 Kings 1:30–39). God visited Solomon, asking him to reveal his most intimate heart's desire. Instead of requesting wealth, popularity, and man's favor, Solomon petitioned God for wisdom.

And God said to Solomon: "Because this was in your heart, and you have not asked riches or wealth or honor or the life of your enemies, nor have you asked long life—but have asked wisdom and knowledge for yourself, that you may judge My people over whom I have made you king—wisdom and knowledge are granted to you; and I will give you riches and wealth and honor, such as none of the kings have had who were before you, nor shall any after you have the like."

—2 Chronicles 1:11–12

Solomon wrote the first twenty-nine chapters in Proverbs and penned Ecclesiastes—books identified as biblical *wisdom literature*. Proverbs consists of thirty-one chapters, the last two added by an unknown person (perhaps King Hezekiah). The Proverbs teach practical wisdom principles for daily living. Throughout the book, three words are consistently emphasized: *knowledge* is mentioned forty-three times, *understanding* is referred to fifty-five times, and the word *wisdom* is emphasized fifty-four times. These three key words unlock Solomon's wisdom doors for spiritual, emotional, mental, and financial increase. Following Solomon's three-step pattern will move a person from average to above average. Solomon knew:

- Knowledge is the accumulation of facts.
- Understanding is the arrangement of facts.
- Wisdom is the application of those facts.

Parents, educators, and teachers can impart knowledge by reading books to their children or students (or recommending books to read), through personal example, and by direct teaching. Knowledge can also be received through personal life experiences. Knowledge without understanding, however, is like a computer with a hard drive filled with information that is never turned on. We can brag about the gigabytes of information, but until the information is accessed and printed from the laptop, it's just a computer collecting information. You must proceed from information to illumination, or understanding.

Understanding is the ability to place information (or facts) received through study and personal experience in a proper arrangement. If we learn and do not put into practice all we have learned, our knowledge becomes like faith without action—it is dead (James 2:17). One hundred students can sit under a teacher and gain knowledge, but not everyone gains understanding of how to activate the information or make it work in life situations. For example, all smokers have knowledge that smoking is a habit that can eventually cause cancer. This is medically documented. Yet some smokers don't think cancer will ever affect them. This is not a lack of knowledge but a lack of understanding.

Christ encountered an *understanding challenge* among His listeners. Often those who heard His parables failed to understand their meanings. His personal disciples often assembled to ask Christ to explain the understanding (the story within the story). In Matthew 13:13, Christ said, "Therefore I speak to them in parables, because seeing they do not see, and hearing they do not hear, nor do they understand." The Greek word for *understand* in this passage means, "to put something together and comprehend it mentally." A person can hear a parable but not get the meaning.

Once we have received understanding and can grasp the meaning and purpose of our information, then we must learn to *apply* that information. This leads to Solomon's third key—the necessity of wisdom. True wisdom is the ability to apply the facts in order to help people and things properly function in their natural and divine order.

There are two types of wisdom: *carnal* (human) and *spiritual* (godly). Israel has used human wisdom on numerous occasions during previous wars. During a battle in Israel in the 1940s, an Arab army controlled a town. Armed with one cannon and two small live shells, the Jewish leader noticed a truck carrying metal pipes that had wrecked. There were also a number of wheels from old wagons lying nearby. An Israeli had an idea to create fake cannons. He and several others built several fake cannons and at night placed them around the city. The only real cannon was put on a hill overlooking the town. In the morning the Jewish man called the Arab leader inside the city, threatening to attack the town if he did not surrender it. The Arab replied, "You Jews don't have any weapons." The man ordered the first of the only two missiles they had to be fired, which hit the wall. The Arab leader looked over the wall and saw numerous cannons, not realizing they were fake ones. He surrendered the city![1]

On another occasion, the Egyptian navy sent a large warship toward Israel's city of Haifa. The Jews had no naval ships but possessed an empty shell of a ship docked in the port. They concocted the idea of creating fake papier-maché missiles and guns on the ship's deck and painting the ship as a decoy to intercept the Egyptian vessel. By the time the Egyptian ship arrived, they saw an unexpected sight—the Israelis had a ship with large missiles! A group of Israeli soldiers intercepted the Egyptians in a small boat, demanding the captain surrender or be "blown out of the water" by Israel's new ship. The Egyptians' war vessel was surrendered. This is an example of carnal wisdom used for a positive purpose, to defeat an adversary.[2]

True spiritual wisdom is the ability to solve life's problems by activating the principles and promises in the Word of God. This is "wisdom from above," which comes to us through the greatest teacher, the Holy Spirit. With His help we can apply the Word to a particular situation, thus creating a solution or finding the needed answer to the problem. Devout Jews understand the importance of wisdom and recognize that using the wisdom principles revealed in the Book of Proverbs will build character, integrity, and honesty—three power triplets needed to truly succeed in family matters, relationships, and business.

We see one example of Solomon's wisdom in 1 Kings 3:16–28. Two women approached Solomon with one child, both claiming to be the child's mother. One pointed to the other, saying, "She rolled over on her child last night, killing it, and now she's saying my child is hers." The other woman repeated the same story, accusing her adversary of accidentally killing her child, then saying the living infant was hers.

Solomon observed the situation and then requested a sword. He said, "I will cut the child in half, and you can both have half of the child."

Immediately, one woman yelled, "No, don't do it. Just give her the child; I don't want to see the child die!" Solomon handed the child to the woman who had cried out. After all, only the real mother would want her child to live—even if another woman raised it. This was a manifestation of spiritual wisdom.

PROVERBS AND THE WISDOM PRINCIPLES

It is common for Jewish sages to address their students as "my son." Solomon's wisdom principles were often addressed in this manner. Various proverbs begin by saying, "My son," then proceed to give these instructions:

- My son, hear the instruction of your father—Proverbs 1:8.

- My son, if sinners entice you [to sin], don't consent—Proverbs 1:10.

- My son, do not walk in the way with them [sinners]—Proverbs 1:15.

- My son, receive my words and treasure my commands—Proverbs 2:1.

- My son, don't forget God's laws and keep His commandments—Proverbs 3:1.

- My son, don't despise God's chastening and correction—Proverbs 3:11.

- My son, don't let the commandments depart from your eyes—Proverbs 3:21.

Solomon is clear that a wise son and a wise man would not consent to unwise advice or follow the ungodly lifestyle of a sinner. He advises the believer not to forget the commandments and not to despise correction when wrong decisions are made. These statements contradict the loose morals of many American teenagers who yield under peer pressure and follow the latest trends, experimenting with drugs and alcohol. Although many have been raised in a righteous family, eventually they forget godly instructions and rebel against correction. These careless actions are ignorance on steroids.

SOLOMON: TRUTH OR CONSEQUENCES

Having experienced abundant wealth, fame, success, and blessings, Solomon provided words of wisdom for future generations about the severe consequences of violating God's commandments and wisdom principles: you can follow truth, or you can rebel and pay the consequences.

The Violation	The Wisdom Principle	The Biblical Consequence
Being immoral with a woman	Proverbs 5:3–10	You lose your honor, and others will get your wealth.
Too much time sleeping	Proverbs 6:10–11	You will live in poverty, always wanting.
Getting money by doing evil	Proverbs 10:2–3	You eventually lose your substance.
Cosigning a note	Proverbs 11:15	It will come back to bite you.
Having a stingy attitude	Proverbs 11:24	It will tend to lead to poverty.
Provoking family to anger	Proverbs 11:29	You will inherit the wind (a storm in the home).
Getting money without labor	Proverbs 13:11	Your finances will slowly deteriorate.
Not listening to reproof	Proverbs 13:18	You will receive poverty and shame.
Taking too much	Proverbs 14:23	It will make you impoverished or in need.
Being too slothful	Proverbs 19:15	You will suffer hunger.
Rejecting the cry of the poor	Proverbs 21:13	He will cry himself and not be heard.
Loving pleasure	Proverbs 21:17	He will not be successful or rich.
Drunkenness and overeating	Proverbs 23:21	You will have poverty, become drowsy, and live in rags.
Trying to get rich quick	Proverbs 28:22	It's an evil inclination that actually creates poverty.

SOLOMON SAYS

Solomon understood that receiving a reward for your labor was linked to certain *dos* and *don'ts*. As a child I played a game called, "Simon says." Forget what Simon said, and let's discover what Solomon says.

Solomon says: Get up, you sluggard.

> How long will you slumber, O sluggard?
> When will you rise from your sleep?
> A little sleep, a little slumber,
> A little folding of the hands to sleep—
> So shall your poverty come on you like a prowler,
> And your need like an armed man.
>
> —Proverbs 6:9–11

Solomon warned against the danger of being a "sluggard" (Prov. 13:4; 26:16). A sluggard is a mentally and physically lazy individual. A sluggard continually procrastinates, putting off until later what should be done now (Prov. 20:4). A sluggard stays up late, sleeps in late, and is always running late for school, work, and appointments (Prov. 6:9). Sluggards are about as easy to motivate as a sleeping elephant. Sluggards will always lack and never make their financial ends meet. They are people who always dream about doing and having and getting but never do, have, or get (Prov. 13:4). The way to defeat slothfulness is to develop diligence:

> The soul of a lazy man desires, and has nothing;
> But the soul of the diligent shall be made rich.
>
> —Proverbs 13:4

Solomon says: Be diligent and you'll find gold.

> Keep your heart with all diligence,
> For out of it spring the issues of life.
>
> —Proverbs 4:23

The common Hebrew word *diligent* is unique. It is *charuwts* and can allude to digging for gold or a threshing sledge with sharp teeth that digs into the field. The picture is going after something with determination, passion, and skill with a final goal (getting the gold, getting a harvest) in mind. Diligence is such an important virtue that the person who develops it can stand before kings (Prov. 22:29).

Diligence has a twin named persistence. Our society wants to eat three meals a day and lose weight, exercise while resting in the recliner watching TV, lose pounds while sleeping, and get a paycheck without working hard.

Solomon says, "He who has a slack hand becomes poor, but the hand of the diligent makes rich" (Prov. 10:4). The reason some Americans are not diligent at work is that too many are working at jobs they do not enjoy. The most diligent workers are those who birthed the business (or ministry) or those who are paid well for their abilities and take to heart their desire to see growth and results. A good financial reward motivates gifted and diligent workers to pursue positive results and financial increase in their workplace.

If there is one word to sum up the Jewish way of life in the business realm it is *diligence*. Some people work *harder*, and others work *smarter*. Working eighteen hours a day for six days every week may win you the "He worked the hardest and the longest" award, but you'll never receive the "He worked the smartest" award. Working eighteen hours a day for six consecutive days will eventually put you in bed for a long unwanted rest or a wooden box for a permanent *vacation*.

I can recall a time when I preached continually every night for three to as high as eleven consecutive weeks. I once ministered nightly for four months without a break. By the conclusion of the fourth month, my nerves were tingling and my body was so tired I was unable to personally pray for seekers at the altar. I was working *hard* but not working *smart*. Today, however, through our weekly telecast *Manna-fest*, the Internet, books, CDs, DVDs, and our *Voice of Evangelism* magazine, I can reach more people around the world in thirty days than I previously reached in twenty-five years of ministering in local churches. That is working smarter.

According to Solomon:

- The diligent will not deal with others by being slack and idle with their work—Proverbs 10:4.

- The diligent will keep his job, but a lazy person will always lose his—Proverbs 12:24.

- The diligent will always follow through, but the slothful will do a halfway job—Proverbs 12:27.

- The diligent plan for their futures with financial prosperity in mind—Proverbs 21:5.

- The diligent and skillful will stand before great men and kings—Proverbs 22:29.

- The diligent will take account, keep good records, and know their business—Proverbs 27:23.

It is difficult to be diligent without a dream, a vision, or a goal. See it, set it, secure it, and succeed with it.

Solomon says: Learn to hold your tongue.

It is not always *what* you say but *how* you say it and the *tone* by which it is said. More irreparable damage has been inflicted through careless words during a heated argument than any one single form of conflict.

Solomon taught: "Death and life are in the power of the tongue" (Prov. 18:21). He mentions the tongue nineteen times in Proverbs, often warning of its destructive power (Prov. 25:23), and reveals that: "Whoever guards his mouth and tongue keeps his soul from troubles" (Prov. 21:23). The New Testament writer James gave a discourse on the danger of an uncontrolled tongue, saying it is a small thing that creates fire (James 3:5–6). He taught that believers should not make oaths but should answer with a simple yes or no (James 5:12). In other words, keep your conversation truthful, brief, and to the point. Soft answers can turn away anger (Prov. 15:1).

Some wisdom advice: *If you don't want it read, don't write it. If you don't want it repeated, don't say it; and if you don't want it seen, don't show it.* Political enemies dig through college papers, old photographs, and interview close friends to discover any written or spoken comment that could be used against the opposing candidate. Politicians have lost their offices by careless words spoken at the wrong time. Solomon says that wisdom includes watching your conversation, because once your words are out, they cannot be recalled. Proverbs 17:27 says, "He who has knowledge spares his words, and a man of understanding is of a calm spirit."

Throughout Proverbs, Solomon revealed the power of the tongue and the effects of words:

- Men are seduced by the flattering words of a woman—Proverbs 6:24.

- The words of a just person are like pure silver—Proverbs 10:20.

- Those who speak rashly are like a person swinging a sword—Proverbs 12:18.

- Those who are righteous will always speak knowledge—Proverbs 15:2.

- Those who mock the poor will themselves be punished—Proverbs 17:5.

- Life and death are released through the power of words—Proverbs 18:21.

- A person who can control what he says will prevent trouble—Proverbs 21:23.

- A sincere rebuke is better than the false flattery of a person—Proverbs 28:23.

Solomon's guidelines for wisdom were birthed out of his own spiritual and human experiences. He was recognized as the world's wealthiest man, and kings and queens sought an occasion to sit under his instruction, hear his proverbs, and discover his wisdom secrets.

Solomon says: Clean your ears out so you can hear me now.

Solomon said to *hear* (Prov. 4:1), to *keep* (Prov. 7:1), and *not to forget* (Prov. 3:1) the instructions and commandments of God. All knowledge begins with hearing. There are two forms of hearing—one with your outer ears and another with your inner spirit. Everyone has ears to hear, but some need spiritual understanding after hearing.

For example, five hundred people can fill up a church and hear the same message. Afterward, ask them what they learned or what they received; some will explain it clearly, while others will admit, "I didn't get anything out of it." Yet, they all heard the same thing. This example illustrates the three types of *ears*. They are:

- *Clean ears*—those who clearly hear the truth, receive it, and follow through with the instructions

- *Cluttered ears*—those who can't receive the information because of preconceived traditions or biases

- *Critical ears*—those who refuse to hear because they have a critical attitude toward the message or messenger

Knowledge enters the mind through reading and hearing. You must *clean your ears out*, removing hindrances and preconceived ideas that block God's Word from making the eighteen-inch drop from your head to your heart. Then, keep (or preserve) what you hear by guarding your heart with all diligence (Prov. 4:23). Christ taught that the adversary attempts to steal from you the Word of God that you hear before the seed can take root and bring forth results (Mark 4:15–17). The third step is to always remember the rules and never forget that the *lack of wisdom* prevents you from following wisdom. The Hebrews were warned that after settling in the Promised Land, they should never forget that it was God and His covenant that gave them the power to get wealth (Deut. 8:17–18). Eight times Moses warned the people not to forget their covenant (Deut 4:9, 23, 31; 6:12; 8:11, 14, 19; 25:19).

Solomon knew that knowledge begins by hearing, understanding begins by doing, and wisdom manifests through diligence.

What I've Learned From Wealthy Believers

Having ministered in more than thirty-five states and ten foreign countries, I have personally met thousands of Christians whom secular business executives would classify as wealthy by American standards. Some own personal businesses, are presidents and vice presidents of corporations, or enjoy high-paying executive careers in major cities. While I have never sought after personal wealth or favors from prominent friends, I have learned many principles of conduct and operational skills practiced by devout believers. I have incorporated several key concepts in this section I call: "Perry's insights from his friends' hindsight," or, "What I learned after they found it out the hard way!"

Perry's Insight #1: **Become a specialist.**

If you sense a particular direction or inspiration for your life, then study from those who have been where you want to go. Study their success and their failures. This is Solomon's first step—collecting information or knowledge. You should gain abundant knowledge until people seek you out and choose to pay you for your expertise.

My father maintained a large file of magazines, sermons, and articles by great preachers from the 1940s to the 1960s. After entering the ministry, I spent hundreds of hours studying the lives and messages of great men and women who went before me—their sermons, methods, gifts, successes, and even their failures. My goal was to repeat the success but guard against the failures. After more than thirty-three years of ministry and more than forty thousand hours of Bible study, I have been labeled by many as a leading prophetic minister and teacher of the Hebrew roots of Christianity. This is not a self-acclaimed title but observations from those who have known me for many years. I focused on two themes—prophecy and Hebrew roots—and have maintained a clear vision to this day.

If you are to become a *specialist* in any field, you need a *passion* for your dream and a *burden* if you accept a calling from God to enter the ministry. In the business world, executives will pay you for the problems you solve—not the ones you make! "Discretion will preserve you; understanding will keep you" (Prov. 2:11). Bosses are less likely to fire the person whose knowledge is valuable for increasing growth and income. "He who has knowledge spares his words, and a man of understanding is of a calm spirit" (Prov. 17:27). Pursue with a passion the things that excite you and capture your imagination.

Perry's Insight #2: **Make wise investments and purchases.**

The best investment is one that carries a positive return. Too much money is wasted on high-priced items that will be sold in a future yard sale for a few dollars. However, when spending substantial amounts of money, the buyer should consider the future value or resale value of the items purchased.

One of my hobbies is attending community auctions, usually two or three times a year. I will only purchase something if I can use it or if it will maintain and increase in value. My youngest sister, Melanie, has sold some of my auction items on her eBay site just for fun. I once purchased several old toys, including about fifty Hot Wheels cars for $70. Melanie sold the cars for nearly $500. Because of my focus on ministry, I do not have time to sell items such as this, but I give Melanie a commission after the sale.

If you are investing in stocks, bonds, or treasuries, never depend solely upon the words of one person. Study and learn the inside information on investments, and be informed before putting large sums of money into the market. "Give instruction to a wise man, and he will be still wiser; teach a just man, and he will increase in learning" (Prov. 9:9). Information brings knowledge, and knowledge increases understanding. Don't forget that if it is too good to be true, it probably is.

Perry's Insight #3: **Create a home business.**

Home computers and Internet sites make it easy to run a small business from home. In fact, billions of dollars flow through the Internet each year, and the amount is increasing. For example, one man purchases old magazines with pictures of old guitars. Using his home computer, he frames these pictures and sells them. I was stunned when his wife said he averaged about $100,000 a year doing this as a side job.

Multilevel marketing ideas are popular, but people must be cautious not to become so consumed in this form of business that they forget to attend church and cease to have quality family time. Just as God gave Moses the plans for the tabernacle and David the plans for the temple, He also provided the wealth for these sacred edifices. The Hebrews seized the gold and silver from the Egyptians (Ps. 105:37), and David acquired additional spoils through his war efforts (1 Chron. 28:11–19). With an inspired idea, some start-up money, and diligence, a person can create income in today's marketplace using the Internet.

Perry's Insight #4: **Contacts can save money.**

Years ago we evaluated the yearly expenses of our ministry and saw where hundreds of thousands of dollars were spent for mailers and boxes for our tape club and our daily orders. I contacted an Arab businessman from Israel who for many years had assisted Christian networks with their special love-gift offers. He was able to travel oversees and hire a box company to provide the mailers, saving the ministry over $80,000 in one major shipment.

This savings provided additional income that was applied to two television contracts on two major stations. Instead of sending money to pay a box bill, we were pleased to invest in reaching hundreds of thousands of more people through our weekly *Manna-fest* telecast.

I have learned that God brings *kingdom connections* into your life—a person who holds a key to unlock a door of opportunity that you need. These connectors link people with people, people with places, and people with the same purpose. Christ said that when we give to others, "with the same measure that you use, it will be measured back to you" (Luke 6:38).

For centuries, Jewish businesses have worked in cooperation with other Jewish sources and understand the concept of what I call a *unified brotherhood for economic purposes*. When items are needed for factories, clothing shops, jewelry, or silver artisans, Jews know other Jewish associates who can provide the resources. Someone often has the solution to your situation, the answers to your questions, and the provision for your passion. "Do not forsake your own friend or your father's friend" (Prov. 27:10). Learn to keep and make quality friends of good character.

Perry's Insight #5: **Your gifts can create what you need.**

God uses natural and spiritual gifts in your life to bless others, including your family. Both Joseph and Daniel could interpret strange prophetic dreams, and their unique gifts brought them before kings. David had a natural ability to use a slingshot, and his gift led him to battle, slaying Goliath and making David an instant national hero. Each of us has a unique gift, or gifts, that can be released to bless us and be a blessing to others.

At one time, my grandfather wrote or had copyrights on hundreds of songs! Noted country gospel singer Ricky Van Shelton recorded one of his songs. I never realized I carried the DNA of songwriting until a friend helped *pull it out of me*. She is a fabulous songwriter, and as we teamed up, I could create the words, and she provided the melody. The first song we ever wrote was "Close to the Cross, but Far From the Blood." Years after we wrote it, it was recorded by the McKameys, a nationally recognized gospel group. During a Sunday service in Tampa, Florida, in the early 1990s, I was suddenly inspired with a chorus, "Let the veil down; let the praise go up." Later, Keith Dudley added verses to the chorus, and this inspiring song was recorded by Judy Jacobs and has been heard around the world.

Soon, noted gospel singers began requesting to hear and record our songs. Such remarkable singers as Karen Wheaton, John Starnes, Mike Purkey, Gold City Quartet, and numerous others have recorded our songs. Several years ago, imagine my shock when I opened an envelope from ASCAP music and saw a royalty check with my name on it for over $4,000—for just one song! This gift was hidden, until pushed to the surface by a person operating in the same gift.

Years ago, I hired a young woman on staff to assist with answering e-mails, letters, and phone calls. Weeks later my wife said, "Did you know she is a great singer?" I didn't, but I eventually heard her and her husband at our local church. We invited this couple to minister at our main convention and later *twisted her arm* to record a gospel CD. This CD was such an inspiration to the body of Christ that she has produced four others, each with dynamic songs and vocals. She is my little girl's favorite gospel singer. Thus, Gina Bean has blessed thousands with her music, and the income from her and her husband's, Larry, music helps provide for their needs and ministry. Proverbs 18:16 says, "A man's gift makes room for him, and brings him before great men."

Perry's Insight #6: **Don't compare yourself with others.**

One of the biggest mistakes we make is when we compare what we are doing with what others are accomplishing. The Bible says it is not wise to compare ourselves with others (2 Cor. 10:12). Ministers often compare the attendance in their church with other congregations in the community. This is unwise. If you are not experiencing results or a surge of growth as others are, you will tend to feel that you are failing and will not see the other successes you may be accomplishing. It is not wise, because growth, increase, and blessings occur at certain seasons during your life cycle, and your growth season may be delayed for a time in the future.

In ancient Israel, David was anointed king as a teenager when King Saul was still on Israel's throne. David patiently waited several years, allowing his *season* to arrive, before being exalted as king. When you see what others are accomplishing, you tend to copy their methods, which don't always work in your own situation. Be content where you are as you move forward each day with the vision and dream growing in you. Prosperity and success do not come instantly, like winning some jackpot, but they are cultivated daily like flowers in a garden, needing water and sunlight.

Perry's Insight #7: Don't build without counting the cost.

In Luke 14:28, Christ said, "For which of you, intending to build a tower, does not sit down first and count the cost, whether he has enough to finish it." I have built two major ministry offices—one is twenty-five thousand square feet, and the latest is forty-five thousand square feet. When understanding our need for expansion, I remembered the words of Christ to "count the cost." I took a lesson from Solomon. His father, David, set aside a portion of the gold and silver for the sacred furniture long before Solomon began the building process (1 Chron. 28:11–19). I began setting aside additional income solely for the preparation of the new building(s). By doing this, we only borrowed $100,000 on one occasion. Both edifices were completed and dedicated debt free.

The same rule is used when purchasing our television airtime, which totals over three million dollars a year. A year in advance, we begin setting aside increments of income to provide payment for one year of airtime. This relieves the stress and burden of paying monthly bills and being concerned if a financial shortfall occurs. I have also followed the instruction of two other scriptures related to the business aspect of our ministry. First, Paul wrote not to be slothful in business but fervent in spirit; serving the Lord (Rom. 12:11). Second, we are told to owe no man anything, but to love one another (Rom. 13:8). Solomon says, "The borrower is servant to the lender" (Prov. 22:7). Most families have a home mortgage and a car payment. However, excessive debt will burden you under chains of heaviness. Don't make major financial decisions linked with borrowing or debt, and don't build unless you first count the cost and can pay the bills.

Working From a Dream

You were once a dream in the hearts of your mother and father. Your birth fulfilled that dream, and as you grew, their dreams grew. Late at night as they tucked you into bed, they dreamed about your future, your destiny. Where would you attend college? Whom would you marry? Would they enjoy grandchildren, and how old would *they* be when the grandkids were lying there where you lay?

Now *you* are dreaming the same dreams your parents dreamed, except you have new dreams for a new generation in time and history. How will you fulfill the dream for your future that you see in your mind but don't see before your eyes? The fulfillment of your dream is a process similar to growing and harvesting from a garden. It is a four-part process:

1. You must *seed* it—by planting the dream or vision in your spirit and mind.

2. Then, you must *feed* it—by energizing the dream and vision with the Word of God.

3. You must *weed* it—by removing doubts, unbelief, and all hindrances and distractions.

4. Finally, you can *eat* it—this is the end result, to enjoy the fruit of your labors.

THE INVESTMENTS OF ANCIENT ISRAEL

The definition of wealth has changed throughout secular history. When examining the Torah and Jewish history, we discover that God defined three main commodities that the Hebrews began to amass as personal investments early in their history, thereby securing them for future generations. They were gold, livestock, and land.

Gold

Throughout history gold has endured as a proven commodity, especially during difficult economic times. Gold has been traded in nugget form and made into jewelry and coinage. In ancient cultures, much of the local gold was hidden in the temples of the gods. These were rather safe locations, since it was assumed that the populations feared the wrath of the gods and would never enter the sacred edifices to steal from the temple coffers.

History reveals that empires have actually invaded one another for the purpose of accumulating the other nation's gold or material wealth. This occurred twice in Israel's history—first, when the Babylonians marched to Jerusalem and stole the gold and silver temple vessels, and again in A.D. 70 when the Roman Tenth Legion raided the sacred temple and shipped the wealth of God's house back to Rome. In his book *War Cycles—Peace Cycles*, author Richard Kelly Hoskins notes that the four major empires of biblical prophecy initiated wars with one another to cancel their own debts with the nation they invaded and to seize their gold and silver. Media Persia invaded Babylon, and later the Greeks overtook the Medes and Persians. Years later the Romans overpowered the Greeks, forming the Roman Empire. Each empire was heavily taxed and relieved or canceled their tax burden and debts by invading and defeating their creditors.[3] From the beginning of time, gold has continually maintained its attraction as a precious metal.

In modern times, gold as a commodity rises in value during difficult economic times. In 1999, a friend suggested that in a few years gold would sell for over $1,000 an ounce. After studying the significance of gold, my wife and I cashed in a special retirement bond to purchase several one-ounce old gold coins from a coin dealer. We purchased them for $265 each. Years later, the same coin was valued at more than $1,050.

Usually when gold rises, silver follows. In the late 1990s a gentleman gave our ministry hundreds of one-ounce silver rounds to sell and fund missionary trips. I held on to them for a time, eventually selling them at $4.25 a coin, thus supporting two major missionary outreaches. Had we waited for a few years, the coins could have sold for $15 per coin—a threefold increase. This would have provided two additional missionary trips (including inflation costs for overseas travel). During the past several years, gold alone has outperformed the DOW, SNP, and the NASDAQ.

Livestock

In the Creation story, the only animals God mentions by name three times are cattle (Gen. 1:24–26). The same is true in the account of the Flood. God said to bring in "cattle after their kind" into the ark (Gen. 6:20, KJV). Abraham was very rich in "livestock, in silver, and in gold" (Gen. 13:2). Jacob was interested in investing in cattle when working with Laban (Gen. 30:29–43). When the Israelites moved to Egypt in time of famine, they took their cattle with them (Gen. 46:6). God protected the cattle of the Israelites when the plague struck Egypt (Exod. 9:4–7), and they departed Egypt with "very much cattle" (Exod. 12:38, KJV). Why were cattle the premier livestock investments among the Jewish people?

An ox (or bull) is a male cow, and the basic term *cow*, or *cattle*, usually refers to the female. Oxen were provided as sacrifices for peace offerings (Num. 7:7–83). The ox does not produce milk; the female cow does. In

Scripture, the land of Bashan in northern Israel was noted for its numerous cattle. Israel was a land of "milk and honey," a phrase indicating prosperity, but also indicating that milk was a necessary commodity for the Hebrew people.

Land investments

God promised Abraham, Isaac, and Jacob a large piece of property in the heart of the Middle East about the size of New Jersey, today called *Israel*. This land holds seven different types of topography that would appeal to every type of living individual. For example:

- You can snow ski on Mount Hermon in the northern Golan Heights.

- You can swim and fish in the Sea of Galilee in northern Israel.

- You can enjoy the beach and sun on the Mediterranean coastline at Tel Aviv.

- You can float in the Dead Sea or enjoy a spa in the Judean wilderness.

- You can visit a beautiful farm in the valley of Megiddo.

- You can travel twenty-five hundred feet in elevation to the sacred city of Jerusalem.

- You can enjoy the rugged, limestone mountains in the central part of the nation.

The land of Israel has it all! Few nations in the entire Middle East have the selection of land forms, lakes, rivers, and farms that Israel has. Israel was to be an "everlasting possession" for Abraham's descendants (Gen. 13:15; 15:18), with God Himself setting the boundaries—"from the river of Egypt to the great river, the River Euphrates" (Gen. 15:18). In Deuteronomy alone, more than twenty-five passages identify the land as belonging to God, who gave the land to Israel as their inheritance. Only when Israel broke their covenant with God were they "plucked off" the land and scattered among the Gentile nations (Deut. 28:63–68).

Any new nation needs a *founding document*, and for Israel it was the

Torah. It needs *a government*, and for Israel it was the prophets, priests, and kings under the leadership of God—the ultimate theocracy. Above all, it needs a *land*, and God provided the needed real estate. Land in general is a powerful investment. Consider the material, agricultural, and financial benefits rooted in land:

- Food grows on the land.
- Minerals are buried under the land.
- Gold, silver, and gemstones are mined from the land.
- Animals graze and feed off the land.
- Fruit trees produce on the land.
- Wood is collected from the land.
- Streams and rivers flow through the land.
- Wells of water and aquifers are under the land.
- Houses are built on the land.
- Flowers bloom on the land.
- Vegetables are grown on the land.

Real estate prices certainly fluctuate; however, history reveals that a person cannot go wrong by owning a quality piece of property that can be farmed, used for grazing livestock, or built upon in the future.

My Italian grandfather was a hardworking man who, as my grandmother teased, "had so many irons in the fire that none of them were hot!" He was a coal miner, songwriter, and magazine publisher, and still found time to pastor a church in Gorman, Maryland, which he constructed in 1959. He lived in Davis, West Virginia, a small community of about seven hundred people. During his lifetime he purchased several pieces of real estate, along with apartments, turning them into six pieces of rental property. Often I was with him when he went from apartment to apartment making minor repairs and talking to the renters. As a child, I recall him saying, "If you invest in anything, invest in land. People always need land and a place to live. You can never go wrong having property, if it is good property."

Granddad retired at age seventy-nine and lived to be eighty-four years old. Until his departure, he received monthly income from five apartments and continually kept them rented. The rentals assisted his income and helped during tax season. I saw, however, the greatest benefit after he passed away.

Grandmother was eventually able to sell all of the property, live off the income, and leave her two daughters some additional money in her will after passing at age eighty-six. Granddad always wanted to ensure that his loving wife of sixty-seven years would be cared for if he departed first.

When we first moved to Cleveland, Tennessee, a real estate specialist showed me a massive piece of land. Pointing to an empty field, he predicted, "Twenty years from now an interstate exit will be here. The town will be coming this way with shops and gas stations. If you would borrow the money to purchase the land now, in twenty years you will be a multimillionaire and will not have to receive an offering because you can live off the income." At that time, I could hardly afford a car and house payment. Smiling, I thanked him for his advice and went on with my ministry. Twenty-eight years passed. The interstate exit exists, along with seven hotels and three convenience stores surrounded by four restaurants. Recently, that formerly $2,000-an-acre property was selling for $100,000 to $300,000 an acre. In fact, the large parcel he suggested I purchase recently sold for an estimated $5,000,000 dollars.

In the 1980s, a Christian man from North Carolina sold a piece of property for $90,000, giving the income to his church's building program. After much prayer, he was impressed to purchase another piece of property. He did an examination for minerals that might be under the land. He was amazed to discover that titanium was present, and a Japanese company was interested in purchasing the property from him. His potential profit was millions of dollars.

LAND—A GENERATIONAL COMMODITY

Many early households in ancient Israel farmed small portions of land that were passed down from generation to generation. The family clan (called *mishpachah*) usually consisted of several generations who shared the same ancestry, living in the same house or sharing farming responsibilities on the same property. If the family farm was sold due to economic distress, God provided a method to redeem the land back to the original family. Called the Jubilee, this cycle of redemption occurred every fifty years (Lev. 25). By proving an original deed of ownership, the land could revert back to the original family. This provided a method to secure a family inheritance from generation to generation. Hebrew slaves were also permitted to return to their families during the Jubilee cycle.

If a family home was sold due to financial misfortune, the sellers had one year in which to redeem it back. If they failed to do so, then the buyer could place his family name on the deed, passing the home on from generation to generation (Lev. 25:30–31). If a Hebrew brother was suffering economically, fellow Hebrews were to assist and provide for him without charging any interest rates on borrowed money or food (Lev. 25:35–37). Taking collateral from the poor was forbidden (Deut. 24:12–13). Many homes would never be foreclosed if a nation practiced assisting the needy and allowing borrowing without interest rates!

Since it was God who blessed the patriarchs with gold (and silver), cattle, and land, this should be an example of the three main commodities for long-term investments. In the past, the enemies of Israel seized their gold, stole their cattle, and occupied their land only to have God regather the Jews back to Israel, restoring the land, cattle, and wealth. The everlasting land grant given to the Jews was established in Abraham and reaffirmed from generation to generation. It was again confirmed in 1948 when Israel was reestablished as a nation.

THE ULTIMATE KEY TO PROSPERITY

Books have been written attempting to explain the amazing success secrets of the Jewish people. However, many authors missed the golden key that unlocks the door of Jewish success—that devout Jews who follow the instructions God laid out in the Scriptures have a unique covenant with God that includes wealth, prosperity, and blessing. These covenant blessings are contingent upon their submission to perform and carry out God's orders.

Human poverty is more than the circumstances of our upbringing or surroundings. It is often a result of generations who are void of understanding and who fail to receive the life-changing redemptive covenant through Christ. The Lord's commandments for practical, moral, and social living are not just for trial-and-error living. Redemption from a life of sin can actually increase your years of living on Earth by breaking unhealthy habits and changing bad attitudes. For example, many inner cities are reeling in a poverty cycle due to addictions and habits. Solomon wrote:

For the drunkard and the glutton will come to poverty, and drowsiness will clothe a man with rags.

—Proverbs 23:21

Poverty and shame will come to him who disdains correction, but he who regards a rebuke will be honored.

—Proverbs 13:18

I believe the reason poverty rules so many lives is because people have never entered into a life-changing covenant of redemption provided through the new covenant. Christ's redemptive covenant can bring deliverance from expensive habits and addictions, and it reforms the human thinking and spirit. The foundation of God's life principles is penned in the Torah.

- The civil and judicial laws instruct us on our relationship with others.
- The moral laws instruct us on our personal conduct.
- The sacrificial laws instruct us on how to put God first in our spiritual life.

How we treat others is a reflection of our character. How we treat ourselves is a reflection of our convictions. How we treat the blessing and favor of God is a reflection of our covenant relationship with Him. Spiritual blessings have conditions. One of the significant conditions to receiving the fullness of blessings from biblical covenants is the willingness to forgive those who have wronged you. If a blood sacrifice was the spiritual DNA of a covenant, then forgiveness is the artery that keeps the lifeblood flowing.

THE SEASON OF *TESHUVAH*

Forgiveness is a major theme in Judaism. In the New Testament, Christ, Paul, and others emphasized that in order to experience spiritual and material blessings and an abundant life, we must willingly forgive those with whom we have an offense. Most Christians are unaware of a season the Jews call *Teshuvah*—a word that comes from the Hebrew root word *shuv*, meaning to *turn* or *repent*.

The Jewish civil New Year always begins in the fall, in either September or October. The last month on the civil calendar is Elul. The season of Teshuvah begins on the first day of Elul and continues for forty days, concluding on the Day of Atonement, celebrated on the tenth day of the Jewish month Tishri.

The concept of Teshuvah originated with Moses. According to the Jewish *Midrash*, Moses was on Mount Sinai for forty days receiving the commandments and learning the oral law (Exod. 24:13–18). He returned to the camp of Israel on the seventeenth day of Tammuz and broke the stone tablets (Exod. 32:19). According to tradition, Moses remained in the camp another forty days until he had burned the golden calf, grinding it up and making the people drink the water (v. 20). After rearranging the tribes in their order, God instructed Moses to ascend the mountain again on the first day of Elul. A shofar (trumpet) was sounded throughout the camp, warning the people not to go near the mountain and not to err again. God ascended in the trumpet blasts, as it is said: "God went up in a blast, the Lord in the sound of the shofar."[4] Thus, the forty days of Teshuvah commemorate the second trip Moses made to the top of the mountain, where he spent another forty days as God revealed His commandments for the second time (Exod. 34:28).

The forty days of Teshuvah are divided into two parts. The first part consists of the twenty-nine days in the month of Elul. Each day a shofar is sounded, reminding the Jewish people to repent. During Moses's first trip, the people became weary of waiting for him and built the golden calf. The second time, the trumpet blasts reminded them that God was in their midst and watching their actions. During the twenty-nine days of Elul, the Jewish people follow several customs.

1. The people recite special prayers, called *Selichot*, to ask God's forgiveness. These prayers are recited in some communities early in the morning, and in older communities, during the week before Rosh Hashanah.

2. Letters are written to correct wrongs and ask for forgiveness from others. Often at the conclusion of the letters, the wish "May you be inscribed in the Book of Life" is penned.

The first part of Teshuvah deals with *personal* repentance toward God and man. The final ten days, which begin on the first day of Tishri, the

Jewish New Year, point the people to a time of *national* repentance. If each individual repents, then the entire nation is prepared to face God on the Day of Atonement (on Tishri 10) and receive a clear verdict of "forgiven." The ten days from Tishri 1 to Tishri 10, called the *Days of Awe*, begin with the New Year (Feast of Trumpets) and conclude with the Day of Atonement. Thus, the fortieth day of Teshuvah concludes on the Day of Atonement, when God has sealed the decisions for His people for the coming year.

It is believed that during these ten days, the gates of heaven are opened to hear the petitions and prayers of the people. It is taught that there are three groups to be examined by the Lord—the totally righteous, the totally unrighteous, and those who are neither righteous nor unrighteous but are living somewhere in between. Based upon prayers of repentance (and forgiving others), God's mercy is manifest on the Day of Atonement and sins are remitted.[5]

Some Christians point out, and rightfully so, that we should not wait for a special *season* to repent of sin. This is correct, and a believer should not even go to bed at night until he corrects his errors or repents of any wrongdoing (Eph. 4:26). However, churches often need a set time when the entire body comes together for a season of reflection, repentance, and cleansing, removing old attitudes and initiating a fresh start. Teshuvah provides a set time on God's calendar for drawing nearer to God, forgiving others, and seeking His favor. Torah-observant Jews also believe a person should repent if he or she sins. However, they believe that from Elul 1 to Tishri 10, forgiveness is more *readily acceptable* since God once pardoned the entire nation of Israel *all at once* in Moses's time. Therefore Elul is considered a month of heavenly compassion.

THE NEED FOR SEASONS OF REPENTANCE

The central theme of redemption is God's forgiveness being released through His mercy toward the repentant sinner. Christians should be fully aware of the emphasis the New Testament places upon forgiving others of their trespasses and their sins toward us. The Torah reveals that abundant blessings are released upon those who have been forgiven of their sins and who are willing to choose a righteous lifestyle by following the spiritual and moral Torah Code. Blessings were promised on their children, their crops, and their livestock, and the defeat of their enemies was assured (Deut. 28:1–14). The New Testament is clear that God's blessings for the individual believer are conditional upon our willingness to follow the new covenant teaching and be willing to forgive others as Christ forgave us (Matt. 6:12–15). Our blessings include forgiveness of sins, answered prayer, financial increase, and the spiritual impartation of righteousness, peace, and joy (Rom. 14:17). Christ said it this way:

> But seek first the kingdom of God and His righteousness, and all these things shall be added to you.
>
> —MATTHEW 6:33

Righteousness cannot be earned, but it is imputed by faith in the redemptive covenant provided by Christ. There is more to wealth than bank accounts, and more to prosperity than owning multiple homes.

SOLOMON'S FINAL DISCOVERY

Solomon's final discovery before his death may come as a surprise to many. After building the most fabulous temple perhaps in history, amassing wealth, and experiencing fame and prosperity, Solomon came to the end of his life with an astonishing statement: "All is vanity." He realized all of his wealth would be left for his son, and not even Solomon knew what type of character he would have (Eccles. 2:19). We could sum up Solomon's attitude by saying, "Enjoy every moment of your life, because you won't take your possessions with you." God has a covenant of blessing for those who follow His precepts. However, keep in mind that there are many things more important than amassing land, gold, and silver. They are:

■ Assuring that your entire family enters a redemptive covenant through the Messiah

■ You, and your family, enjoying good health and living long, full lives

■ Knowing that your grandchildren (future seed) are being raised in the admonition of the Lord and the new covenant

- Having peace to sleep each night and having joy with the type of work you do

- Making friends who love you for who you are and not what you have or what you can do for them

- Learning to walk in forgiveness, and dying in peace knowing where you are going before you arrive

If you are redeemed by the Messiah, have healthy children, can pay your bills and sleep at night, have friends who love you, and enjoy your job, *then you are successful in life*. You are truly prosperous.

What *God* Knew

As part of the covenant blessing and as a motivation for following the laws of God, the Almighty established a covenant of wealth with the Hebrew nation. This provided for their personal and national financial security and demonstrated to surrounding pagan nations that the abundant blessings on their land, livestock, fruit trees, and harvest cycles were visible proof of the care and love the Hebrew God had for His people.

What Devout *Jews* Know

The Torah and the wisdom literature are filled with solid, practical wisdom, instruction, and counsel for daily living and to help one make the right choices. Devout Jews continually read and study these guidelines and principles, teaching them to their children.

What *Christians* Should Know

John wrote, "I pray that you may prosper in all things and be in health, just as your soul prospers" (3 John 2). By walking in purity and righteousness and putting God's kingdom first, your personal needs will be met (Matt. 6:31–33). Prosperity is one branch on the covenant tree. Believers should study the wisdom literature in Proverbs and apply the principles, which will bring forth fruit on the tree. Always remember: money is simply a tool for accomplishing dreams and visions and is to be used as a resource for your family. When you are blessed, never forget it was God who gave you the power to "get wealth."

Chapter 11

THE INFLUENCE OF HEBREW BIBLICAL PROPHECY ON WORLD LEADERS

CODE 11:
The Hebrew Scriptures reveal future world events.

Blessed be the name of God forever and ever,
For wisdom and might are His.
And He changes the times and the seasons;
He removes kings and raises up kings;
He gives wisdom to the wise
And knowledge to those who have understanding.
—Daniel 2:20–21

W ORLD LEADERS HAVE MADE MAJOR DECISIONS IN REACTION to what they read in ancient biblical prophecies. Prophecy is when God prewrites the headlines using inspiration, dreams, visions, or divine visitations, revealing future events often thousands of years before they occur. Prophecy is what makes the Bible different from the other sacred oracles of world religions. For example, what would you do if you read your name in the Bible and it revealed your destiny long before you were born?

NAMED TWO HUNDRED YEARS BEFORE HIS BIRTH

Twenty-seven centuries ago in the time of King Hezekiah, the prophet Isaiah predicted that the Babylonian army would invade Judea, march to Jerusalem, destroy the temple, and steal the priceless temple treasures. Later, Jeremiah predicted the Jews would remain captive in Babylon for seventy years before returning to Israel (Jer. 25:11). One hundred forty years before the Babylonians' arrival, Isaiah predicted a man named Cyrus would rise to power and release the Jews from Babylon, permitting their return to Israel. Isaiah predicted:

> Who says of Cyrus, "He is My shepherd,
> And he shall perform all My pleasure,
> Saying to Jerusalem, 'You shall be built,'
> And to the temple, 'Your foundation shall be laid.'"

> Thus says the LORD to His anointed,
> To Cyrus, whose right hand I have held—
> To subdue nations before him
> And loose the armor of kings,
> To open before him the double doors,
> So that the gates will not be shut.
>
> —ISAIAH 44:28–45:1

When Isaiah wrote this, Cyrus was not yet born. Years later, Nebuchadnezzar, the king of Babylon, invaded Israel, conquering Jews from Judea. For seventy years the Babylonians enslaved the Jews, until Persian invaders shut off the water, dug under the city, and overthrew the Babylonians in one night. Two leaders, Darius, a Mede, and Cyrus, a Persian, now ruled from the Babylonian throne.

Jewish history reveals that after the Persian invasion, the Hebrew prophet Daniel opened the scroll of the prophet Isaiah and showed Cyrus a 140-year-old prophecy that predicted Cyrus's name and his preordained God-given assignment. Josephus recorded Cyrus's reaction when he read his own name in the Hebrew scroll:

> Thus saith Cyrus the king: Since God Almighty has appointed me to be king of the inhabited earth, I believe He is that God of which the nation of the Israelites worship; for indeed He foretold my name by the prophets and that I should build a house in Jerusalem in the country of Judea.[1]

This amazing prophecy motivated Cyrus to act it out. He permitted the Jews to return to Israel to rebuild their temple and to restore the sacred vessels Nebuchadnezzar had seized seventy years prior. Two prophecies from Isaiah, a Hebrew prophet, transformed the course of Israel's history!

THE GENERAL'S DREAM SAVED JERUSALEM

A second example concerns a Greek general. After two hundred years of Persian rule, the Greeks overthrew the Persians, capturing Babylon. The new global leader was Alexander the Great, military king of the Grecian Empire. His armies marched from Egypt to India. After conquering Syria and Tyre, he sent a letter to Jaddua, the Jewish high priest in Jerusalem, asking for provisions. The priest replied that he supported Darius the Median king while he was still living. Alexander was furious and eventually marched to Jerusalem to kill the high priest. Fearful, Jaddua called for prayer and sacrifices. In a dream, Jaddua saw everyone wearing white, and him wearing his high priest garments, going out to meet Alexander.

Jaddua instructed the people to wear white, and he would meet Alexander and his army in his priestly apparel. Alexander arrived, encountering the huge Jewish procession led by the colorful high priest. Alexander saluted the high priest as the Jews surrounded him. When the soldiers questioned why he, Alexander the Great, should salute a simple Jewish priest, he answered:

> "...I saw this very person in a dream, in this very habit, when I was in Dios in Macedonia, who, when I was considering with myself how I might obtain the dominion of Asia, exhorted me to make no delay, but bodily to pass over the sea thither, for that he would conduct my army, and would give me dominion over the Persians..."[2]

Afterward, the high priest rolled open the scroll of Daniel and showed Alexander an amazing prophecy, hundreds of years old, predicting through prophetic symbolism his destiny as a world leader:

> And when the Book of Daniel was showed him wherein Daniel declared that one of the Greeks should destroy the empire of the Persians, he supposed that himself was the person intended.[3]

Alexander then stopped taxes until the seventh year and gave Jews in Media and Persia ability to make their own laws.

The biblical prophecy prevented the death of the priest and another possible destruction of Jerusalem by Alexander. Twice, ancient world leaders' decisions were influenced by the biblical prophecies written hundreds of years before they were fulfilled.

DANIEL'S PROPHECY INSPIRES A REVOLT

Cyrus and Alexander reacted positively to the Jews because the Hebrew prophets foretold of their destiny and their rise to power. Another example occurred when a wicked leader, Antiochus Epiphanes, invaded Jerusalem in 167 B.C. and stopped the sacrifices and prevented Jewish circumcision, Sabbath worship, and Jews celebrating the feasts. Daniel had predicted such a person would rise and would have dominion for forty-two months. Inspired by this prediction, a Jewish family called the Maccabees fought against the ungodly Greeks. After years of fighting, the Jewish temple was cleansed on the twenty-fifth of Kislev, three years to the day it was defiled by Antiochus. Josephus wrote:

> And this desolation came to pass according to the prophecy of Daniel, which was given four hundred and eight years before; for he declared that the Macedonians would dissolve that worship [for some time].[4]

The Jewish uprising against their enemies was inspired from their interpretation of a 408-year-old prophecy from a Hebrew prophet!

Throughout history, Christians have read the Books of Daniel and Revelation, which reveal events to occur before or during the revealing and return of the Messiah. This includes numerous *signs*—the rise of a man called the

Antichrist, a time identified as the *Tribulation*, and other predicted events. Since the first century, well-meaning Christians have attempted to interpret these signs and apply them to their generation. Several early fathers taught that Nero was the Antichrist. After ten persecutions against Christianity by ten Roman emperors, the theology was changed, and by the fifth century, some fathers began teaching that the kingdom of God would come to Earth during a one-thousand-year rule of the Roman church. In A.D. 999, many Christians in Europe sold their possessions, donning white robes and making a pilgrimage to the Holy Land to stand on the Mount of Olives in Jerusalem and await Christ's return. When there was a no *show*, the Crusades restored hope that soon faded with the Islamic conquest of Jerusalem. Then in the 1800s a renewed interest in prophetic teaching emerged.

For nineteen hundred years, the scholars, fathers, and teachers had all seemed to miss the most important key to biblical prophecy and the return of the Messiah-King. The key was Israel. No major prophecy concerning the return and rule of the Messiah could be fulfilled until Israel was first a nation and Jerusalem was in the hands of the Jews. Numerous predictions by the Hebrew prophets Isaiah, Ezekiel, Daniel, and Zechariah reveal this. The picture became clearer in the late 1800s.

1917 AND THE JERUSALEM MIRACLE

In 1886, a Dr. Guinness began calculating various timeframes using biblical numbers from the Book of Daniel and exchanging their normal meaning of prophetic days into prophetic years. He calculated that the timeframes of 1,260 and 2,520 were not days but prophetic years, and he began calculating the times of the Gentiles mentioned in prophecy, which was a clue to the return of the Messiah. His calculations indicated the *times of the Gentiles* began with Muhammad in A.D. 622 and would conclude in or around 1917. He predicted that 1917 would be the "most important and momentous of all the cycle of years."[5] These predictions were written and made known throughout the Christian community in the late 1800s.

It was at the conclusion of World War I in 1917 that a Christian British general, Edmund "the Bull" Allenby, took Jerusalem, ending thirteen centuries of Islamic rule, including four hundred years of Turkish occupation (1517–1917). The Turks had said that the water of the Nile River must flow to Palestine before they would ever lose Jerusalem. Of course, this would be impossible. However, when the British began laying twelve-inch pipes to pump water from Egypt to supply water for the British, the suspicious Turks became discouraged.

Strangely, the Muslims had a prophecy attributed to tenth-century poet Ibn Khasri that said: "The man who will conquer Jerusalem and redeem it from the infidel for all time to come will enter the Holy City humbly on foot, and his name is God's Prophet."[6]

John Hilton was a mechanic in the British Royal Flying Corps. After he attended church on a Sunday morning in June 1917, the clergyman saw Hilton's military uniform and made a strange prediction. The minister informed Hilton that he had been reading the Bible from Isaiah 31 and believed that *aeroplanes* would be used to deliver Jerusalem to the British. Months later, prior to the invasion of the old city of Jerusalem, General Allenby wired London for advice, and the reply was the same scripture the minister had studied, found in Isaiah 31:4–5 (KJV):

> For thus hath the LORD spoken unto me, Like as the lion and the young lion roaring on his prey, when a multitude of shepherds is called forth against him, he will not be afraid of their voice, nor abase himself for the noise of them: so shall the LORD of hosts come down to fight for mount Zion, and for the hill thereof. As birds flying, so will the LORD of hosts defend Jerusalem; defending also he will deliver it; and passing over he will preserve it.

After receiving the wire, Allenby called for planes to fly low over Jerusalem, dropping leaflets warning the Turks. When the Turks heard and read the name Allenby, which could be—and was—misread as *Allah en Nebi*, translated in Arabic as *Allah* (God), *Nebi* (prophet), the Turks surrendered the keys of the city to Allenby, whom Arab Christians were calling "God's prophet," on December 9, 1917. Two days later, Allenby and several military commanders entered the Jaffa Gate and walked into the city on foot. The combination of Allenby's name and taking the city on foot fulfilled the predictions of a tenth-century Islamic poet. Allenby's method of sparing the city from destruction was inspired from a biblical Hebrew prophet. Jerusalem's liberation from four hundred years of Turkish rule also occurred during a Jewish festival on the Jewish calendar—the first day of Hanukkah![7]

In 1917, a new "ism" had risen on the earth out of the Russian Revolution. The bear of Communism had come out of hibernation and was loose on the earth. For seventy years, the atheistic Communist doctrine had brainwashed the masses and oppressed free thinkers. After nearly seventy years, another prophetic cycle began that would push the bear back in his cave—at least for a while.

THE EAGLE, THE IRON SICKLE, AND THE POPE

Three men, Ronald Reagan (the eagle), Mikhail Gorbachev (the iron sickle), and Karol Joseph Wojtyla (Pope John Paul II), will go down as legends in world history for being the trio that, working together, helped to bring about the greatest political changes in modern history—the collapse and demise of Communism in the Soviet Union and the Eastern European states.

Ronald Reagan—the eagle

Most Americans are unaware of a personal prophecy given to Ronald Reagan while he was governor of California, which predicted his future destiny as president. According to the book *Reagan, Inside Out*, the story begins in California on a beautiful October day in 1970.[8] Herbert E. Ellingwood, Governor Reagan's legal affairs secretary, had invited several guests to visit the governor. Among them were celebrity Pat Boone, Mr. Harald Bredesen, and a minister, George Otis. Boone was a longtime friend of the Reagans, and at the time the governor was running for reelection.

According to those present, the conversations included a discussion on Bible prophecy and the Holy Spirit's move in the Last Days. After some time, Ellingwood led the group toward the front door, and the final good-byes were being said. One of the ministers spoke up and asked, "Governor, do you mind if we take a moment and pray for you and Mrs. Reagan?"

Immediately Reagan replied, "We would appreciate that," as his countenance turned rather serious. The group formed a circle, joining hands as Reagan bowed his head. Prayer was immediately offered asking for God's blessings. Suddenly in the middle of the prayer, the unexpected occurred. George Otis recalled what transpired:

> The Holy Spirit came upon me, and I knew it. In fact, I was embarrassed. There was this pulsing in my arm, and my hand—the one holding Governor Reagan's hand—was shaking. I didn't know what to do. I just didn't want this to be happening. I can remember that even as I was speaking, I was working, you know, tensing my muscles and concentrating, and doing everything I could to stop that shaking.[9]

At that moment Otis's prayer changed completely from a basic prayer of blessing to a more steady and intent word. The Holy Spirit–inspired words coming from Otis's mouth spoke directly to Reagan, addressing him as, "My son," and recognizing his role as leader in a state that was the size of many nations on earth. His "labor" was described as "pleasing." Suddenly the following words were spoken: "If you walk uprightly before Me, you will reside at 1600 Pennsylvania Avenue."[10] Everyone knew that 1600 Pennsylvania Avenue was the address of the White House, the home of America's presidents.

Ten years passed, and in 1980, against all odds, Governor Reagan ran for president. Political analysts were critical, saying he was "too old to make clear mental decisions and, if elected, could die in office." Others said he was incompetent and just an actor. Despite the objections, Reagan won and was reelected for a second term. He not only lived to be seventy-eight, but he passed the age of ninety! The prophetic word came to pass.

Ten years before his election as president, God revealed His will for Ronald Reagan. Reagan was a dedicated Christian who loved the Bible. Familiar with biblical prophecy, he sometimes privately consulted key ministers to ask for their opinions on how certain world events would play into the prophetic scenarios of Scripture.

Mikhail Gorbachev—the iron sickle

On the opposite end of the globe, behind the iron curtain of the Soviet Union, another *setup* was unfolding in the very stronghold of Communism. It was predicted on two different occasions.

Sixty-two years before the rise of Communism, a man named Dr. Hudson Taylor was ministering. Taylor was a missionary to China. It has been written concerning Taylor: "For forty years the sun never rose on China, but Hudson Taylor was on his knees praying for the salvation of the Chinese."[11]

In 1855, during one of his furloughs to England, Taylor was preaching, when suddenly he stopped. He stood speechless for a time with his eyes closed. When he began to speak he explained:

> I have just seen a vision. I saw in this vision a great war that will encompass the whole world. I saw this war recess and then start again, actually being two wars. After this, I saw much unrest and revolts that will affect many nations. I saw in some places spiritual awakenings. In Russia, I saw there will come a general all-encompassing spiritual awakening so great that there could never be another like it. From Russia, I saw the awakening spread to many European countries. Then I saw an all-out awakening followed by the coming of Christ.[12]

Sixty-two years after Hudson's vision, the Russian Revolution birthed Communism. This anti-God system grew like a poison vine, choking to death individual faith in God. For almost seventy years, the sword of godless Communism was dripping with the blood of Christian martyrs and Communist resisters. None in the West ever comprehended the possibility that the iron curtain could melt and a period of religious freedom would rise like steam from hot water.

Since a true Communist must be a confessed atheist, Western Christians reasoned it impossible for Soviet Christians to ever see their chains of oppression fall off. Yet a few underground believers in the unregistered Pentecostal church were aware of an inspired prediction given in the 1930s revealing that in the future, religious freedom would come again. That prophetic word was guarded by leaders in the underground church for more than fifty years. Several years ago, while visiting Russia, the old prophecy was told directly to Rev. Lovell Carey, former world missions director for the Church of God, Cleveland, Tennessee.

1930 prophecy concerning "Mikhail"

Lovell was in Russia shortly after the fall of Communism. He met with one of the bishops of the unregistered Pentecostal church, Bishop Fedatov. According to the bishop, in the 1930s a Christian woman gave an unusual prophetic word under the inspiration of the Holy Spirit. It said that in the future a person would arise in the Soviet Union whose name would be *Mikhail*. He would have a mark on his forehead. She predicted that during his time, freedom to worship and revival would come. However, this freedom would only be for a short time; then repression would begin.

Fifty years later, this prediction would be fulfilled. Mikhail Gorbachev became the leader of the Soviet Union! Words like *glasnost* became globally recognized. A lesser-known part of the story concerning Mr. Gorbachev reveals the timing of the Almighty's hand in raising up men in leadership.

Christian mother influences Mikhail

Lavon Riley was a tour operator from Texas. In the late 1980s, Mr. Riley planned a trip to Russia, traveling with a planeload of Christians. Underneath their plane were thousands of Bibles. Upon his arrival, it was difficult to get clearance for the Bibles, but after a detailed visit with customs personnel and a special permit, the army came with trucks and delivered the Bibles directly to the churches.

Lavon personally told me that during this trip, the KGB called him into their offices. Great fear overwhelmed him. The KGB proceeded to tell him they were aware of his every step, even producing a file four inches thick giving minute details of every trip Lavon had ever made in Russia. It turned out that the meeting was not intended to arrest or interrogate him but to demonstrate to him that a *new Russia* existed that would allow more religious freedom. A permit was granted to Lavon by the third man under Gorbachev to bring as many Bibles into Russia as Lavon desired!

It was at this time that Lavon learned that the mother of Mikhail Gorbachev was an Orthodox Christian. She had prayed for Mikhail for many years that he would become a leader in Russia. He also learned that for Mikhail's birthdays, his mother would make a special cake, at times placing certain scriptures on it. This was confirmed when Gorbachev appeared on the *Hour of Power* with Robert Schuller, October 22, 2000, and spoke about his mother's prayers, stating that "practically all" his family were Christians.

While Mikhail has kept a close tie to the Russian Orthodox Church, none can deny that *perestroika* created an atmosphere of coexistence that opened the door to freedom of religious expression without repression. Apparently the predestined purpose of Gorbachev was twofold—to bring religious freedom to the Soviet Union (Russia) and to allow the Soviet Jews to immigrate back to Israel. This action was a direct fulfillment of ancient biblical prophecies concerning the return of the Jews from the north country back to Israel (Jer. 31:8).

The *prophetic* role of Karol Wojtyla—the pope

On May 18, 1920, Karol Joseph Wojtyla was born in Wadowice, Poland. During the Nazi occupation of Poland, Karol pursued studies working as a stonecutter to hold a work permit, thus keeping him from being deported or imprisoned. He joined the UNIA, a Christian democratic underground group. Jewish organizations such as B'nai B'rith and others testified that he helped Jews find refuge from the Nazis. In 1942 he began studying for the priesthood and was ordained a priest on November 1, 1946. By 1967 he was elevated to cardinal, and on October 16, 1978, at age fifty-eight, Karol Wojtyla was elected pope and chose the title of John Paul II.

TWO ASSASSINATION ATTEMPTS

Oddly, both Reagan and the pope survived assassination attempts on their lives in the same year! On May 13, 1981, the pope was greeting a crowd at Vatican Square in Rome, Italy. As he leaned over to kiss a statue of the Virgin Mary, a Turkish terrorist fired a gun, striking the pope in the abdomen. He slumped into the arms of his secretary, blood pouring from the wound. Despite losing six pints of blood, John Paul II survived. The pope realized he had been shot on the sixty-four-year anniversary of the famous Marion apparition known as "Our Lady of Fatima," an alleged apparition of the Virgin Mary that appeared to three children in Fatima, Portugal, on May 13, 1917 (the same year of the Communist Revolution). Because of this strange coincidence, the pope credited Our Lady of Fatima (the Virgin Mary) with sparing his life and dedicated the remaining time of his papacy to her "immaculate heart."

It was also in 1981 that President Reagan was speaking at a luncheon at the Hilton Hotel in Washington DC. As he exited a side door, waving at the reporters, a young man named John Hinckley fired six shots at the president. A single bullet ricocheted off the limo door and entered Reagan's chest just one inch from his heart. Reagan told several Secret Service agents that he gave credit to God for protecting his life.

These two assassination attempts helped bond a special relationship between the president and the pope. In June of 1982, President Reagan flew to the Vatican to have a personal meeting with Pope John Paul II. Years later, their private discussion was made public. Both men discussed their assassination attempts and agreed that God had spared their lives for a special and specific purpose. Both men discussed the terrible scourge of Communism and how the oppressive regime had destroyed personal freedoms and faith in God for millions of people who desired freedom. At that moment, both men pledged to work together to help spread freedom throughout Communist nations.

Reagan did more than just talk about freedom. Three weeks after the meeting, he signed a secretive National Security Directive to purchase and send into Poland the necessary equipment, including copy machines, fax machines, and other electronic equipment, to assist the Solidarity Movement in Poland. This group would organize protests that would be aired via satellite around the world and would unite a large following of Polish workers.

The plan worked. Just as Communism captured the minds of the common people during the 1917 revolution, it was the common workers of Poland who took the keys of freedom and unshackled their bands of iron. The impact of their uprising soon spread to Romania, Bulgaria, and Germany, where the world watched stunned as the infamous Berlin wall was dismantled by the German people! Before Reagan departed from office, the Berlin wall had crumbled, the Soviet Union had unraveled, and the icy cold war had melted. According to a report in *TIME* magazine dated February 24, 1992, the coalition forged between Reagan and the Vatican consisted of a five-part strategy "that was aimed at bringing about the collapse of the Soviet Economy, fraying the ties that bound the USSR to its client states in the Warsaw Pact and forcing reform inside the Soviet empire."[13] Both Reagan and Gorbachev admitted the vital role the pope played in the collapse of Communism in Eastern Europe.

Few non-Catholics understand one of the unseen motivations of the pope's decision to become directly involved in liberating the Eastern bloc Communist countries, especially the Soviet Union. His spiritual inspiration hinged upon a prophecy that was given through an alleged apparition of the Virgin Mary in 1917.

The Prophecy of Fatima

Pope John Paul II credited the Virgin Mary for sparing his life. One year after his near-death experience, the pope traveled to a famous Catholic shrine in Fatima, Portugal, and presented one of the bullets used in the attack to be placed in the crown of the statue of Our Lady of Fatima as a token of gratitude to her for saving his life. The pope pledged himself to Mary and gave himself to her message, especially the message of Fatima. His personal motto was *Totus tuus sum Maria*, meaning, "Mary, I am all yours." At the same time on May 13, 1982, the pope prayed before the statue of our Lady of Fatima and consecrated the world to her, based on the promise from 1917, which said: "If my wishes are fulfilled…my immaculate heart will triumph, Russia will be converted, and there will be peace." The pope, along with most traditional European Catholics, was very aware of the prophecies given in Fatima, Portugal, in 1917 concerning the future fall of Communism. Because the pope's life was spared on the anniversary of the Fatima visitation, the Pope felt compelled to help fulfill the "wishes of the virgin Mary," proclaimed at Fatima, that Russia would be converted.[14]

From that moment it became the goal of the pope to see Communism fall in the European Eastern bloc, including the Soviet Union. The pope would receive help from the eagle of America (Reagan) and from a leader living under the iron sickle, Mikhail Gorbachev. These examples reveal the power of prophecy to inspire decisions with global ramifications.

Prophecy Motivates the Jews

From the destruction of the temple and Jerusalem in A.D. 70, the Jews were nineteen centuries without a homeland. Their future situation had been predicted by the prophet Hosea:

> For the children of Israel shall abide many days without king or prince, without sacrifice or sacred pillar, without ephod or teraphim. Afterward the children of Israel shall return and seek the LORD their God and David their king. They shall fear the LORD and His goodness in the latter days.
>
> —HOSEA 3:4–5

There are several other biblical prophecies related to future events in the nation of Israel, which include the following:

- A time of great trouble would come in which Jews would be near extinction—Daniel 12:1.

- God would breathe on the Jews and bring them up from their spiritual graves—Ezekiel 37:9–13.

- Israel would again be restored in just one day as a nation—Isaiah 66:8.

- Jerusalem would be built up before the Messiah returns—Psalm 102:16.

- Jews would return to Israel from the nations where they were scattered—Jeremiah 29:14.

- Once restored, Israel would blossom and fill the world with fruit—Isaiah 27:6.

- The latter rains would return, causing the desert to blossom—Joel 2:23–24.

- Hebrew (the pure language) would again be spoken in Israel—Zephaniah 3:9.

- Surrounded by enemies, Israel would survive—Zechariah 12:2–9.

The biblical prophecies predicting a Jewish return to Israel have always reminded and motivated devout Jews and rabbis to keep the *Zionist* vision of a Jewish homeland alive when there was no homeland. Rabbis knew the promise: God will "…gather together the dispersed of Judah from the four corners of the earth" (Isa. 11:12). They looked for a leader to fulfill these expectations. When the French emperor Napoleon conquered Poland and Russia, his decisions to tear down the walls of the Jewish ghettos and remove the laws of injustice against the Jews, plus restore a Jewish council (Sanhedrin), gained the attention of the Jews. Marching to Jerusalem, he declared his intent to reestablish Jewish sovereignty over the Holy Land. Many Jews were convinced that Napoleon was introducing a new messianic era. Some Hassidic

Jews believed the French leader would help restore Israel and help introduce the final redemption. Of course, Napoleon met his Waterloo, and the Jews remained in Europe without the redemption of their promised homeland. The late 1800s saw a new stirring for the restoration of Israel as a Jewish state.

In 1886, Theodor Herzl wrote an inspiring book, *The Jewish State*, which stirred up great interest on the Jewish homeland question.[15] Through his efforts, the First Zionist Congress was held in Basel, Switzerland, one year later. Thus a *Zionist movement* for the restoration of a Jewish homeland in Palestine began to take root.

When World War I concluded, a Jewish chemist, Dr. Chaim Weizmann, had assisted the British in developing a new system for providing acetone, a chemical needed to make ammunition. Without it, the British would have lost the war. Following the war, Weizmann gained favor with the British government and convinced the British foreign secretary, Arthur James Balfour, to contact Lord Rothschild, a wealthy English financier, to help the Jewish settlement with a declaration, which read:

> Dear Lord Rothschild,
>
> I have much pleasure in conveying to you, on behalf of His Majesty's Government, the following declaration of sympathy with the Jewish Zionist aspirations which has been submitted to, and approved by, the Cabinet.
>
> His Majesty's Government views with favour the establishment in Palestine of a national home for the Jewish people, and will use their best endeavours to facilitate the achievement of this object, it being clearly understood that nothing shall be done which may prejudice the civil and religious rights of existing non-Jewish communities in Palestine, or the rights and political status enjoyed by Jews in any other country.
>
> I should be grateful if you would bring this declaration to the knowledge of the Zionist Federation.
>
> Yours,
> Arthur James Balfour

Within one month of this declaration Jerusalem fell into British hands.[16] The restoration for a new Jewish state had begun. Little did the Jews know that their most difficult time lay ahead twenty-two years in the future.

THE HOLOCAUST PROPHECIES

In Moses's closing days, he warned Israel of a future time when great distress and trouble would overwhelm Israel because as a nation they would turn from God's ways and follow the manner of the idolatrous, heathen nations. The people were put on divine notice about what to expect during these dark seasons. Moses warned:

> Because you did not serve the LORD your God with joy and gladness of heart, for the abundance of everything, therefore you shall serve your enemies, whom the LORD will send against you, in hunger, in thirst, in nakedness, and in need of everything; and He will put a yoke of iron on your neck until He has destroyed you.... You shall be left few in number, whereas you were as the stars of heaven in multitude, because you would not obey the voice of the LORD your God.... Your life shall hang in doubt before you; you shall fear day and night, and have no assurance of life. In the morning you shall say, "Oh, that it were evening!" And at evening you shall say, "Oh, that it were morning!" because of the fear which terrifies your heart, and because of the sight which your eyes see.
>
> —DEUTERONOMY 28:47–48, 62, 66–67

There is one seven-year period in Jewish history that fulfilled every detail of Moses's warning—and that was the Nazi holocaust. During the reign of Hitler, about six million Jews perished. Another Hebrew prophet, Ezekiel, caught a vision called the "valley of dry bones" (Ezek. 37). Ezekiel saw a large field with a multitude of disjointed, separated bones scattered in open graves. As Ezekiel wondered in amazement, God breathed upon the bones, causing a shaking and a coming together bone to bone. Soon Ezekiel saw a great army rising from the graveyard to return back to Israel (Ezek. 37:21–24). They would no longer be divided between northern and southern tribes but would be one nation. Ezekiel saw the national resurrection of Israel from the graveyard of Gentile nations.

In the 1940s in the midst of possible annihilation, Moses's prediction of great trouble and Ezekiel's prophecy of a national resurrection gave the Jewish Holocaust survivors hope of returning to their original land. In 1986, I met a group of Jewish Holocaust survivors at the Renaissance Hotel Ballroom. These elderly women showed me their arms, which were tattooed with a number. During our discussion, I asked them about Ezekiel's prophecy, and amazingly they agreed that the valley of dry bones was a prediction of how the Jews would survive the Holocaust and come back from the dead to live and build a nation. One said that this was the one biblical prediction that gave a glimmer of hope in a dark time.

After the Jews were dispersed in A.D. 70, scattered among the Gentile nations, and without a home, God kept His covenant to Abraham and brought the seed of Abraham back to the land promised to Abraham. In 1967, during the Six-Day War, the covenant of David for the city of Jerusalem was remembered as the Jews reunited east and west Jerusalem under one Jewish covering. Thus Jerusalem became the united capital of Israel. This historic event reminds me of Psalm 102:16: "For the LORD shall build up Zion; He shall appear in His glory." Our generation has witnessed the return of the Jews from the four corners of the earth back to their land. The desert Isaiah saw is now blossoming like a rose and filling the world with produce. The ancient prophecies have prophesied about Israel, preserved Israel, and produced a reborn Israel—all because God cannot go back on what He has promised. It would be good if all world leaders would pay more attention to the words of the Hebrew prophets.

WHAT *God* KNEW

God is able to prove to the world that His written words found in the Holy Scriptures are the only true divine revelation on Earth, because they contain prophecy. One-third of the Old Testament prophecies have not yet occurred, and there are 318 New Testament predictions concerning the return of Christ. It is prophecy that accurately reveals the future of nations, Israel, and believers in the new covenant.

WHAT DEVOUT *Jews* KNOW

Jews who have studied the Torah and the prophets are aware of the numerous predictions that foretold of Israel's times of tribulation. They are also taught of God's eternal favor on Israel if the people will turn to God and follow His commandments. According to prophecy, Israel will never be destroyed as a nation, and the Jewish people will endure into the messianic kingdom.

WHAT *Christians* SHOULD KNOW

Some Christians have little interest in studying biblical prophecy, as they perceive the subject as negative and rather depressing. However, with so much of Scripture being prophetic, and with the fact that believers will one day live and rule from Jerusalem, it would be a mistake to avoid understanding what the Bible says about the future—since you are going there!

Chapter 12

IMPART BEFORE YOU DEPART

> ## CODE 12:
> *Blessings are generational—leave a heritage, and pass on a legacy.*

By faith Isaac blessed Jacob and Esau concerning things to come. By faith Jacob, when he was dying, blessed each of the sons of Joseph, and worshiped, leaning on the top of his staff.
—HEBREWS 11:20–21

JONATHAN EDWARDS WAS MARRIED IN 1727. EDWARDS WAS ONE of the American colonies' most noted and respected early preachers. His classic message, "Sinners in the Hands of an Angry God," was so convicting that the unrepentant sitting under his preaching would cry out in anguish, dropping to the floor. Yet many are unaware that in his private life, Edwards was a very loving, compassionate man who spent quality personal time with his family.

Edwards was blessed with eleven children. When he was at home, Edwards had a special chair that he alone sat in. In the evenings, Edwards would sit down with his children for one hour each day. The smaller ones would sit in his lap, and the older ones would spend quality time conversing with their dad. Edwards took time to pray a special blessing over each child.

To prove that Edwards's prayers and blessings were effective, in 1900 A. E. Winship tracked down fourteen hundred descendants of Jonathan Edwards.[1] In his published study, Winship revealed that the one marriage of Edwards produced an amazing lineage, including 285 college graduates on the Edwards family tree. His lineage produced:

- Three hundred preachers
- Thirteen noted authors
- Thirteen college presidents
- Sixty-five college professors
- One hundred lawyers and a dean of a law school
- Thirty judges
- Fifty-six physicians and a dean of a medical school
- Eighty holders of public office
- Three United States senators
- One vice president of the United States
- One comptroller of the United States Treasury[2]

The spiritual seeds of faith, hope, and love planted into the hearts of the Edwards children blossomed into a family tree, producing numerous generations of spiritual fruit. Is it possible that today's families can begin planting a family tree, nourishing a generational seed that will become a legacy of righteousness? The first four generations of Hebrew fathers prove this is possible.

First Generation—Planting the Seed

Abraham was childless, but he began a future nation with a dream and a seed. God gave him the *promise* of a nation, and he gave God the *person* to form the nation—a seed son named Isaac. Abraham was a spiritual pioneer blazing the trail to new lands, digging wells, building herds, and amassing gold and silver (Gen. 13:2). In his old age, he sent his servant to find a bride for his son. Eleazar's caravan headed to Syria with ten camels loaded down with gold, silver, and jewels as a bridal gift for an unknown, unseen woman of destiny (Gen. 24:10). The servant confessed, "The LORD has blessed my master greatly, and he has become great; and He has given him flocks and herds, silver and gold, male and female servants, and camels and donkeys" (v. 35). Abraham planted the seed of the nation, and Isaac watered the seed to begin a family tree.

SECOND GENERATION—WATERING THE TREE

After Abraham's death, his son Isaac received not only the wealth of Abraham but also an additional measure of the covenant blessing. Abraham encountered famine in the Promised Land, which forced his family to move to Egypt for provisions (Gen. 12:10). Years later, a great famine struck in Isaac's time. However, the covenant blessing on Isaac was at a new level. Instead of going to Egypt for provision, Isaac redug the wells of Abraham and used the water, sowing his seed in the time of famine, and he received a one-hundredfold return (Gen. 26:12). Isaac used the water of his father to survive the famine. We also read: "And the man waxed great, and went forward, and grew until he became very great" (v. 13, KJV). Abraham was *great* (Gen. 24:35), but Isaac was *very great!*

The blessings on the second generation exceeded the blessings on the first generation. Abraham was the root, Isaac was the trunk, and his son Jacob was the first branch on the family tree. The roots of the covenant were deep, and the tree was unshakable. The water of the Spirit and the light of the Word sustained the growth of the tree as the third generation began to take form.

THIRD GENERATION—GROWING THE TREE

As the time of Isaac's departure drew near, he spoke a special covenant blessing upon his son Jacob. Esau, the firstborn, was expecting to receive the blessing. Instead, Jacob pretended to be Esau, tricking his father in order to receive Esau's blessing. The Bible records the words of Isaac's blessing on Jacob:

> Therefore may God give you of the dew of heaven, of the fatness of the earth, and plenty of grain and wine. Let peoples serve you, and nations bow down to you. Be master over your brethren, and let your mother's sons bow down to you. Cursed be everyone who curses you, and blessed be those who bless you!
>
> —GENESIS 27:28–29

Esau became angry, and a death threat was upon Jacob. He fled from home heading to Syria to live with his mother's brother, Laban. He entered Syria with nothing, but twenty years later he returned to the Promised Land with abundant wealth, especially flocks and herds of livestock. God blessed Jacob in all he did, and he told Laban: "For what you had before I came was little, and it has increased to a great amount; the LORD has blessed you since my coming" (Gen. 30:30). Laban even admitted that God had blessed his farm because a special blessing followed Jacob (v. 27).

After twenty years of hard work, Jacob had two wives, twelve children, and massive flocks of animals when he returned to the Promised Land to meet Esau. Jacob was uncertain if his reception would be peaceful or end in the death of his family. For security purposes, Jacob divided his family into two groups and crossed the Jordan River, coming face-to-face with his twin (Gen. 33).

After a weeping reunion, Jacob offered Esau a special gift of choice animals from his abundant flock. Esau responded, "I have enough, my brother; keep what you have for yourself" (Gen. 33:9). Jacob demanded that Esau accept the gift, and confessed: "Take my blessing that is brought to thee...because I have enough" (v. 11). The gift included:

- Two hundred female goats
- Twenty male goats
- Two hundred female rams
- Twenty male rams
- Thirty female camels and colts
- Ten bulls
- Twenty female donkeys
- Ten male donkeys

Jacob fled from home with nothing but his father's spoken blessing. After twenty years, Jacob had such abundance he was trying to give some of it away. Esau, on the other hand, was so blessed he didn't have room enough to receive the blessing. What brought such abundance in the lives of these descendants of Abraham? In Jacob's case, the answer is fourfold:

- Jacob worked hard during all types of circumstances, including the cold and heat (Gen. 31:40).

- Jacob was loyal to his assignment, even when he was mistreated (Gen. 31:7).

- Jacob was focused on what he wanted (Rachel) and allowed nothing to prevent him from getting it.

- Jacob was under a special generational covenant blessing through his father Isaac (Gen. 27:27).

These same four principles—hard work, loyalty to the vision, determination, and walking in a covenant relationship with God—can release God's favor in your life. Jacob was obsessed with his dream. He wanted Rachel for his wife, and this desire became his motivation for working. You may have a goodly heritage, but God cannot bless the hands of a lazy person who is not consistent in following a dream or vision or fulfilling the purposes of God. The blessings that God had placed upon Jacob were recognized by those for whom he worked. Laban realized, "The Lord has blessed me for your sake" (Gen. 30:27). Laban knew he had little when Jacob arrived, but twenty years later God had blessed the hard work of Jacob, and now both Laban and Jacob were enjoying the fruits of Jacob's labor.

Jacob's wives, Leah and Rachel, confessed that their father had spent their inheritance, leaving them with nothing. Laban had "completely consumed [their] money" (Gen. 31:15). They realized God's blessings were with Jacob, and they departed from their father's house to journey to the Promised Land, with little concern for the personal inheritance they would never receive. The blessings on Jacob had multiplied far beyond the level of Abraham and Isaac. There were now twelve branches on the family tree, and fruit (spiritual and material prosperity) was beginning to be seen.

FOURTH GENERATION—PROTECTING THE TREE

Seventy souls came from the loins of Jacob (Exod. 1:5). These seventy included his twelve sons, their children, and their children's children. Jacob's twelve sons were called the *sons of Jacob* and, eventually, the *children of Israel* (v. 1). This large family became the nation of Israel. During a global famine, Jacob had to move the family to Egypt to protect the *family tree*. He knew there was a time to stay in one place and a time to move on to another.

Jacob's sons were the fourth generation from Abraham. In any business or family, the fourth generation is the most critical for the legacy to continue. For example, Moses was the first generation out of Egypt, and Joshua was the second. Joshua had elders who had seen the great works of the Lord. However, there arose another generation (fourth generation) that "did not know the Lord nor the work which He had done for Israel" (Judg. 2:10). This (fourth) generation went into apostasy, resulting in judges and deliverers being raised up to break their captivity and return them back to the Torah.

Jacob's children were taken to Egypt to be preserved and protected from starvation. The Jewish family tree began with Abraham's seed, Isaac's watering, Jacob branching out, and, by the time they journeyed to Egypt, a new nation, Israel, was in the earth. At the end of their extended stay in Egypt, they departed with an estimated 1.5 million people, and they carried out the gold and silver of the Egyptians with them (Ps. 105:37).

This was the Jewish legacy. From Exodus 1 to Deuteronomy 34 the story begins and ends with Moses, but the Exodus from Egypt is still remembered each year at Passover. Moses's name is spoken somewhere every day when the Torah is studied, and the roots of the family tree are continually expanding, especially since there are Christian branches now grafted into the family tree of Israel that Paul speaks about in Romans 11!

The Hebrew roots run deep in the soil of the Torah, and the Gentile branches that have been grafted are being nourished by those roots. Paul reminded the Gentiles: "Remember that you do not support the root, but the root supports you" (Rom. 11:18). Christians share the same heritage of Jewish people. The Jews are a natural seed of Abraham, and the Christians are a spiritual seed (Gal. 3:29).

GOD PLANS FOR GENERATIONAL BLESSINGS

When God makes a covenant with a person or a nation, He is a long-term planner and thinks generationally. Covenants always carry a promise to you and your seed (Gen. 9:9), which are the first and second generations. Then it expands to your children's children (Ps. 128:6)—the third generation—and those who are afar off (Acts 2:39), which speaks of a continual blessing. God looks so far into the future that David wrote:

> He hath remembered his covenant for ever, the word which he commanded to a thousand generations. Which covenant he made with Abraham, and his oath unto Isaac; and confirmed the same unto Jacob for a law, and to Israel for an everlasting covenant.
>
> —Psalm 105:8–10, kjv

David understood the covenant of Abraham and also received a special covenant promise from God. The Almighty made a powerful covenant to bless the descendants of David from generation to generation.

Scripture indicates that David was a man after God's own heart. He became Israel's second king and captured the stronghold of Jebus (Jerusalem), making it Israel's capital. David and his mighty men were also responsible for destroying a race of giants (1 Chron. 20:4–8). His love and passion for God brought great favor and wonderful covenant promises for David and his descendants who would follow after God:

> And your house and your kingdom shall be established forever before you. Your throne shall be established forever.
>
> —2 Samuel 7:16

> Then I will establish the throne of your kingdom over Israel forever, as I promised David your father, saying, "You shall not fail to have a man on the throne of Israel."
>
> —1 Kings 9:5

> Your seed I will establish forever, and build up your throne to all generations.
>
> —Psalm 89:4

> The Lord has sworn in truth to David;
> He will not turn from it:
> "I will set upon your throne the fruit of your body.
> If your sons will keep My covenant
> And My testimony which I shall teach them,
> Their sons also shall sit upon your throne forevermore."
>
> —Psalm 132:11–12

The Lord promised a Davidic dynasty. David was one of Israel's greatest men, but he carried a mark against his name etched by his adulterous affair with a married woman. This sin opened the door for a rebellion among David's sons. Adonijah began a family feud (1 Kings 2). Amnon raped his half sister (2 Sam. 13), and Absalom was the *hippie* on the run stirring up a rebellion against David (2 Sam. 13). David's advantage was his humility and willingness to repent when confronted with his own disobedience. David knew of God's faithfulness when he wrote:

> My covenant I will not break,
> Nor alter the word that has gone out of My lips.
> —Psalm 89:34

> He remembers His covenant forever,
> The word which He commanded, for a thousand generations.
> —Psalm 105:8

PASSING ON THE COVENANT FAVOR

The effects of a generational covenant can be seen in the kings who sat on the throne of Israel. Eighty-six years following David's death, a descendant named Abijam took the throne. We read, "His heart was not loyal to the Lord his God, as was the heart of his father David" (1 Kings 15:3). Then we read these amazing words:

> Nevertheless for David's sake the Lord his God gave him a lamp in Jerusalem, by setting up his son after him and by establishing Jerusalem.
> —1 Kings 15:4

God could have stripped the throne from under this king or removed him by an uprising. God, however, chose to keep the king in his position because of His promise to His servant David. The same story is repeated in 2 Kings 8, about one hundred fifty-six years after David's death. A king named Jehoram came to power. His wife was Athaliah, the wicked daughter of the infamous King Ahab. Jehoram "did evil in the sight of the Lord" (2 Kings 8:18). Yet God's mercy prevailed, as we read:

> Yet the LORD would not destroy Judah, for the sake of His servant David, as He promised him to give a lamp to him and his sons forever.
>
> —2 KINGS 8:19

By now, David's body had already turned to dust. However, God had not forgotten His promise to David. He preserved the seed of David, Jehoram, not because he was good or righteous, but because God cannot lie, and He was faithful to keep the word spoken to His servant.

The power of the Davidic covenant continued for three hundred thirteen years following David's death through another descendant of David, King Hezekiah. The prophet Isaiah pronounced a sudden death sentence on the king. Hezekiah humbled himself, facing the temple and praying for God's mercy. The Lord sent a second word through Isaiah saying that He would extend the king's life for fifteen more years (2 Kings 20:5–6). The Lord also revealed to the king:

> Thus says the LORD, the God of David your father: "I have heard your prayer....I will deliver you and this city from the hand of the king of Assyria; and I will defend this city for My own sake, and for the sake of My servant David."
>
> —2 KINGS 20:5–6

More than three hundred years after his burial, God was still talking about David, just as He continually spoke about "My servant Moses" and "My friend Abraham." God's covenants carry on from generation to generation, not because His people always obey His Word, and not because they are always living right—but because when He speaks an everlasting covenant, it is *everlasting*. God promised the land to the Jews and promised Jerusalem to the seed of David, also the Jews.

Some Christians will counter by saying, "How can you teach that the Jews have any covenant with God, when numerous Jews are atheists and agnostics, and some actually have animosity toward Christians?" First, some covenants are unconditional, and others are conditional. The Jews are promised the land of Israel and Jerusalem, and these promises were sealed with Abraham and David, as we have written. God kept His Word for Abraham's and David's sake, not because His chosen ethnic people were walking in complete obedience (although Paul wrote in Romans 11 that there is a remnant who obeys the covenant).

In fact, Israel was held to a higher accountability than all other nations because they were accountable for the knowledge they have. When they walked in the covenant, they were blessed above all nations. However, when they mingled with idolatry, forgot the Sabbath, built graven images, and forsook the covenant, they were taken into captivity to other tribes and nations. Paul reveals that in time to come: "All Israel will be saved" (Rom. 11:26). God honors His *unconditional* covenants not because people are good, but because He is good and true to His Word, just as He was with the descendants of David.

Second, God cannot go back on His written or spoken Word. When He insisted on destroying Israel for worshiping the golden calf, Moses reminded God of His covenant with Abraham, Isaac, and Jacob, and suddenly God repented (changed His mind) and preserved the Israelites (Exod. 32). God is bound to His covenant.

There is also a difference between a Jewish covenant for the land of Israel, the city of Jerusalem, and the promised agricultural blessings on the land and a redemptive covenant that releases a person from his or her sins, imparting eternal life. That covenant was ratified through Christ and must be entered into by faith in the judicial mercy provided through Christ's death and resurrection. If anyone follows the moral-judicial-ethical principles and the wisdom proverbs of Solomon, these principles will work and affect their lives.

SO WHY AM I IN A MESS AND NOT BEING BLESSED?

When we understand the blessing found in a covenant relationship with God, why do some believers appear to walk in peace, joy, health, prosperity, and successful family relations, and others are...well...continually going from one mess to another? There are four common, simple explanations that can be given:

The DNA

With the increase in DNA testing and technology, some individuals believe their "bad luck in life" is somehow linked to a set of bad genes or some moral failure that was encoded in the DNA of a parent or grandparent.

Therefore, their reasoning for continual failure is a "bad set of genes." Some who are not familiar with the concept of redemption through Christ are unaware that they can receive a spiritual "blood transfusion" through the new covenant that can erase their past and bring new life for their future!

Wrong patterns

Wrong habits form wrong patterns, and wrong patterns can lead to bondages. If you continually stay up late and sleep in late, you become sluggish and lazy. You can be late for work, late for school, and eventually get fired or fail the grade. You can spend weekends wasting time and money on things that don't benefit you in the long term. Perhaps you've formed some bad habits that you need to break.

Wrong thinking

Stinking thinking leads to smelly decisions. In the Bible, Moses sent twelve spies to check out the Promised Land for forty days. Ten returned and reported on the walled cities and giants, but two men had tasted the grapes and said, "We are able to possess the land." All Israel believed the negative report of ten who said, "We can't," instead of the report of the two who said, "We can." As a result, Israel wandered for forty years in the wilderness because of their unbelief!

Wrong relationships

What would your life have been like if you (as a man) had Delilah as your hairdresser or Bathsheba as your personal trainer at the gym? What if you were following Lot's wife when she stopped to look back? What if Judas was your personal bookkeeper, and Pharaoh was your boss? I would say these are classified as "friends to avoid."

Wrong relationships will diminish your light and pull you into the slime.

Everyone wants an explanation of what he or she didn't understand and usually gets it from those who love explaining things they themselves don't understand. There are numerous reasons why Christians struggle and encounter opposition and difficult times. Some of it comes with the territory. The good news is that the act of redemption, called *regeneration* (Titus 3:5), through Christ is supernatural and can change character weakness in a person. Following God's Word will help you develop new patterns and new friendships (relationships) and, of course, will stop the stinking thinking by renewing your mind in the Word and through the Holy Spirit (Rom. 12:2). The favor of God is released to you through obedience to God.

UNDERSTANDING PERSONAL FAVOR FROM GOD

The Hebrew word for favor is *chen*, which is the same word for *grace*. In the New Testament, the words *favor* and *grace* are the same word and are defined as, "that which causes delight or favorable regard toward."

From a practical perspective, there is a difference in the function of grace and favor. Grace is unearned merit, but favor can be earned through acts of kindness. For example, Christ's grace cannot be earned, but it is free for the asking. Yet, favor is a multiplication of grace upon a person.

> For You, O LORD, will bless the righteous;
> With favor You will surround him as with a shield.
>
> —PSALM 5:12

> For whoever finds me finds life,
> And obtains favor from the LORD.
>
> —PROVERBS 8:35

> Good understanding gains favor,
> But the way of the unfaithful is hard.
>
> —PROVERBS 13:15

> Fools mock at sin,
> But among the upright there is favor.
>
> —PROVERBS 14:9

> He who finds a wife finds a good thing,
> And obtains favor from the LORD.
>
> —PROVERBS 18:22

Grace is free and unearned, but we can, through our actions and obedience, gain the unique favor of God, as He is pleased with our obedience.

IMPART BEFORE YOU DEPART

The ability to impart to another is as old as Jacob blessing his sons. When Abraham thought he was dying, he began thinking of his son Isaac. When

Isaac felt he was dying, he was thinking about his sons, Esau and Jacob. When Jacob was dying, he called his sons and began blessing them. When Moses knew he was about to depart, he insured Israel's future by laying hands on Joshua, thereby transferring the anointing. The prophet Elijah imparted to Elisha before he departed to heaven. Paul began grooming Timothy, and even Christ spoke to His disciples, raising His hands to bless them before ascending to heaven.

Some failed to transfer the blessing forward. Joshua never named a successor before he died, and two generations later, Israel entered into apostasy. Elisha received a double portion of Elijah, but he never transferred the anointing to another prophet. Elisha died and took the power he had to his grave.

The reason for raising your children and grandchildren in truth and righteousness is so that you can leave a heritage, a spiritual legacy that can be passed on.

BUILDING LEGACIES

There are three things you can impart to your descendants before you depart this life besides leaving their names to receive material possessions in a will.

1. A *heritage*—something that's not material, such as traditions, handed down from one generation to the next

2. A *legacy*—passing on a good name, including corporations, teams, and goods continually used

3. A *dynasty*—a succession of rulers, or a group maintaining power from the same family line

Being a fourth-generation minister, I am a part of a heritage of ministry. As God continues to bless our ministry, we can create a legacy of ministry to pass on to the next generation. When older Americans speak of the famed Kennedy family, they think of Joe, JFK, Bobby, and Ted. This clan had been labeled a political dynasty. If another Bush (such as Jeb) were to be elected president, the family could be viewed as the *Bush dynasty*. Dynasties can be interrupted when a leader in the line dies in disrepute or publicly destroys their integrity, thereby disgracing the family name.

Legacies are built when a name brand, such as Coca-Cola, continues its success from generation to generation. Coke memorabilia is valued as highly as any other name-brand memorabilia in the world. It's all in the name!

Sports teams have been labeled *America's team* or an *American dynasty*. One such team that has formed a dynasty is the New England Patriots. The 2004 team became the second team in NFL history to appear in and win three Super Bowls in a four-year span. The 2007 season was considered by football fans the greatest season for any team in the history of the NFL since the time when the season was expanded from fourteen games to sixteen games in 1978. The Patriots brought home eighteen straight wins in the season and set or tied sixteen NFL records.[3] A win at the 2007 Super Bowl would have catapulted them to a level no other NFL team had ever experienced.

I attended two of the Patriots Super Bowl games and watched in Phoenix, believing they were headed for a fourth historic win. The game became the most exciting game in pro football history. In the final minutes, the underdog team, the New York Giants, took the lead, literally shocking the Patriot fans. The Patriots sealed their season with eighteen amazing wins and only one loss.

After the after-game gala, I spoke briefly with Robert and Myra Kraft, the owners of the team. I remember congratulating Mr. Kraft on a great season and encouraging him for the future, as I was sure they would again end up on top. He said something very profound that I will always remember. He said, "People will not be talking about the record-breaking undefeated season, but they will always remember the one loss at the Super Bowl." Later his comments reminded me of a statement made by a fellow minister many years ago: "People will always remember two things about you: your entrance and your exit—your first impression and your last, your beginning and your ending."

Names are the umbilical cord giving life to a legacy or a dynasty. Look at the following names, and think about the first impression that comes to your mind:

- Abraham Lincoln
- Adolf Hitler
- Marilyn Monroe
- John F. Kennedy
- Ronald Reagan

■ Bill Clinton

Let's see if my first impressions in any way match your first impressions.

■ Abraham Lincoln—great legacy as the president who broke slavery during the Civil War
■ Adolf Hitler—an evil dictator, World War II, and the instigator of the Jewish Holocaust
■ Marilyn Monroe—Famous actress whose life was cut short
■ John F. Kennedy—the Cuban missile crisis and a popular president assassinated in Dallas, Texas
■ Ronald Reagan—a great president promoting the fall of Communism and the Berlin wall
■ Bill Clinton—president whose unwise moral decisions destroyed his legacy

This is why Solomon wrote: "A good name is to be chosen rather than great riches, loving favor rather than silver and gold" (Prov. 22:1). People always connect your name to your deeds and your deeds with your name.

DESTROYING YOUR POTENTIAL

In 1946 a Baptist magazine printed an article on the young men who would impact their generation. They listed Bron Clifford and Chuck Templeton, both in their early twenties and both drawing crowds of eight to ten thousand in their meetings. Omitted from the list was another young minister named Billy Graham. Ten years later, Clifford had died of cirrhosis of the liver, and Templeton had left the ministry for a sports commentator job. The two men who had been expected to make the greatest impact for God's kingdom fell off the radar. The unnamed third Baptist minister, Billy Graham, became a worldwide legend. Billy proved that it is not how fast you come out of the starting block but how you finish the race that matters.[4] Even the turtle made it to Noah's ark by persistence and commitment.

What Are the Greatest Gifts
You Can Leave With Your Family?

Years ago I met a couple in their sixties who eventually moved to our community to be close to our ministry. The woman's previous husband, who had passed away, was quite wealthy, and over many years she had amassed several millions of dollars in jewelry. She had owned collectible stores and was a collector of limited edition dolls and arts objects. Her collections were so large that she filled up the attic, several rooms, and the garage—all filled with expensive memorabilia. She was a strong prayer warrior who loved God's Word. One morning I was stunned to hear that she had passed away.

Weeks later an estate auction was conducted in our town. It took two full days with two auctioneers going continually to move all of the items from her estate. The auction fans from our town said that never in the history of Cleveland had they ever seen so much available from one home at one auction. During the auction, her son came to me and said, "Mom would have a fit to see these limited edition items going so cheaply." I reminded him that his momma was with the Lord (2 Cor. 5:8; 12:1–4), and where she was she didn't miss any of the *stuff* that remained behind. I shared the following story with him.

Years ago this same woman handed me a check to purchase a new dockable television camera to take to Israel for taping television programs. Hundreds of programs, video, and DVD specials on biblical and prophetic themes had been taped with the camera she purchased. Countless numbers of people from around the world had been educated in life-changing spiritual truth, and many had turned their lives over to Christ. As I shared this story with her son, I rejoiced that although she left her earthly possessions behind, every time we use the digital camera her memory lives on, and she continues to build on her heavenly reward (1 Cor. 3:8, 14).

Proverbs 13:22 says, "A good man leaves an inheritance to his children's children." Often people leave great financial wealth for their children who live undisciplined lives and waste their inheritance, just as Solomon wrote in Proverbs 20:21: "An inheritance gained hastily at the beginning will not be blessed at the end." While children would rather have additional cash, a new car, or more *stuff*, there are greater inheritances to leave than earthly possessions.

How to Leave Your Legacy

Leave a spiritual legacy. When you depart, leave such a good name in the community that your children will be proud they carry that name. Those who leave a legacy are spoken well of, often many years after they have passed. A spiritual legacy is your history as viewed through His story, the story of your walk with the Lord and the blessings you experienced in life. I hear people tell stories of men and women of faith whom they never met, but these faithful names have lived on long after the people are gone. Make your footprints large enough for someone to follow, and make sure they go straight, not veering to the left or the right.

Leave stories that can be passed down from generation to generation. When we take a vacation, my wife will say, "We're making memories." The stories my father told yesterday are the stories I will tell my children tomorrow. Every night before going to bed, my little girl will lie beside me, saying, "Dad, tell me a story." Instead of the "big bad wolf," I relate stories of personal experiences and blessings of God that I have seen.

Leave plenty of pictures

When a home burns down, the main item people miss are their pictures, which cannot be replaced. Keep them in a fireproof safe or file cabinet. Get them out during major holidays and holy days when the family is together. Look at how everyone has changed, and tell a little story about the places you remember. Always take a video camera with you on major holidays and events. This will provide future generations with visual pictures of family members they may have never met.

Leave a financial legacy

There are individuals of great wealth who could leave continuous legacies by building Bible schools, mentoring schools, an orphanage, or a drug rehab center, or by providing for the poor and needy or assisting a ministry or church. These are the legacies that carry continual rewards because they change lives for generations long after each person has departed this life. In this way, people continue to build up their *heavenly accounts* as their work continues.

Leave a good name

A good name is maintained in life by treating people with respect, by being honest and forthright in your business ventures, and by maintaining moral character. At times humans fail in one or more of these areas, and the family name gets *dragged through the mud*. When this occurs, it takes time to restore credibility.

Years ago my mother gave me a plaque that sits in my office, which reads:

STONE

You got it from your father, it was all he had to give,
So it's yours to use and cherish for as long as you may live.
If you lose the watch he gave you, it can always be replaced.
But a black mark on your name, Son, can never be erased.
It was clean the day you took it, and a worthy name to bear.
When he got it from his father there was no dishonor there.
So make sure you guard it wisely, after all is said and done,
You'll be glad the name is spotless when you give it to your son.

This simple poem is a reminder and a motivation to me that, by God's grace, I must maintain integrity so that when my name is mentioned, people will know a true man of God has passed among them. A good name will outlast your lifetime, and a bad name will long be remembered as well.

LEAVE A SPIRITUAL LEGACY

I love hearing people talk about their parents, grandparents, and ancestors and how their prayer lives were so strong and their walks with God so straight that they prayed diseases out of bodies, food on an empty table, and snatched souls from the brink of premature death. These are true legacies! Moses almost lost his legacy when he smote the rock and was prevented from entering the Promised Land. David carried a dark mark on his name because of his affair with Bathsheba, although he repented and died a victorious warrior. Had Christ not interceded, Peter could have ruined his future by cursing and denying the Savior. Samson broke his Nazirite vow, but he made one final comeback at the end of his life and made it into the Hall of Faith in Hebrews 11. We still read of the feats of these men because they left spiritual *legacies* for future generations. Begin a legacy by:

- Reading the Word of God to your children and grandchildren and letting them see you studying God's Word

- Leading the family in prayers of blessing, protection, and favor, and prayers on the Sabbath, over the meals, and so on

- Allowing your family to see, by your example, the proper way to respect and treat others

- Being an example by guarding your conversation, never being critical or mean-spirited

- Showing the love of Christ by feeding the poor, caring for the needy, and getting your family involved in service

- Setting the example by taking the family to a house of worship and being involved in kingdom work

You know someone has made an impact when that person's family still misses him or her years after he or she has passed away. That person left a legacy, evidenced by others who repeat that person's testimonies and the stories of that person's life generations after that person's death.

THE JEWISH LEGACY

Mark Twain, in an 1899 quote from *Harper's Magazine*, summed it up best when he said:

If the statistics are right, the Jews constitute but one percent of the human race. It suggests a nebulous dim puff of star dust lost in the blaze of the Milky Way. Properly the Jew ought hardly to be heard of, but he is heard of, has always been heard of. He is as prominent on the planet as any other people, and his commercial importance is extravagantly out of proportion to the smallness of his bulk. His contributions to the world's list of great names in literature, science, art, music, finance, medicine, and abstruse learning are also way out of proportion to the weakness of his numbers. He has made a marvelous fight in the world, in all the ages; and has done it with his hands tied behind him. He could be vain of himself, and be excused for it. The Egyptian, the Babylonian, and the Persian rose, filled the planet with sound and splendor, then faded to dream-stuff and passed away; the Greek and the Roman followed, and made a vast noise, and they are gone; other peoples have sprung up and held their torch high for a time, but it burned out, and they sit in twilight now, or have vanished. The Jew saw them all, beat them all, and is now what he always was, exhibiting no decadence, no infirmities of age, no weakening of his parts, no slowing of his energies, no dulling of his alert and aggressive mind. All things are mortal but the Jew; all other forces pass, but he remains. What is the secret of his immortality?[5]

Twain asked the question, "What is the secret?"

I have asked, "What is the code of the Jews?" It is clear that God alone selected Abraham for a new nation and revealed the code of heaven to an earthly people. The covenants were sealed in blood, and out of the seed of Abraham came another nation of destiny, which the Jewish apostles identify as the church, born out of a blood covenant ratified and sealed through Christ's own sufferings. The church must understand the Jew, and the Jews must understand that true Christians love Israel and the Jewish people. We are from the same tree.

■ ■ ■ ✡ ■ ■ ■

Appendix

MEANINGS OF IMPORTANT JEWISH TERMS AND WORDS

Abraham — the patriarch and father of the Hebrews who lived 1700 to 2000 B.C.

Ashkenazi Jews — descendants from the medieval Jewish communities from the land on both sides of the Rhine in Germany

bar (or bat) mitzvah — a Hebrew word meaning a religious ceremony for a Jewish boy and girl reaching age thirteen

bar — a Hebrew word meaning "a son of"

bat — a Hebrew word meaning "a daughter of"

b'rit — Hebrew word for *covenant*, the relationship and agreement between God and His people

brit milah — the Hebrew term for the Jewish ritual of circumcising a male child on the eighth day after his birth

Canaan Land — the ancient name of Israel prior to Abraham's descendants possessing the land and naming it Israel

cantor — from Latin, meaning "one who sings"; a chanter/singer of the liturgical materials in a synagogue

Chumash — a word describing the five books of Moses (Torah) bound in a book and not in a scroll

Days of Awe — ten days from Feast of Trumpets to the Day of Atonement

dreidel — the four-sided top that is used to play a game during Hanukkah

gadol — a Hebrew word meaning "large or great"; often used referring to a Torah scholar of a certain prominence

Gemara — applied to the Babylonian Talmud and the work of generations in completing the *Mishna* to produce the Talmud

Gentiles — a term used to refer to non-Jews, also called *goy*

Hadassah — the Jewish name for Esther, mentioned in the Book of Esther

Haftorah — a selection from the Book of the Prophets (*Nevi'im*), recited after the Torah portion on the Sabbath or on festivals

Hashem — a word meaning "The Name"

Israel — a name given to Jacob that later identified the sons of Jacob and was given to the land where they lived

Jew — traditionally a person with a Jewish lineage or one who adheres to Judaism

Judaism — the religion of devout Jews who follow the philosophy and traditions of the Torah, with cultural roots in Israel

kaddish — a classical Jewish prayer recited at the end of each major section of each liturgical service

kevah — a fixed time, fixed words, or prayers

kippah — a Jewish head covering worn for worship, when studying the Torah, or at other times

Kohen (or Cohen) — an Israelite priest from the tribe of Levi who ministered in the tabernacle and the temple in Jerusalem

kosher — meaning "fit or ritually correct"; Jewish dietary laws based upon the Torah

Luchot — meaning "tables" or "tablets," referring to the Ten Commandments

matzah — Jewish unleavened bread used during Passover

menorah — the seven-branched golden candelabra used in the temple; a nine-branched menorah is used during Hanukkah.

Midrash — the Jewish commentaries written to interpret the Hebrew Scriptures in a thorough manner

mishpat — law from the Torah that can be rationalized

Notes

INTRODUCTION

1. As referenced in Harry MacArthur, DD, "Why You Can't Rub Out the Jew!" *Voice of Calvary*, reprinted in *The Biblical Evangelist*, http://www.messiah3.org/cantruboutjew.htm (accessed October 30, 2008).

2. SimpletoRemember.com, "Jewish Quotes," http://www.simpletoremember.com/vitals/quotes.htm (accessed September 3. 2008).

3. Ebo Quansah, "A Heart for Israel! Revealed: Why US Loves Israel," *Ghanaian Times*, October 1, 2008, http://www.newtimesonline.com/content/view/17945/268/ (accessed October 31, 2008).

4. Jinfo.org, "Jewish Nobel Peace Prize Winners," http://www.jinfo.org/Nobels_Peace.html (accessed October 31, 2008).

5. David M. Kohl and Barbara J. Newton, "Questions Generation X Is Asking About Finance and Investments," *Farm Business Management Update*, Virginia Cooperative Extension, December 1999, referencing November 1999 *USA Today* news article, http://www.ext.vt.edu/news/periodicals/fmu/1999-12/genX.html (accessed October 31, 2008).

6. Dr. Gerhard Falk, "Jewish-American Literature," Jbuff.com, http://www.jbuff.com/c021501.htm (accessed October 31, 2008).

7. John Leo, "A Big Mess on Campus," *U.S. News & World Report*, May 19, 2002, http://www.usnews.com/usnews/opinion/articles/020527/archive_020870_2.htm (accessed October 31, 2008).

8. "Intelligence of Jews and of Jewish Israelis," http://sq.4mg.com/IQ-Jews.htm (accessed October 31, 2008).

9. Steve Sailer, "IQ and Disease: The Curious Case of the Ashkenazi Jews," VDARE.com, http://www.vdare.com/Sailer/050605_iq.htm (accessed October 31, 2008).

10. Steven Silbiger, *The Jewish Phenomenon: Seven Keys to Enduring Wealth of a People* (Atlanta, GA: Longstreet Press, 2000), quoted in "Money, Class, and Power," http://www.jewishtribalreview.org/21money.htm (accessed October 31, 2008).

11. The Jewish Scriptures are called the Tanakh. This name is a Hebrew acronym for the three divisions of the Hebrew Scriptures: The Torah (the first five books of Moses—Genesis through Deuteronomy), the Nevi'im (Prophets), and Kutuvim (Writings), or TaNaK.

Chapter 1
Living by Heaven's Rule Book

1. Flavius Josephus, *Antiquities of the Jews*, book 1, chapter 2, section 3, http://bible.crosswalk.com/History/BC/FlaviusJosephus/?book=Ant_1&chapter=2 (accessed October 31, 2008).

2. Jacob's name was changed by God to Israel. Following this change, his sons were no longer identified as just the sons of Jacob, but the children of Israel (Gen. 32:32), a term found 630 times in the 1611 King James translation of the Bible.

3. Tour Egypt, "Egypt Mythology," http://interoz.com/egypt/gods1.htm (accessed September 4, 2008).

4. The AishDas Society, "Pamphlet 9—The Letters of the Torah," *Torat Emet*, http://www.aishdas.org/toratemet/en_pamphlet9.html (accessed September 4, 2008).

5. For more information on the genetic studies of the tribe of Levi, see a report by Rabbi Yaakov Kleiman, "The DNA Chain of Tradition," Jewish Genes & Genealogy, http://www.cohen-levi.org/ (accessed September 4, 2008).

6. David Goldstein, *Jacob's Legacy* (New Haven, CT: Yale University Press, 2008).

7. The Talmud is a commentary of Jewish discussion concerning the oral law as it relates to Jewish law, ethics, customs, and history. It attempts to clarify parts of the Torah that may not be clear. There is both a Jerusalem and Babylonian Talmud.

8. The three fall feasts are Trumpets, Atonement, and Tabernacles. Numerous prophetic teachers believe that Trumpets is a picture of the gathering of the church (1 Thess. 4:16–17; Eph. 1:9–10), Atonement is a picture of the coming great tribulation (Matt. 24:21), and Tabernacles is a picture of the coming thousand-year reign of the Messiah (Rev. 20:4).

Chapter 2
The Secret in the Covenant

1. W. E. Vine, *Vine's Expository Dictionary of Old and New Testament Words* (Nashville, TN: Thomas Nelson, 1997).

2. Ibid., 52–53.

3. The word *signet* comes from the Latin *signum*, meaning "sign." The ancient seals on the rings were often made of agate, carnelian, or sardonyx. The ring was worn on the little finger. Documents were often rolled as a scroll (or folded flat), with small leather straps tied around them. Hot wax was poured directly on the parchment, and the seal on the ring impressed on the document. Many seals have been found throughout the years in archeological excavations throughout the Middle East.

4. Rabbi Shira Milgrom, "Covenanting," Weekly Torah Commentaries, MyJewishLearning.com, http://www.myjewishlearning.com/texts/Weekly_Torah_Commentary/lekhlkha_uahc5762.htm (accessed September 4, 2008).

5. H. Clay Trumbull, *The Blood Covenant* (Kirkwood, MO: Impact Books, 1975), 6, 10.

6. Ibid., 16–17.

7. Ibid., 37–38.

8. Ibid., 317.

9. Abraham was one hundred when Isaac was born, and Sarah was ninety. Therefore Abraham was seventy-five when he left for Canaan (Gen. 12:4), and Sarah would have been ten years younger, or about sixty-five years of age. Isaac was not born until approximately twenty-five years after Abraham first received the promise (Gen. 17:17).

10. Wikipedia.org, "Bar and Bat Mitzvah," http://en.wikipedia.org/wki/Bar_mitzvah (accessed September 4, 200).

11. Massoume Price, "Rituals of Circumcision," Iran Chamber Society, http://www.iranchamber.com/culture/articles/rituals_of_circumcision.php (accessed November 4, 2008).

12. *British Journal of Cancer* 19, no. 2 (June 1965): 217–226.

13. H. L. Wilmington, *Wilmington's Guide to the Bible* (Wheaton, IL: Tyndale House, 1981), 817.

14. Ishmael was born when Abraham was eighty-six years of age (Gen. 16:16). Isaac was born when Abraham was one hundred (Gen. 21:5) and Sarah was ninety (Gen. 17:17). Ishmael was thirteen when he was circumcised by Abraham (Gen. 17:25). Isaac was born one year later (Gen. 17:21). After Isaac was weaned, Abraham made a feast, during which Ishmael mocked Isaac (Gen. 21:8–9). Isaac would have been about two years of age, making Ishmael fifteen to sixteen years of age when he was cast out of the home.

15. The four references are Exodus 19:5; Deuteronomy 14:2; 26:18; and Psalm 135:4.

CHAPTER 3
SECRETS OF THE HEBREW ALPHABET AND WORDS

1. John Parkhurst, *A Hebrew Lexicon* (London: William Baynes & Paternoster Row, 1728 [Julian Calendar]), viii, Preface, third paragraph.

2. Josephus, *Antiquities of the Jews*, book 1, chapter 1, section 4, http://bible.crosswalk.com/History/BC/FlaviusJosephus/?book=Ant_1&chapter=1 (accessed November 7, 2008).

3. Ibid.

4. Origen, *Against Celsus*, book 5, chapter 30, http://www.ccel.org/ccel/schaff/anf04.vi.ix.v.xxx.html (accessed November 7, 2008).

5. Ibid., chapter 31, http://www.ccel.org/ccel/schaff/anf04.vi.ix.v.xxxi.html (accessed November 7, 2008).

6. The entire Old Testament was written in the Hebrew language, with the exception of portions of Daniel and Ezra, which were written in Aramaic (Dan. 2:4–7:28).

7. Marvin R. Wilson, *Our Father Abraham: Jewish Roots of the Christian Faith* (Grand Rapids, MI: Wm B. Eerdmans Publishing, 1989), 128.

8. Ibid., 130–131.

9. Ibid., 136.

10. AncientScripts.com, "Hebrew," http://www.ancientscripts.com/hebrew.html (accessed September 4, 2008).

11. Hebrew4Christians.com, "Birkat Kohanim—The Priestly Blessing," http://www.hebrew4christians.com/Blessings/Synagogue_Blessings/Priestly_Blessing/priestly_blessing.html (accessed September 4, 2008).

12. Mount Ophel (2 Chron. 27:3), Mount Zion (Ps. 48:2), and Mount Moriah (2 Chron. 3:1) are three hills that join together to form the area from the southern to the northern slopes where the old city of Jerusalem with its walls now sits. Mount Moriah is the highest peak, where the first and second Jewish Temples once sat.

13. Navigating the Bible II, "Torah," http://bible.ort.org/books/torahd5.asp (accessed September 8, 2008).

14. Avram Yehoshua, "The Alef-Tav," http://www.seedofabraham.net/jat.htm (accessed November 10, 2008).

15. Rabbi Benjamin Blech, *The Secret of Hebrew Words* (Nothvale, NJ: Jason Aronson, Inc., 1991).

16. Rabbi Mendy Hecht, "How Is a Torah Made?" AskMoses.com, http://www.askmoses.com/article/698,2200336/How-is-a-Torah-Made.html (accessed September 4, 2008).

17. Blech, *The Secrets of Hebrew Words*, Preface, ix.

18. Ibid., 174.

19. HisSheep.org, "Cosmic Signs and Last Days Prophecy," http://www.hissheep.org/special/prophecy/cosmic_signs_and_last_days_prophecy.html (accessed November 10, 2008).

20. GreatSite.com, "English Bible History," http://greatsite.com/timeline-english-bible-history/index.html (accessed November 10, 2008).

21. Rabbi Louis Jacobs, "The Tetragrammaton," MyJewishLearning.com, http://www.myjewishlearning.com/ideas_belief/god/Overview_About_God/God_Speaking_Gillman/God_Names_CohnSherbok/Tetragrammaton_.htm (accessed September 5, 2008).

22. *Mishna, Sotah* 6:6; *Tamid* 7:2; and *Yoma* 6:2.

23. Finis Jennings Dake, *Dake's Annotated Reference Bible* (Lawrenceville, GA: Dake Bible Sales, 1976), s.v. "Genesis," 52.

CHAPTER 4
GOD'S FEASTS, SABBATHS, AND SPECIAL FAMILY CELEBRATIONS

1. Paul J. Achtemeier, ed., *HarperCollins Bible Dictionary* (New York: HarperOne, 1996), 901.

2. *The Talmud*, Sanhedrin 21b.

3. Josephus, *Antiquities of the Jews*, book 12, chapter 7, section 7, http://bible.crosswalk.com/History/BC/FlaviusJosephus/?book=Ant_12&chapter=10&s= (accessed November 11, 2008).

4. AskMoses.com, "What Do the Hebrew Letters on a Dreidel Mean?" http://www.askmoses.com/en/article/99,41308/What-do-the-Hebrew-letters-on-a-Dreidel-mean.html (accessed November 11, 2008).

5. Gideon Weitzman, *In Those Days, at This Time* (Jerusalem: Grow Publications).

6. According to the book *Numbers in Scripture* by E. W. Bullinger, "Man's pulse beats on the seven-day principle, for Dr. Stratton points out that for six days out of seven, it [the heart] beats faster in the morning than in the evening, while on the seventh day it beats slower." [E. W. Bullinger, *Numbers in Scripture: Its Supernatural Design and Spiritual Significance* (Grand Rapids, MI: Kregel Publications, 1967).]

7. The prayer prayed over the candles is: "Blessed are You, Eternal One our God, Ruling Presence of the Universe, Who makes us holy with mitzvoth and gives us the mitzvah of lighting the Sabbath lights."

8. ReligionFacts.com, "Shabbat: The Sabbath," http://www.religionfacts.com/judaism/holidays/shabbat.htm (accessed September 5, 2008).

9. There are 24 hours in 1 day, with 7 days in 1 week, totaling 168 hours in 1 week. With just 2 hours a week in worship and study, it leaves 166 hours.

CHAPTER 5
THE MEANINGS AND PURPOSES OF JEWISH LIFE CYCLES

1. Simcha Kling, *The People and Its Land* (New York: USY Publishing, 1988), 31.

2. James Strong, *Strong's Exhaustive Concordance of the Bible* (Peabody, MA: Hendrickson Publishers, updated version 2007), s.v. "nuwd," OT:5110.

3. NYU.edu, "How Much Time Do Kids Spend With Dad?" *USA Today* (magazine), August 2000, http://www.nyu.edu/fas/cassr/yeung/spendwithdad.pdf (accessed September 5, 2008).

4. Alfred Edersheim, *Sketches of Jewish Social Life* (Henderson, NE: Henderson Publishers, 1994), 99–100.

5. Ibid., 100–101.

6. *Israel Today* magazine, April 2003, no. 51, 12.

7. Examples of Jewish toys are found at such Web sites as www.oytoys.com/.

8. Shaunti Feldhann and Lisa A. Rice, *For Parents Only* (Sisters, OR: Multnomah Books, 2007), 24.

9. Blech, *The Secrets of Hebrew Words*, 153.

10. *Israel Today* magazine, October 2003, no. 57, 12.

11. David Popenoe, "Life Without Father," *Mensight*, TheMensCenter.com, excerpted from David Popenoe, *Life Without Father* (n.p.: Free Press, 1996), viewed at http://mensightmagazine.com/Articles/Popenoe/nofathers.htm (accessed September 25, 2008).

12. Wikipedia.org, "World War I Casualties," http://en.wikipedia.org/wiki/World_War_I_casualties (accessed November 11, 2008).

13. Wikipedia.org, "Hitler Youth," http://en.wikipedia.org/wiki/Hitler_Youth (accessed September 5, 2008).

14. Ibid.

15. Vine, *Vine's Expository Dictionary of Old and New Testament Words*, 200.

16. *Israel Today* magazine, February 2005, no. 73, 12.

17. *Israel Today* magazine, April 2005, no. 75, 12.

18. *Israel Today* magazine, February 2003, no. 49, 12.

19. Wilson, *Our Father Abraham*.

20. Theador H. Gaster, *Customs and Folkways of Jewish Life* (New York: William Sloane Associates Publishers, 1955), 14.

21. William Barclay, *Educational Ideals in the Ancient World* (Grand Rapids, MI: Baker Book House, 1977), 12–13.

22. Wilson, *Our Father Abraham, Jewish Roots of the Christian Faith*, 308.

23. Kamran Sedighian and Andishe Sedighian, "Use of Background Music in Electronic Learning Environments," University of British Columbia, Canada, http://www.cs.ubc.ca/labs/egems/kamran7.doc (accessed September 8, 2008).

24. Peggy Peck, "ASH: Daily Doses of Bach and Breathing Lower Blood Pressure," MedPageToday.com, May 23, 2008, http://www.medpagetoday.com/MeetingCoverage/ASH/9597 (accessed September 8, 2008).

25. Francis Rauscher et al., "Music and Spatial Task Performance," Nature 365, no. 611 (October 14, 1993), viewed at http://www.uwosh.edu/departments/psychology/rauscher/Nature93.pdf (accessed September 8, 2008).

CHAPTER 6
NAMES ARE PROPHETIC AND CAN REVEAL A CHILD'S DESTINY

1. Meaning of names was obtained from Behindthename.com, http://www.behindthename.com (accessed September 8, 2008).

2. In Hebrew, the word *chabod* is translated as "glory," such as the "glory of God." It alludes to the tangible presence of God, such as the cloud that entered the temple and the priests could not minister because of the "weight" of God's glory. The letter *I* in front of *chabod*, or *I-chabod* in the English Bible means, "no" glory. The ark was taken in battle and the glory of God was now departed from Israel.

CHAPTER 7
BIBLICAL SECRETS FOR A WOMAN WHO WANTS A CHILD

1. Rajeev Agarwal, "Stress and Pollution Are Major Cause of Infertility Among Urban Couples," Bio-Medicine.org, http://www.bio-medicine.org/medicine-news/Stress-and-Pollution-are-Major-Cause-of-Infertility-Among-Urban-Couples-12395-1/ (accessed September 8, 2008).

2. Landrum Shettles and David Rorvik, *How to Choose the Sex of Your Baby: The Method Best Supported by Scientific Evidence* (St. Charles, MO: Main Street Books, 1996).

3. Although not confirmed from a reputable source, this ancient Chinese gender chart is said to now reside in the Beijing Institute of Science. See Chinese Birth Calendar, http://www.chinesebirthcalendar.org/ (accessed November 12, 2008).

4. Additional infertility facts may be accessed at www.lovetoknow.com.

CHAPTER 8
LESSONS FROM THE MEZUZAH FOR
MARKING YOUR HOUSE FOR GOD

1. Information about the Jewish traditions of the tefillin is adapted from "Getting Ready for the Bar-Mitzvah—The Tefillin (Phylacteries)," Jewish Celebrations, http://www.mazornet.com/jewishcl/Celebrations/mitzvah/Orthodox/Tefillin.htm (accessed September 10, 2008).

CHAPTER 9
AMAZING HEALTH SECRETS OF KOSHER
DIET FOODS FROM THE HOLY LAND

1. For more information about the specific Jewish kosher requirements, see "How Do I Know It's Kosher? An OU Kosher Primer," Orthodox Union, http://www.ou.org/kosher/primer.html (accessed September 10, 2008).

2. Much of the information in this chapter regarding foods from the Holy Land has been adapted from George Mataljan's comprehensive Web site, The World's Healthiest Foods, and can be accessed at http://www.whfoods.com/.

3. George Mataljan, "Whole Wheat," The World's Healthiest Foods, http://www.whfoods.com/genpage.php?tname=foodspice&dbid=66#summary (accessed September 10, 2008).

4. George Mataljan, "Barley," The World's Healthiest Foods, http://www.whfoods.com/genpage.php?tname=foodspice&dbid=127#foodspicename (accessed September 10, 2008).

5. George Mataljan, "Grapes," The World's Healthiest Foods, http://www.whfoods.com/genpage.php?tname=foodspice&dbid=40#foodspicename (accessed September 10, 2008).

6. George Mataljan, "Figs," The World's Healthiest Foods, http://www.whfoods.com/genpage.php?tname=foodspice&dbid=24#foodspicename (accessed September 10, 2008).

7. Joe and Teresa Graedon, "Pomegranates Have Many Health Benefits," People's Pharmacy, HealthCentral.com, November 7, 2005, http://www.healthcentral.com/peoplespharmacy/408/61202_2.html (accessed September 10, 2008).

8. Wordpress.com, "The Healthiest Oil," November 6, 2007, http://foodishealth.wordpress.com/2007/11/06/olive-oil/ (accessed November 13, 2008).

9. Julie Ann, "The Many Health Benefits of Honey," LifeScript Connect Network, July 27, 2007, http://www.lifescript.com/channels/healthy_living/Life_Tips/the_many_health_benefits_of_honey.asp?page=1&trans=1 (accessed September 10, 2008).

10. HealingDaily.com, "Olive Oil's Health Benefits," http://www.healingdaily.com/detoxification-diet/olive-oil.htm (accessed September 10, 2008).

11. Judaism 101, "Kashrut: Jewish Dietary Laws," http://www.jewfaq.org/kashrut.htm#Fats (accessed September 10, 2008).

12. Annie B. Bond, "Vinegar Kills Bacteria, Mold, and Germs," Healthy & Green Living, May 5, 1999, http://www.care2.com/greenliving/vinegar-kills-bacteria-mold-germs.html (accessed September 10, 2008).

13. S. I. McMillen, None of These Diseases (Grand Rapids, MI: Fleming H. Revell Co., 1993), 11.

14. Wilmington, Wilmington's Guide to the Bible, 816–817.

CHAPTER 10
THE SPIRITUAL PRINCIPLES OF WEALTH AND PROSPERITY

1. This story was related to me verbally by my Israeli friend and travel guide Gideon Shor.

2. Ibid.

3. Richard Kelly Hoskins, War Cycles—Peace Cycles (Lynchburg, VA: Virginia Publishing Company, 2000).

4. The Midrash, Tehillim 47:6.

5. The information on Teshuvah is from the author's detailed book on the seasons of Teshuvah: Perry Stone, The Forty Days of Teshuvah (Cleveland, TN: Voice of Evangelism, 2006).

CHAPTER 11
THE INFLUENCE OF HEBREW
BIBLICAL PROPHECY ON WORLD LEADERS

1. Josephus, Antiquities of the Jews, book 11, chapter 1, section 1, http://bible.crosswalk.com/History/BC/FlaviusJosephus/?book=Ant_11&chapter=3&s= (accessed November 14, 2008).

2. Ibid., book 11, chapter 8, section 5, http://bible.crosswalk.com/History/BC/FlaviusJosephus/?book=Ant_12&chapter=2&s= (accessed November 14, 2008).

3. Ibid.

4. Ibid., book 12, chapter 7, section 6, http://bible.crosswalk.com/History/BC/FlaviusJosephus/?book=Ant_12&chapter=10 (accessed November 14, 2008).

5. Dr. and Mrs. H. Grattan Guinness, Light for the Last Days (n.p.: 1886), as referenced in "The Long Promised Regathering of Israel, Part II," The Herald, vol. 5, no. 11, June 1, 1922, http://www.heraldmag.org/archives/1922_6.htm#_Toc517748597 (accessed November 17, 2008).

6. Henry James Forman, The Story of Prophecy (New York: Tudor Publishing Co., 1940), 95.

7. This story was related to the author by Jewish guides during a visit to Israel. Additional information can be obtained from Isracast.com, "Dec. 1917—General Allenby Enters Jerusalem," http://www.isracast.com/article.aspx?ID=763&t=Dec .-1917---General-Allenby-Enters-Jerusalem (accessed November 17, 2008).

8. Bob Slosser, *Reagan, Inside Out* (New York: W Pub Group, 1984).

9. Ibid., as quoted in Bob Slosser, "The Prophecy," CBN.com, http://www.cbn .com/spirituallife/BibleStudyAndTheology/discipleship/Slosser_ReaganProphecy .aspx (accessed November 17, 2008).

10. Ibid.

11. Dr. and Mrs. Howard Taylor, *Hudson Taylor's Spiritual Secret* (Chicago, IL: Moody Press, 1983).

12. On one of his furloughs in the 1850s to England, Hudson Taylor was preaching when he suddenly stopped and just stood for a period of time with his eyes closed. When he started to speak again, he explained that he had seen a vision. This vision was taken from an article published in Finland in 1945, titled "Spiritual Revival." There are several Web sites that contain portions of this vision, including Bill Somers, "Judgments in the Earth," Appendix G, http://www.etpv.org/bills_page/ judgment.html (accessed September 16, 2008).

13. Carl Bernstein, "The Holy Alliance," *TIME*, February 24, 1992, http://www .time.com/time/magazine/article/0,9171,974931-2,00.html (accessed September 16, 2008).

14. Slosser, *Reagan, Inside Out*.

15. Theodor Herzl, *The Jewish State* [*Der Judenstaat*] (Germany: Herzl Press, 1970).

16. Israel Ministry of Public Affairs, "The Balfour Declaration," November 2, 1917, http://www.mfa.gov.il/MFA/Peace%20Process/Guide%20to%20the%20 Peace%20Process/The%20Balfour%20Declaration (accessed September 15, 2008).

CHAPTER 12
IMPART BEFORE YOU DEPART

1. A. E. Winship, *Jukes-Edwards: A Study in Education and Heredity* (New York: Hard Press, 2006). Also available as a Google book, http://books.google.com/books ?id=gKMXAAAAYAAJ&printsec=frontcover&dq=Jukes-Edwards:+A+Study+in +Education+and+Heredity#PPA1,M1 (accessed September 15, 2008).

2. Ibid.

3. "New England Patriots Winning Streaks," http://www.allthingsbillbelichick .com/thestreak.htm (accessed September 16, 2008).

4. Steve Farrar, *Finishing Strong* (Sisters, OR: Multnomah, 2000).

5. Mark Twain, "Concerning the Jews…" *Harper's Magazine*, September 1899, viewed at Ohr Somayach, http://ohr.edu/judaism/concern/concerna.htm (accessed September 16, 2008).

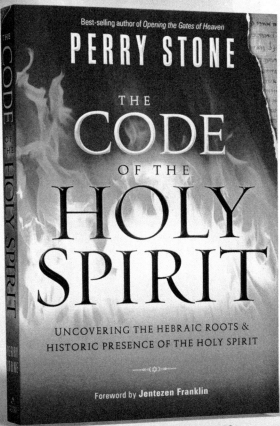